D1386530

The Good of the Novel

EDITED BY
Liam McIlvanney and Ray Ryan

faber and faber

First published in 2011
by Faber and Faber Ltd
Bloomsbury House
74–77 Great Russell Street
London WC1B 3DA

Typeset by Faber and Faber Ltd
Printed in England by CPI Mackays, Chatham

A CIP record for this book
is available from the British Library

ISBN 978–0–571–23086–0

10 9 8 7 6 5 4 3 2 1

Contents

Introduction

The Good of the Novel is a collection of specially commissioned essays on the contemporary Anglophone novel. The book brings together some of the most strenuous and perceptive critics of the present moment and puts them in contact with some of the finest novels of the past three decades. The book starts from the conviction that the job of the critic is evaluation, and that what needs to be evaluated is primarily the technique of the writer. The essays in this volume are avowedly evaluative; that is, they attempt to consider novels as novels.

'Real novels are as rare / As winter thunder or a polar bear' is W. H. Auden's jocular proposition in 'Letter to Lord Byron'. Real critics are rare too, and it might be thought that the digital revolutions of the late twentieth century have made them still rarer. Now that anyone who wishes to can review a book on Amazon, who any longer defers to the critic's expertise? Where are the pundits who can establish a writer's reputation, as Kenneth Tynan helped to establish Samuel Beckett's? If the authority of the literary critic has been dissipated by the internet, it has also been sabotaged by the academy's retreat into theoretical obscurantism. The result is a demise of critical authority that has been both celebrated – in books like Jeff Gomez's *Print is Dead* (2007) – and lamented, most notably in Rónán McDonald's *The Death of the Critic* (2007).

This project is motivated partly by the sense that, as books like Terry Eagleton's *After Theory* (2004) and Valentine Cunningham's *Reading After Theory* (2001) postulate, we are emerging from a period of heavily theoretical criticism and that, as a result, what might be called the novelness of novels is coming back into focus. The loosening of the theoretical grip has coincided with a reinvigoration of evaluative literary criticism, notably in the form of the long review-essay. The past decade and a half has seen the emergence of a number of strong evaluative critics (some of them novelists themselves), writing in magazines like the *London Review of Books*, the *Times Literary Supplement*, the *New Republic* and the *New York Review of Books*.

This is, in fact, a very good period for literary criticism. It may be that reports of the critic's death have been exaggerated. It is not true, for one thing, that the internet is intrinsically hostile to critical authority. There is plenty of rigorous, discriminating criticism in online journals like *Salon* and *Slate*, as well as on literary blogs and e-zines. Nor have university English Departments altogether abandoned the practice of evaluative criticism. There is no shortage of literary academics – John Mullan, Helen Vendler, John Carey – who eschew the 'jargon o' the schools' (in Robert Burns's phrase) to engage a general audience. But if it is true, as Martin Amis argues in *The War Against Cliché*, and McDonald in *The Death of the Critic*, that the days when literary criticism seemed a practice of indisputable cultural centrality are over, it remains equally true that there is presently at work in Britain and America a group of literary journalists and academics committed to the evaluative criticism of fiction, to a criticism that approaches novels as novels.

Much of the most interesting and rewarding criticism of recent years has been preoccupied with the question of 'novelness', with what is distinctive and indigenous to the novel form. The debate has been shaped by the appearance of a number of highly publicised novels that have seemed, in interesting ways, to be aping other cultural forms – novels that aspire to journalism, biography, history, 'prose television' and so forth. The list would include David Foster Wallace's *Infinite Jest*, Don DeLillo's

Underworld, Jonathan Franzen's *The Corrections*, Tom Wolfe's *A Man in Full*, Richard Powers's *The Time of Our Singing* and Zadie Smith's *White Teeth*. These are books which bombard the reader with data, with unassimilated nuggets of arcane information. Gordon Burn has described them as 'data-processing machines', 'big, brick-like novels which also double as encyclopaedias'. They are novels which appear to share the belief of Eric Packer in DeLillo's *Cosmopolis* that 'data itself was soulful and glowing'. Their frenetically proliferating narratives and compulsive purveyance of information has led James Wood to coin the term 'hysterical realism' to describe their procedures.

The attractions of 'hysterical realism' have only increased in the wake of the 9/11 terrorist attacks on New York and Washington, and the related pressure on novelists to make their work somehow 'equal to' the historical moment it inhabits. The danger of this imperative – and its potentially catastrophic effect on the economy of the novel – is evident in the recent career of Nicholson Baker. Baker's forte as a novelist has been the ingenious and suggestive microanalysis of everyday objects and activities. This is the 'sluggish' novel par excellence, slowing down perception until the familiar discloses its strangeness. In books like *The Mezzanine* and *A Box of Matches*, Baker opens new areas of experience, changes the way we look at things. By contrast, his 2004 novel *Checkpoint*, in which two men in a hotel room discuss means of assassinating President Bush, is a tickertape of received opinion. There is almost nothing in the book that you couldn't find more pithily expressed in the op-ed columns of a broadsheet newspaper. In this sense, it is less a novel than a tissue of disposable journalistic 'positions'. In courting social and political 'relevance', in seeking to make his novel equal to its historical moment, Baker dissipates its force. Nor is this simply a question of politics. Baker's earlier writing is much more intelligently political than *Checkpoint*. In *Checkpoint* you either agree or disagree with Baker's conclusions, and you know in culties with Franzen's first two novels is that their documentary ambition – their aim to function as working scale-models of the contemporary American city – overwhelmed their ability to communicate the lives of believable human beings. In this sense, Franzen's focus on the Lambert family in *The Corrections* represents a contraction of scope, but also an enlargement of sympathy. It's as if Franzen has come to share the novelistic premise of Graham Greene in *Our Man in Havana*: 'I can't believe in anything bigger than a home, or anything vaguer than a human being.' At one point in *The Twenty-Seventh City*, a character reflecting on the political conspiracy which animates that novel observes that 'individuals were vectors, not origins'. The problem with Franzen's first two novels is that the author himself appears to second this perception. By the third novel, the correction has been made. When Chip Lambert dismisses his parents as 'vectors of corporate advertising' for wearing their cruise-line shoulder-bags, we are meant to laugh at his priggishness.

The novels of Franzen and Baker, and of DeLillo, Tom Wolfe, Zadie Smith and others, have focused recent criticism on the question of when a novel is most novelistic, and when a novel stops being a novel and becomes something else – novelised history, novelised biography, novelised journalism. In pursuing this concern with the distinctive virtues of the novel – with what Robert Macfarlane has called 'the mandate of the novel' – recent critics owe a great deal to the critical formulations of Milan Kundera, particularly in the essays collected in *The Art of the Novel* (1988), *Testaments Betrayed* (1995) and *The Curtain* (2007). In these essays, Kundera disparages all forms of novelised journalism and novelised history, and argues that: 'The sole *raison d'être* of a novel is to discover what only the novel can discover. A novel that does not discover a hitherto unknown segment of existence is immoral. Knowledge is the novel's only morality.'

It is worth asking, then, what this novelistic knowledge might look like. What is it that the novel knows? What kinds of truth can the novel tell? What is it about the language used in a novel that creates a world different from that of drama or poetry? What distinguishes fictional prose from journalism, biography, or non-fictional prose? And how does a particular novel exemplify this? In seeking answers to such questions, *The Good of the Novel* will not be dogmatic or prescriptive. To theorise about a genre as fluid, capacious and protean as the novel is to risk incoherence or banality. Each novel sets the terms of its own reception, makes its own demands of its readers. As Amit Chaudhuri argues here, the reading of a single novel can realign one's entire aesthetic. Each novel writes its own constitution. Moreover, as both Mikhail Bakhtin and Kundera have emphasised, the novel is the one genre that can accommodate all others. Poetry, drama, shopping lists, recipes, personal letters, legal depositions, newspaper reports: everything can be incorporated in the novel's capacious maw. How definitive can one be in identifying the characteristics of such a genre? How does one evaluate such multifariousness?

For all that, the novel as a form is amenable to study. The novel has a history, a tradition, a generic profile. It has characteristic procedures and protocols; it has distinctive faculties and virtues. Perhaps we can even follow Kundera in talking of 'the spirit of the novel'. One can say, for one thing, that the truth of fiction cannot be rendered in any other form; it cannot be abstracted or codified, turned into a thesis or proposition. Novelistic truth is not data, not reportage, not documentary, not philosophical tenet, not political slogan. Novelistic truth is dramatic, which means above all that it has to do with character, and with what the Scottish philosopher John Macmurray calls 'persons in relation'. In exploring character, the novel's key strength is the disclosure of human interiority. To the question, what does the novel do?, we might most pertinently answer: the novel does character, and the novel does interiority. In Bellow's *Seize the Day*, it does Tommy Wilhelm's lengthy, baffled, outraged, complicated internal response to the poem Dr Tamkin has just shown him, before he responds: 'Nice. Very nice. Have you been writing long?'

The novel also does character and interiority in a specific way. It tends to be anti-heroic in its characterisation. The novelistic hero is rarely heroic, rarely has the finish and consistency of the epic hero, the tragic hero, the action hero. When most novelistic, the world of the novel is one of compromise, shortcomings, inexactitude – a comic world, in other words. As this suggests, 'novelness' is partly a question of perspective, of a writer's orientation towards his or her material. The novelistic approach is humorous, relativistic, sardonic and sceptical, which is why a poem like Byron's *Don Juan* – with its irreverence, its joyous detonation of pious abstractions, its overtly 'anti-poetic' animus – can be more 'novelistic' than many a novel. A good novel's truths are never portentously explicit or categorical. In forwarding its own truths, the novel will rely on the implicit – on patterns of imagery, on parallel episodes whose significance is nowhere made explicit but remains unstated, open-ended. The novel's truths are not reducible to a formulation, a proposition. They are partial, provisional. The novel represents a distinctive kind of ontology. The novel's wisdom is the 'wisdom of uncertainty'.

All this is intended less as a manifesto than a rough working definition of the kinds of principles and categories that preoccupy many of the contributors to *The Good of the Novel*. Questions as to what the novel does and what kinds of truth the novel tells are best answered in practice, and this is what *The Good of the Novel* aims to do, by bringing some of the strongest critics of the present moment into contact with some of the finest novels of the past three decades. While André Gide's ambition to 'strip the novel of every element that does not specifically belong to the novel' remains an impossible goal for the novelist, it provides a good working rule for the critic. How good are these novels? What kind of good are they? What do these novels achieve that couldn't be achieved in any other genre? These are the questions we aim to address in *The Good of the Novel*.

1 Ian McEwan, *Atonement*

JAMES WOOD

There is something fishy from the start. A group of peculiarly named characters – Pierrot, Lola, Briony, Jackson, Leon – gather in a Surrey country house in 1935. But the country house is a bit of a fake – it is barely forty years old – and the characters themselves have an aura of the inauthentic. They say rather literary-sounding things like: 'I knew some grammar school types at Oxford and some of them were damned clever.' Or: 'He's got a first-rate mind, so I don't know what the hell he's doing, messing about in the flower beds.' The village constable is a kind of fake, too – a 'kindly old man with a waxed moustache whose wife kept hens and delivered fresh eggs on her bicycle'. (Well, of course.) The author's prose is rich, studied, sometimes carefully pretentious – 'the long grass was already stalked by the leonine yellow of high summer' – but always very careful, very 'good':

> The drawing room which had transfixed her that morning with its brilliant parallelograms of light was now in gloom, lit by a single lamp near the fireplace. The open French windows framed a greenish sky, and against that, in silhouette at some distance, the familiar head and shoulders of her brother. As she made her way across the room she heard the tinkle of ice cubes against his glass, and as she stepped out she smelled the pennyroyal, camomile and feverfew crushed underfoot, and headier now than in the morning.

Meanwhile, the author also subtly flags the fact that though the *mise en scène* is 1935, the scene of the writing is nearer to home: 'But Jackson had wet the bed, as troubled small boys far from home will, and was obliged *by current theory* to carry his sheets and pyjamas down to the laundry and wash them himself, by hand.' (My italics.) One of the characters, Paul Marshall, is described in the style of a *Boys' Own* annual: 'only fractions of an inch kept him from cruel good looks'. Cruel good looks, eh? The same could be said for the entire first section of *Atonement*: only fractions of an inch keep the writing from sounding quite real.

Those are of course deliberate fractions. In the same year that our strangely named crowd assembles in Sussex, the critic Cyril Connolly published a polished plaint called 'More About the Modern Novel', in which he proposed banning 'whole landscapes' from the modern novel, including the following: 'reception of love-letters by either sex . . . all allusion to illness or suicide (except insanity), all quotations, all mentions of genius, promise, writing, painting, sculpting, art, poetry, and the phrases "I like your stuff". "What's his stuff like?", "damned good", "Let me make you some coffee", all young men with ambition or young women with emotion, all remarks like "Darling, I've found the most wonderful cottage" (flat, castle), "Ask me any other time, dearest, only please – just this once – not now", "Love you – of course I love you" (don't love you) – and "It's not that, it's only that I feel so terribly tired." Forbidden names: Hugo, Peter, Sebastian, Adrian, Ivor, Julian, Pamela, Chloe, Enid, Inez, Miranda, Joanna, Jill, Felicity, Phyllis.' Connolly might as well have been describing the first part of *Atonement*; one suspects that Ian McEwan, who in the third part of this novel will invent a long letter from this same Cyril Connolly, is perfectly familiar with that witty screed from 1935.

It would be fair to say that until the publication of *Atonement* in 2001, Ian McEwan's fictions had been prodigies: they did everything but move us. McEwan had made himself a master of narrative stealth, of the undetonated bomb and the slow-acting detail: the fizzing fact that steadily dissolves throughout a novel and perturbs everything around it. His fictive worlds had always been highly managed climates, with not much room for gratuity, abundance, spaciousness. His books, like detective stories, were always moving forwards. They seemed to shed their sentences rather than to accumulate them. Tidiness, finish, polish, craftsmanship, formal intelligence – these were the words that seemed best to describe his work.

Atonement represents a break with this pattern. McEwan carefully loosens the golden ropes that have sometimes made his fiction feel so craftily imprisoned. This novel has a new spaciousness and amplitude, moving, in its first section, from England in 1935 to, in its second, a remarkable account of the British army's retreat at Dunkirk, and thence to a third chapter set in wartime London. More importantly, McEwan employs this large novel to comment on the type of fiction that he has tended to produce in the past – the sort of controlled and controlling storytelling that insists on artfully tidying up its clean narrative lines and themes, the sort of fiction that always seems to know better than the characters themselves what they are thinking, what they are going to do next. It is perhaps a stretch to claim that *Atonement* is an atonement for fiction's manipulative untruths, not least because finally it seems to be a defense of those untruths. But it is surely a novel explicitly concerned with fiction's fictionality, and keen to examine the question of the novel's responsibility to truth.

These rather abstract anxieties are wonderfully made flesh in the novel's thirteen-year-old heroine, Briony Tallis, who is an ambitious budding writer. The novel opens, amusingly, with her attempt to write a play, *The Trials of Arabella*, and to cast in it her cousins, Pierrot, Jackson, and Lola. McEwan shows a great deal of tact in the patient way he follows the daydreams and furies of this bright little girl. The aimless solipsism of childhood is marvellously caught, as Briony sits and plays with her hands:

She raised one hand and flexed its fingers and wondered, as she had sometimes before, how this thing, this machine for gripping, this fleshy spider on the end of her arm, came to be hers, entirely at her command.

Or did it have some little life of its own? She bent her finger and straightened it. The mystery was in the instance before it moved, the dividing moment between not moving and moving, when her intention took effect. It was like a wave breaking. If she could only find herself at the crest, she thought, she might find the secret of herself, that part of her that was really in charge. She brought her forefinger closer to her face and stared at it, urging it to move. It remained still because she was pretending, she was not entirely serious, and because willing it to move, or being about to move it, was not the same as actually moving it. And when she did crook it finally, the action seemed to start in the finger itself, not in some part of her mind. When did it know to move, when did she know to move it?

Briony's elder sister, Cecilia, has just come down from Cambridge, which she attended with a young man called Robbie Turner. Robbie's status is awkward: the son of the Tallis's cleaning lady, he has been essentially adopted by the wealthier family, who paid for his education. And Cecilia is complicatedly in love with him.

A house party is in the offing: Briony's elder brother Leon and his friend Paul Marshall have arrived from London. But there is a way in which none of these people quite exist for Briony, are indeed just Pierrots for her inner circus: 'was everyone else really as alive as she was?' she muses. 'For example, did her sister really matter to herself, was she as valuable to herself as Briony was? Was being Cecilia just as vivid an affair as being Briony? Did her sister also have a real self concealed behind a breaking wave, and did she spend time thinking about it, with a finger held up to her face?'

Briony is going to learn that indeed her sister does feel as 'valuable to herself' as Briony does. Or rather, she is going to ignore this sympathetic imaginative truth, in a moment for which the rest of her life will be an atonement. From her window, she sees an event which she can barely comprehend. Cecilia and Robbie are standing next to the fountain. Suddenly, Cecilia strips off her clothes and jumps in to retrieve something, while Robbie watches her. Then she puts her clothes back on, and returns to

the house. Robbie also leaves the scene. Briony is oddly stirred
by her witnessing, convinced she has seen some kind of mysterious erotic domination played out. At first, she holds herself
to properly rational standards. She knows she must not judge.
She decides to abandon melodrama, with its easy judgments,
and start the task of writing truthfully and impartially. She can
write the scene from three different perspectives, she realises
with excitement – hers, Cecilia's, and Robbie's:

> from three points of view; her excitement was in the prospect of free-
> dom, of being delivered from the cumbrous struggle between good
> and bad, heroes and villains. None of these three was bad, nor were
> they particularly good. She need not judge. There did not have to be a
> moral. She need only show separate minds, as alive as her own, strug-
> gling with the idea that other minds were equally alive . . . And only in
> a story could you enter these different minds and show how they had
> an equal value.

Sixty years later, McEwan tells us, when Briony is a famous novelist, her work known for its 'amorality', she will remember this
year as a turning point in her literary development.

But of course Briony ignores her own wise perspectivism. A
series of events combine to convince her that Robbie is a sexual menace, an outsider, a predator who must be stopped. She
reads an erotic note that Robbie writes to Cecilia but mistakenly
hands her; and she interrupts Robbie and Cecilia having hurried sex in the library, inferring from their position that Robbie
is forcing Cecilia. So when the fifteen-year-old Lola is molested
in the house's darkened garden, Briony assumes that the shape
she saw was Robbie's, and she testifies against him to the police.
Robbie is duly arrested.

Briony's impulse to judge, to close the case, is inextricable
from her literary impulse, which is to fashion a closed story.
Stories, she has already reflected earlier in the book, are only
stories when they have endings: 'Only when a story was finished, all fates resolved and the whole matter sealed off at both

ends so it resembled, at least in this one respect, every other
finished story in the world, could she feel immune, and ready
to punch holes in the margins, bind the chapters with pieces of
string, paint or draw the cover, and take the finished work to
show to her mother, or her father, when he was home.' There
has to be a 'story' about Robbie, she thinks:

> and this was the story of a man whom everybody liked, but about
> whom the heroine always had her doubts, and finally she was able to
> reveal that he was the incarnation of evil. But wasn't she – that was,
> Briony the writer – supposed to be so worldly now as to be above such
> nursery tale ideas as good and evil? There must be some lofty, god-like
> place from which all people could be judged alike, not pitted against
> each other . . . If such a place existed, she was not worthy of it. She
> could never forgive Robbie his disgusting mind.

What Briony has seen is plotless, because she can make no
hermeneutic sense of it. But she imposes a plot anyway: she
makes it mean. In addition to explicit ruminations like these
on storytelling and fiction, *Atonement*'s first section is carefully
mined with signifiers of fictionality. There is, first of all, as already mentioned, the nagging artificiality of the entire section,
along with the heaped literary allusions, to Austen, Fielding,
Richardson, T. S. Eliot, and so on: McEwan superbly pulls off
that very hardest of tasks, the simultaneous creation of a reality that satisfies as a reality while signaling that it is itself a
fiction. Note, too, that one of the reasons that the writing here
feels so calmly antique, so 'old-fashioned', is that McEwan systematically avails himself of precisely the 'lofty, god-like place
from which all people could be judged alike' so characteristic
of nineteenth-century (especially Tolstoyan) fiction. After all,
McEwan reserves the god-like right to enter, variously, the
minds of Briony, Cecilia, their mother Emily Tallis, and Robbie
Turner. He uses a confident, generalising authorial voice ('in
any case, she was discovering, as had many writers before her,
that not all recognition is helpful'); or an all-knowing 'flash-

forward,' which signals his own control of events ('Briony was hardly to know it then, but this was the project's highest point of fulfillment'); and he fills the section with intimations of foreclosure and clairvoyance: Lola, Jackson and Pierrot are the children of divorce, 'a mundane unravelling that could not be reversed'; Robbie's mother actually works as a part-time clairvoyant, dishing out predictions to the villagers for money; and the Tallis paterfamilias is a London civil servant who has been working in – what else? – something called 'Eventuality Planning'. Indeed, isn't the generally absent Tallis father a kind of omniscient narrator whose calming presence, in an ideal world, might have averted all these nasty unplanned eventualities? 'When her father was home,' Cecilia thinks to herself, 'the household settled around a fixed point . . . he mostly sat in the library. But his presence imposed order and allowed freedom.' Cecilia prefers Fielding to Richardson, she tells Robbie; clearly she needs the forceful, paternal intervention of a Fielding-like narrator: naughty Richardsonian seduction-missives are just what set this mess ticking.

But such a narrator, who at once 'imposed order and allowed freedom', only exists ideally: that is why he is absent. In practice, McEwan seems to be saying, the storyteller can grant his invented people a good deal less freedom than he likes to congratulate himself on. The lofty, god-like perspective is an ideal, and hard to attain in reality. The storyteller will be at worst a Briony – an arch-controller and distorter – or at best a McEwan, more patiently shaping his characters' destinies. We can tell that Briony is applying too much torque to her story, and is thus a 'bad' novelist; but what about McEwan, the 'good' novelist? Perhaps he is just a more efficient version of Briony – one who, like all great storytellers, smothers his obvious manipulation in the subtlest sleight-of-hand?

All this is raised by the first section of *Atonement*, before any of the revelations of part three, which force us to modify our

entire sense of the story. So in this paradox-thick novel, one
of the nicest paradoxes is that it is only through fiction itself
– McEwan's own narration – that we can see how potentially
untruthful and distorting fiction can be (Briony's fictive distortions). Yet, in a further twist, if all fiction is a species of distortion – Briony's *and* McEwan's – why should we believe that
fiction can disinterestedly comment on its own distortions? Fiction can't be its own ombudsman, it seems; postmodern self-
reference of the kind that *Atonement* attempts will always have
the feel of a sick man analysing his former health. McEwan, I
think, sees all this, and wants to get beyond the gesture of certain kinds of self-referential novels, which seem to assume that
merely by flagging their own fictionality – simply by interrupt-
ing their own artifice – they have broken the spell of fictionality.
This is why his novel, for all its late-twentieth-century tricks,
refers to Austen, Fielding and Richardson – to a tradition, early
in the novel's history and before the great developments of realism, that had no illusions about illusion, that was able robustly
to keep in its head the apparent incompatibilities that fiction
is both about the world and makes the world, and that empiri-
cism and idealism can work together.

Atonement, then, is both a postmodern novel and an old-
fashioned one, and it wants to have things both ways. It offers
a critique of the dangers of fiction-making, much as *Pnin* or
The Prime of Miss Jean Brodie do; but, also like those novels, it
bursts out of the implied melancholy of this self-laceration by
the sheer force of its world-making reality, by the power of its
capacity to make palpable, to make real, a fictional world, to
satisfy its ordinarily hungry readers.

The best example of McEwan's desire to want it both ways,
to be both skeptical and affirming, is the way he casts doubt on
the possibility of imaginative sympathy and yet honours it as a
novelistic ideal. It may be an impossible ideal, McEwan seems
to say, but the novelist must continue to strive for it. Certainly,

Atonement has to be seen as a book about the dangers of failing to put oneself in someone else's shoes, that crucial transfer-
ence of sympathy that Adam Smith wrote about long ago in *The
Theory of Moral Sentiments*: 'the source of our fellow-feeling for
the misery of the other . . . is by changing places in fancy with
the sufferer, that we come either to conceive or to be affected
by what he feels.' This is what Briony signally fails to do in the
novel's first section, but it is what McEwan is signally trying to
do in this same section, carefully inhabiting one point-of-view
after another. Emily Tallis, stricken with a migraine, lies in bed
and thinks anxiously about her children – a kind of Mrs Ramsay moment, you might say – yet the reader cannot but notice
that she is in fact a very bad imaginative sympathiser, because
her anxiety and anger get in the way of her sympathy. Reflecting
on Cecilia's time at Cambridge, she thinks about her own comparative lack of education, and then quickly, but unwittingly,
gets resentful:

> When Cecilia came home in July with her finals' result – the nerve of
> the girl to be disappointed with it! – she had no job or skill and still
> had a husband to find and motherhood to confront, and what would
> her bluestocking teachers – the ones with silly nicknames and 'fear-
> some reputations' – have to tell her about that? Those self-important
> women gained local immortality for the blandest, the most timid of
> eccentricities – walking a cat on a dog's lead, riding about on a man's
> bike, being seen with a sandwich in the street. A generation later these
> silly, ignorant ladies would be long dead and still revered at High Table
> and spoken of in lowered voices.

In Adam Smith's terms, Emily is quite unable to 'change places'
with her daughter; in a novelist's or actor's language, she is no
good at 'being' Cecilia. But of course McEwan is himself wonderfully good here at 'being' Emily Tallis, using free indirect
style with perfect poise to inhabit her complicated envy.

Later in the section, as Emily sits by the light, she sees moths
drawn to it, and recalls being told by 'a professor of some science

or another' that 'it was the visual impression of an even deeper darkness beyond the light that drew them in. Even though they might be eaten, they had to obey the instinct that made them seek out the darkest place, on the far side of the light – and in this case it was an illusion. It sounded to her like sophistry, or an explanation for its own sake. How could anyone presume to know the world through the eyes of an insect?' Emily, of course, *would* think this, proving herself very much the mother of impetuous Briony, who, precisely, did not take enough care to see reality from Robbie's or Cecilia's eyes. McEwan knowingly alludes here to a celebrated dilemma in the philosophy of consciousness, most famously raised by Thomas Nagel in 1974 in his essay 'What is it like to be a bat?' Nagel concludes that a human cannot change places with a bat, that imaginative transfer on the part of a human is impossible: 'Insofar as I can imagine this (which is not very far), it tells me only what it would be like for *me* to behave as a bat behaves. But that is not the question. I want to know what it is like for a *bat* to be a bat.' Standing up for novelists, as it were, J. M. Coetzee has his novelist-heroine, Elizabeth Costello, explicitly reply to Nagel in his eponymous novel. Costello says that imagining what it is like to be a bat would simply be the definition of a good novelist. I can imagine being a corpse, says Costello, why can I not then imagine being a bat? (Tolstoy, in an electrifying moment at the end of his novella *Hadji Murad*, imagines what it might be like to have one's head cut off, and for consciousness to persist for a second or two in the brain even as the head has left the body. His imaginative insight foreshadows modern neuroscience, which does indeed suggest that consciousness can continue for a minute or two in a severed head.)

McEwan himself discussed these matters shortly after the terrorist attacks of September 11th, 2001. In an impassioned piece in the *Guardian*, entitled 'Only Love and Then Oblivion', he argued that 'If the hijackers had been able to imagine themselves

into the thoughts and feelings of the passengers, they would
have been unable to proceed. It is hard to be cruel once you permit yourself to enter the mind of your victim. Imagining what
it is like to be someone other than yourself is at the core of our
humanity. It is the essence of compassion, and it is the beginning of morality . . . Among their [the terrorists'] crimes was
a failure of the imagination.' Sounding very like Adam Smith,
McEwan didn't need to say, because it was so deeply implied,
that this sympathy is one of the novelist's great, ideal faculties. One might disagree with his certainty – after all, what if
Mohammed Atta did indeed, and with great relish, imagine being his own victims? – and still be moved by the novelist's great
faith in the powers of the imagination.

The second and third sections of *Atonement* have a very different tone from their predecessor. In Part Two, we have moved
ahead five years, as the narrative follows Robbie Turner re-
treating, along with the rest of the British Expeditionary Force,
through northern France to Dunkirk. We learn that he has been
in prison, that he and Cecilia are ardently corresponding, and
that a remorseful Briony, now eighteen, wants to make amends
by retracting her statement to the police. In the second section,
however, this information is in some way incidental to the extraordinary evocation of the hideous banalities of warfare. In the
third section, we follow Briony as she struggles with her job as a
trainee nurse at a large London hospital during the war. In a gesture of atonement, she has forsworn Cambridge, and dedicated
herself to nursing. Towards the end of this section, she visits her
estranged sister in Balham, and discovers that she is living with
Robbie, who has briefly returned from army service. There is an
awkward, icy encounter between accuser and accused.

The difference in tone is that the writing seems in some almost impalpable way to have 'settled down'. In particular, the
queasy alternation between lyrically fine writing and plainer

description that is characteristic of the first section has here disappeared. The first section, for example, flourished this rather uselessly lacy description of some roast potatoes: 'The undersides held a stickier yellow glow, and here and there a gleaming edge was picked out in nacreous brown, and the occasional filigree lacework that blossomed around a ruptured skin.' That reads like Nabokovian parody, and not much like the McEwan we know from his earlier work, who would run a mile from 'nacreous'; the stylishness has a slightly revolting amorality: all *this* for some roast potatoes? There are patches like this throughout the first section, in which the writer seems to be trying out different levels of stylishness. But in the second and third sections, the same quality of attention, of visual noticing, is now disciplined, thinned of its excess luxury, and made morally strenuous by virtue of its suddenly serious subject. In the third section, Briony, now a nurse in London, is dressing a wound, and here is how McEwan describes it: 'The wound was eighteen inches long, perhaps more, and curved behind his knee. The stitches were clumsy and irregular. Here and there one edge of the ruptured skin rose over the other, revealing its fatty layers, and little obtrusions like miniature bunches of red grapes forced up from the fissure.' Ah – *that* sounds like McEwan. The same quality of noticing that was fussily lavished on the potatoes is strictly lavished on the wound, to tremendous effect: the style seems to be atoning for earlier luxuries.

In general, the prose in these latter sections is recognisably consistent with McEwan's exactitude, especially his precise and systematic use of estrangement. In the second section, again and again the prose presents a kind of metaphorical mirage which, as Robbie dazedly refocuses, melts into horrid reality:

> hanging there, a long way off, about thirty feet above the road, warped by the rising heat, was what looked like a plank of wood, suspended horizontally, with a bulge in its centre . . . A fighter was strafing the length of the column.

At first sight it seemed that an enormous horizontal door was flying up the road. It was a platoon of Welsh Guards in good order, rifles at the slopes, led by a second lieutenant.

A black furry shape that seemed, as he approached, to be moving or pulsing. Suddenly a swarm of bluebottles rose into the air with an angry whining buzz, revealing the rotting corpse beneath.

There were no boats by the jetty. He blinked and looked again. That jetty was made of men, a long file of them, six or eight deep, standing up to their knees.

If the first section was a display, a demonstration of the novelist's consummate freedom to inhabit several characters and of his ability to stretch his prose style into different shapes, the second and third sections are passionately committed to a single point of view, and labour to make us inhabit that vision. Of course, in a novel so involved with fiction's truthfulness, the amazing evocations of Dunkirk and wartime London cannot but fail to share some of the weird but successful doubleness of the novel's first section. Stephen Crane's writing about the Civil War was so vivid that one veteran swore he had fought alongside Crane (who was not alive then) at Antietam. By contrast, McEwan is not shy to credit, in his acknowledgments, the Imperial War Museum; so he is happy to let us have an image of the bespectacled contemporary author doing his research, poring over texts and photographs. We know, then, that the burden is on the author-researcher to *put us there*, to 'do' Dunkirk, to make us inhabit Robbie's wet boots. McEwan succeeds, I think, and makes it seem less like fiction than like a memoir. This is what Aristotle meant when he said that a convincing impossibility is preferable, in poetry, to an unconvincing possibility. Yet this great freedom shows how dangerous fiction can be, and why its transit with 'lies' has historically been so subversive.

And again, steadily, stealthily, McEwan, amidst the proper raising of postmodern doubt and scepticism, is making his own case *for* fiction, is making his own defence of what he does as a novelist. The second section begins thus: 'There were horrors enough, but it was the unexpected detail that threw him and afterwards would not let him go.' And a little later, Robbie thinks to himself: 'No one would ever know what it was like to be here. Without the details there could be no larger picture.' The 'unexpected' or telling detail is one of the elements of modern fiction's power after Flaubert, and sure enough, these two sections are built, systematically, out of telling detail after detail. Briony, tending to a soldier who has lost half his face, 'could see through his missing cheek to his upper and lower molars, and the tongue glistening, and hideously long.' *Hideously long* is worthy of Conrad. McEwan surely wants us to reflect on this word 'detail' when, in the third section, he has Briony meet Cecilia and Robbie. In the course of their painful meeting, Briony reveals what the reader has suspected, that it was Paul Marshall who attacked Lola, and not, as Robbie and Cecilia had always imagined, Danny Hardman, the gardener. 'During the silence that followed, Briony tried to imagine the adjustments that each would be making. Years of seeing it a certain way. And yet, however startling, it was only a detail. Nothing essential was changed by it. Nothing in her own role.' As a legal assessment of her own role as false witness, this may be true, but in every other respect, of course, a 'detail', in this charged context, can never be 'only' a detail. It was a failure to read mere *details*, to take pains – in a literary sense – with detail that led Briony astray in the first place. McEwan, the novelist, would not have made Briony's mistake, one feels.

But then Briony, it seems, is not a very McEwanish kind of writer. The great revelation of the third section, and even more acutely of the fourth section, dated London, 1999, and which I have withheld for so long in an attempt to evoke the experience of reading the novel for the first time, is that Briony not only grew up to be a writer, but that she has written the text we have just read – all of it, because the third section ends: 'BT London, 1999.' In the third section, McEwan invents a letter from Cyril Connolly, in his capacity as editor of *Horizon*, the celebrated little magazine. Connolly has rejected Briony's novel, *Two Figures by a Fountain*. Connolly's letter suggests that Briony has written a rather dreamy, drifting kind of piece in the manner of a sub-Virginia Woolf, from three points of view – Briony's, Cecilia's, and Robbie's – full of lyrical aimlessness ('scores of pages [dedicated] to the quality of light and shade, and to random impressions,' writes Connolly). He suggests that Briony try again, and insert a little more plot and human interest into the narrative. Suddenly the peculiarities of the first section, in particular the lyrical instability of the writing, make sense. (Connolly, the Proustian aesthete, picks out 'the long grass stalked by the leonine yellow of high summer' as especially fine.) It was not simply, then, 'McEwan' writing; it was McEwan writing as Briony. McEwan was impersonating a tyro Virginia Woolf.

In the short fourth section of the novel, set in 1999, Briony is an old and eminent writer, who has just been given a diagnosis of dementia. The novel ends with the lady at her writing desk, at five in the morning, reflecting on the piece of writing she first started in January 1940 (which must have been the piece Connolly saw), and to which she has returned 'half a dozen different' times between then and now. But although we comprehend that what we have just read – the text of the entire novel – was written by Briony, we have no great desire to comprehend that what we have just read was *made up* – i.e. invented – by Briony; McEwan cleverly plays on the complacency of our middlebrow readerly expectation, whereby, with the help of detailed verisimilitude, we always tend to turn fiction into a kind of fact. If we have just read, in section three, that Briony walked to Clapham and saw Robbie and Cecilia there, this must 'really' have happened, yes? – even if Briony admits that *she*, and not McEwan, wrote what we just read. Most of us have no great willingness

to see fiction as invention, but McEwan wants us to turn fiction
back into fiction, as it were, and on the last two pages of his
novel, he lays bare his final secret: Robbie died at Dunkirk on
June 1, 1940, and Cecilia was killed in the same year by a bomb
in Balham. The lovers never united. Briony invented their prosperity as an act of novelistic atonement for her earlier act of
novelistic failure. She never 'really' saw them in Balham. That
was invention, wish-fulfillment. As a girl, she ended their lives,
by falsely testifying; as an adult and novelist, she has brought
them back to life.

There is something moving about this guilty resurrection, especially in the context of the Second World War. The references
to Woolf are not hubristic, for *To the Lighthouse*, that elegy for
the dead of the First World War, circles around and around this
idea of how to mourn both the private dead and the public dead.
In the last section of Woolf's novel, the painter, Lily Briscoe, ef-
fectively brings Mrs Ramsay back to life, by thinking about her
and by painting a representation of her into her picture. The
novel itself achieves a kind of revivifiying of Virginia Woolf's
mother, the model for Mrs Ramsay. Briony has done something
similar in the second and third sections of *Atonement*, and the
desperation of both her guilt and her wish-fulfillment stirs us
in ways we cannot quite describe, not least because, by virtue of
McEwan's delayed revelation, we have ourselves been made part
of Briony's wish-fulfillment, we have become its willing victims,
content to believe, until the very last moment, that Cecilia and
Robbie did not actually die. We wanted them to be alive: we
have been absolutely complicit with Briony's yearning, and the
realisation that we too wanted that 'happy ending' brings on a
kind of guilt, a kind of atonement for the banality of our own
literary impulses.

So McEwan's book pampers our old-fashioned readerly expectations and then dashes them. It says, in effect: 'You wanted
a "good read", didn't you? Well, you've had your good read for

three hundred or so pages. And now? It was all made up. It never happened.' But *Atonement,* of course, is at the same time a very 'good read' in an old-fashioned sense, which is why the novel provokes divergent responses: it alienates some readers, who dislike the trick ending, and who perhaps dislike the revelation of their own complicity in having enjoyed, until that revelation, a good read; yet the novel has of course sold hundreds of thousands of copies, and has been enjoyed by the kind of book clubs that would be wary of, say, *In Between The Sheets* or *The Cement Garden.*

Is this, in fact, a 'trick ending'? Or is it really the only ending such a book could have had? Certainly, if this is a trick ending, then this novel also has a trick beginning and a trick middle. For it never stops being about its own writing – the second and third sections may be less obviously fictive, less obviously artificial and self-reflexive than the first one, but they still raise questions, as we have seen, about the relation between authorial research and invention, between fiction and fact. And the final revelation, to be fair to McEwan, is not much like those moments at the end of certain kinds of postmodern stories when the author writes: 'And then he woke up' or 'Then she put down her pen, and closed the book you have just been reading.' We don't suddenly exclaim, at the end of *Atonement,* 'Oh, it was just a fiction.' We exclaim: 'So, what kind of fiction is this?' Or perhaps, better: 'So, what kind of truth is this?' For the ironies can only pile higher and higher. If Briony invented sections two and three, it would seem that Briony's nice fiction – Cecilia and Robbie reunited – is trying to atone for her nasty fiction (her false witness in section one), one untruth for an original untruth. But why should the 'untruth' of her second and third chapters be morally superior to the untruth she committed in part one? You could say that, in bringing Robbie and Cecilia back to life, she at least did no harm. But in strictly literary terms, just as she forced an ending onto the young lovers in part one by sending

Robbie off to jail, so she has forced an ending onto the older lovers in parts two and three by shaping their destinies. A happy ending still represents the exercise of a God-like power on the part of the author. A story must be closed in order to be a story, and such closure can entail either death or longevity.

Stranger still, if Briony wrote *all three* parts, how do we know she is atoning for anything? Connolly asked for more plot; and she provided it. In our minds, the events of part one have become 'real' while the events, or some of them, of parts two and three have now become 'unreal'. But what if Briony made everything up, from the encounter at the fountain to the encounter in Balham? What if it is all fiction? And of course, it is *all* fiction, for what does it even mean to be talking in this babyish way about Briony's fiction when it was not Briony but someone called Ian McEwan who made all this up anyway?

One final trick, a subtle one, remains. Briony does not exactly say that Robbie and Cecilia died. She says this:

> But now I can no longer think what purpose would be served if, say, I tried to persuade my reader, by direct or indirect means, that Robbie Turner died of septicaemia at Bray dunes on 1 June 1940, or that Cecilia was killed in September of the same year by the bomb that destroyed Balham Underground station. That I never saw them in that year. That my walk across London ended at the church on Clapham Common, and that a cowardly Briony limped back to the hospital, unable to confront her recently bereaved sister.

Surely it must amuse McEwan that thousands, probably millions of readers have chosen to read the passage above as a simple declaration that the lovers died and that Briony fictively prolonged their lives. But what Briony in fact does is float a hypothesis: she says, in effect, what if I tried to convince you that these people died? Would you still believe me? This sounds less like a statement than another potential fiction, as if -Briony is saying: 'You must believe whatever you want to believe. I could take you either way.' Thus for a second time in this book, the revelation of fictionality seduces the reader into separating fact from fiction. In the first example, the revelation that Briony wrote section three (the 'BT 1999' that appears at the end of section three) encourages the reader to think of what he has read as a fiction but a 'real' fiction: Briony may have written what we have just read, but she did really meet the lovers in Balham, we say to ourselves. In the second instance, the revelation that the lovers died in 1940 seduces us once again into turning fiction into fact: ah, we say to ourselves, Briony was lying about the lovers having survived the war; after all, they actually, really – 'actually', 'really' – died. She made it up. (All novels that introduce second and third layers of false fictionality work in this way, it seems, to establish fake distinctions between truth and reality: the second part of *Don Quixote*, for example, forces us to choose between a false Quixote and a 'real' one.)

But Briony merely says, *what if they died?* The same reader who had happily followed Briony's fiction in the second and third sections, who had happily acceded to the happy ending of the good read, now accedes again to Briony's final manipulations – this same reader now longs to make of this revelation yet another kind of easy fact: oh, they *actually* died. But McEwan chooses his words carefully, here – note that little interpolation, 'say' – because he wants this to sound like another possibility, another fiction. None of us, it seems, is really bold enough to confront the fictionality of fiction – we are all middlebrows now. And so is McEwan, whose novel is both manipulative and ample, at once calculating and keen to escape the charge of calculation by accusing itself of the sin before the reader can. *Atonement* prosecutes and defends fiction-making at the same time, and whether readers think this doubleness a blatant contradiction or a necessary paradox will determine their assessment of the novel. The hostile reader may argue that *Atonement* is just a typically manipulative Ian McEwan novel, one in a series of similarly sensational productions, but one that differs

from its predecessors in being anxious about its own manipulations, and which thus incoherently arraigns Briony for the very
faults it too commits. (There is that McEwanish need to tidy up
all loose ends, for instance, to explain to the reader, at the end,
how to read the novel properly – just as Briony loves, as a child,
the experience of neatly binding her notebooks and closing off
her fictions.) The more sympathetic reader may concede the
justice of this complaint, yet also feel that *Atonement* has a bril-
liance and suppleness that do indeed set it apart from his other
work; and this reader may reflect that, anyway, all the writer can
ever do, whether pre-modernist, modernist or post-modernist,
is simultaneously enact and atone for the manipulations of
fiction-making, in an eternally dialectical contradiction.

Don DeLillo, *Underworld* and *Falling Man*

ANDREW O'HAGAN

A Tale of Two Novels

For those who read novels, admiration is very often a wild-eyed precursor to ingratitude. We love our favourite novelists up to the point where the play of their talents overreaches our faith in them, and on that day we feel free to consider the new work an act of betrayal. There is nothing new in this and the process is important in the art of novel-loving. The good novelist will take it on the chin and serve his periods like Picasso. Yet in the nicest circumstances the motions of a novelist to honour and develop their material and their style is the stuff of complicated pleasure. We should avoid missing it if we can and I offer here an instance in Don DeLillo. The fact that DeLillo should risk both our love and our disappointment is a credit to his mother and his old school. It is also a guarantee, I think, of his essential seriousness: he is a senior craftsman, and we go about reading each of his novels in the manner of people with a lot to lose.

ONE: *Underworld*

Once or twice a year you might happen across some radiant and quite unexpected verbal event, some divine turn in the common words, coming from an archangel such as Joan Didion or from some new guy who is tight with his own foreignness. But from Don DeLillo you can count on good sentences by the yard: he knows how to place an idea at the heart of every line, and he can command those sentences to live a life both pretty and profound. In England, you could count on one hand the number of living writers who possess a good combination of tenderness and gravity and who show an interest in imagining the relationship between individuals and the forces of the state, or in distilling the workings of the market, or the effects of the Cold War, the tragedy of nuclear waste, the absurd comedy of modern planning, or the way in which media images so madly intrude on the inner life. Where is the English novelist with the imaginative gumption to enter, subcutaneously, as DeLillo does, into the world of supermarkets, all-night gas stations, denatured submarine bases, hinterland housing projects, food-processing plants, the secret history of the soil beneath you, and the whole underworld of public and private affairs, all wired from the breathing perspective of the new family?

Lionel Trilling once referred to the 'habitual music of Scott Fitzgerald's seriousness'. DeLillo has that too, and he has always been a student of American derangement. Very early in his career he demonstrated the ability to see madness inherent in contemporary ideas of communication and entertainment, and like nobody else, he has detected and followed the weird shadows passing over everyday life in the United States. In his first novel, *Americana*, it was the world of advertising. In that arena of excellent lies he saw how far a country might be steered from itself – very from its decent heart – if commercial energies went wild and free. In the world's most populist country, DeLillo has always been the writer who understands the downside of mass democratic craving; he has written novels about the rock scene (*Great Jones Street*) and has upended the common apprehension of glory that feeds the great American sports (*End Zone*). Mass popularity, the rough hysteria of the common grain, has always fascinated DeLillo, and in most of his books he has led readers back, again and again, to the presence of threat in large groups of people who seem to believe in the same things. Like Elias Canetti or Sinclair Lewis, DeLillo has long drawn on the notion that crowds are often not good together, or that they are vulnerable to forces – some within, plenty without – that are not good for them. In his 1977 novel *Players,* he wrote about the terrorist as a figure who understands the way modern people move, and he examined the manner in which unnoticed lives can be subject to interventions they never suspected. *Libra,* his fictional account of the John F. Kennedy assassination, gave an unbelievably acute sense of how this kind of power had some-how moved from the centre of corporate agencies into the minds of individuals and into the living rooms of every one of us. By the time of *Mao II,* the terrorist had arrived at the place where he could replace the novelist: the man with the bomb, not the pen, was the one who could alter the consciousness of his times in an instant. But as if to contradict this, DeLillo's vision has gathered force with each of his novels, and his finer sense of America's talent for both massive secrecy and mass be-lief comes together in *Underworld.*

Mao II opened with a crowd at Yankee Stadium, and the idea of crowds never left that book alone: 'the future belongs to crowds'. *Underworld* opens in a stadium too, but the sinister sway of the crowd here quickly gives way to the slow move-ments of several individuals, and soon we are wrapped up in the matter of their interconnected yearnings and sufferings. The whole novel is a journey into the repositories of personal memory, on the one hand, and the grave machinations of glo-bal threat, on the other. Never before, on the page, have we been led to consider so deeply our spiritual reliance on the threat of nuclear destruction. Not in this way – with the smallness of lives so appended to the greatness – and not with such grand melody and sadness for the age we have lived through. DeLillo has come up with a Cold War lament, a sore song with which to close down the century, but all in all it is a work of magical res-cue. His novel is like a flying carpet, beneath it Breughel's *The Triumph of Death.* One art work standing inside another. And given this, we might come to feel, if only for the length of a long novel, that we now know the meaning of the term 'mutually assured destruction'. The meaning of art and the meaning of weapons systems are seen to mingle and change places. DeLillo is interested in what art has to say about our vast dying.

But it all starts with Bobby Thomson hitting his great home run – 'the shot heard round the world' – that gives the Giants the pennant. It is 1951, and J. Edgar Hoover shares a box at the New York Polo Grounds with Frank Sinatra, Jackie Gleason, and Toots Shor. The crowd is beneath them, begging for entertainment and its share in a day's triumph. 'All these people,' DeLillo writes, 'formed by language and climate and popular songs and breakfast foods . . . have never had anything in common so much as this, that they are sitting in the furrow of destruction.' And the shrill promise of destruction is whispered into Hoover's ear at the game: an aide comes with the news that the Russians have just tested their first atom bomb. The Director sees skeletons dancing about the field. You get the impression this is the news Hoover has waited for all his life. It means his time has been well spent, the Soviets are indeed a threat, and you can almost imagine him sleeping better at night for the realisation. 'It's not enough,' he reckons, 'to hate your enemy. you have to understand how the two of you bring each other to deep completion.'

Underworld is vastly episodic: locations change from part to part, and so does time, and point of view. But the alternations only add to our sense of how time plays out in the average mind, and they might offer a lesson in how memory lives its own life, coming and going, bringing new stuff in a new way every time. The central figure in the book is a fifty-seven-year-old called Nick Shay. He is from the Bronx, he once had an affair with the wife of his chemistry teacher, who is now an artist, and he goes off to see some sort of installation she has created in the desert. 'The past brings out our patriotism, you know?' she tells him. 'We want to feel an allegiance. It's the one undivided allegiance, to all those people and things.' Her name is Klara Sax. She is working in an area where America once tested its big bombs. She is famous. Nick and Klara, we might imagine, are the love interest, two more-or-less messed-up figures who once tried for love in a Cold War climate. Their love was deceitful and curious and a long time ago, yet it is a small moment of frozen urgency in both their lives. You get the feeling they know how their secret love happened to counterpoint a secret rage in the world around them. (They're intelligent that way.) But they might also represent something else. He works in Waste; she works in Art. They are both concerned about the machinations of Defense. DeLillo gives you the feeling that the intimacy shared by these people is not only gone from them, it has become impossible.

The work she is doing in the desert entails painting old B-52 bombers, and she is given to describing what she does in the following way:

> She said, 'See, we're painting, hand-painting in some cases, putting our puny hands to great weapons systems, to systems that came out of the factories and assembly halls as near alike as possible, millions of components stamped out, repeated endlessly, and we're trying to unrepeat, to find an element of felt life, and maybe there's a sort of survival instinct here, a graffiti instinct – to trespass and declare ourselves, show who we are.'

Klara is an amalgam of New York 60s conceptualist art types, the sort of artist who is into found objects and who makes statements about waste and recycling. Her art and her speech and her memory are very much of a time: they rely on overexcited juxtaposition. Some of this excitement is clearly DeLillo's own. She went to Truman Capote's Black & White Ball and knew she might have stood next to J. Edgar Hoover, and later we hear, from Hoover's point of view, that the anti-war protesters were gathered in force outside the Plaza. DeLillo, like all the most likable conspiracy theorists, is never one to miss a twist.

The Thomson home run is viewed as a moment of innocence, and all around it that day had gathered the portents of doom. And the baseball itself (or a notion of the actual ball) is what beats us back ceaselessly into the past of this novel. The ball disappears, and the boy who caught it and the father he gave it to become characters in this account of contemporary American time. In those days before instant replays, the strike and the home run could only be seen to happen once, and then the event became part of the memory of the crowd. It could only be reproduced in the clear imagination. This is what I mean by innocence: the Thomson homer just happened *once*. In the future, nothing big that happened in public would ever happen just once.

DeLillo's Cold War childhood – the Bronx of those days, the immigrant scene – might be thought to lie buried at the palpitating heart of *Underworld*. The image of the baseball might bring him all the way to the center of his childhood fevers. For Nick Shay, as for millions of American boys and girls, the unfolding détente imposed order on his early life, and the rules of survival, the threat of ruin, offered a structure for living in those years of 'duck and cover' under the school desk.

Nick's colleague Brian has a conversation in the book with a guy called Marvin, who is a dedicated collector of baseball memorabilia. He is more than just a collector, though; he speaks like a trailer-park wizard. He is a seeker of meaning in the people's century, and baseball, the everything of baseball, gives him his big way in.

Brian said, 'I went to a car show and it did something to me.'

'What did it do?'

'Cars from the nineteen-fifties. I don't know.'

'You feel sorry for yourself. You think you're missing something and you don't know what it is. You're lonely inside your life. You have a job and a family and a full executed will, already, at your age, because the whole idea is to die prepared, die legal, with all the papers signed. Die liquid, so they can convert to cash. You used to have the same dimensions as the observable universe. Now you're a lost speck. You look at old cars and you recall a purpose, a destination.'

'It's ridiculous, isn't it? But probably harmless too.'

'Nothing is harmless,' Marvin said. 'You're worried and scared. You see the cold war winding down. This makes it hard for you to breathe.'

Brian pushed through a turnstile from an old ballpark. It creaked sort of lovingly.

Without the dependable threat of the Bomb, Brian, and Nick too, is simply and individually 'the lost man of history'. Nick and Brian have a *fin de siècle* vibe about them. Each of them is packed with all the last-minute notions of the society to which they belong. They are waste experts. We have a fine sense of Shay's emotional sickness: he is full of dread and bad information. He knows that one of the most disastrous ironies of our age is that we may in the end use nuclear weapons for one purpose only – to help in the killing of nuclear waste.

Nick Shay is a man in pursuit of himself, a man who is no accidental American but someone charged with the ominous energies of the age, one who can feel history seeping through the walls of his every room. Despite all this appropriate darkness, *Underworld* contains some of the funniest of DeLillo's writing. Meet Jesse Detwiler, 'a fringe figure in the sixties, a garbage guerrilla who stole and analyzed the household trash of a number of famous people. He issued mock-comintern manifestos about the contents, with personal asides, and the underground press was quick to print this stuff. His activities had a crisp climax when he was arrested for snatching the garbage of J. Edgar Hoover from the rear of the director's house in North Washington.' In a manner we might recognise, Detwiler became sort of famous himself, 'part of a strolling band of tambourine girls and bomb makers, levitators and acid droppers and lost children'.

DeLillo grasps at the counterculture as a tale of America told by an idiot, full not only of sound and fury but also of a special kind of sense, and the kind of sense that would not go down well in a police state. They are a carnivalesque troupe who seek the higher truths, a generation who feel failed by their parents' cars and houses and TVs, and who set out to open up their minds and to run from brutality. The spirit of wrecked shamanism is everywhere evident in *Underworld* – Lenny Bruce appears now and then – and the common, mainstream love of baseball is contrasted with that 60s generation, who sought a new commonality, and who often looked for it in painting and rock music and films.

At one point in the book Klara Sax goes to see a new Eisenstein movie called *Unterwelt*. Long suppressed by the Soviets and the Germans, it is a portrait of strangely gray mutant figures scurrying around in some nether region, living in secret, fighting some powerful unknown quantity. From here DeLillo's narrative itself goes underground, and we find a world there of apocalyptic graffiti artists, young Americans on the verge of something big, fame or destruction. 'You can't tell the difference between a soup can and a car bomb,' thinks Nick's brother Matt, adrift in his own weirdness, 'because they are made by the same people in the same way and ultimately refer to the same thing.'

The book is a furious and gentle montage in itself, an exercise in the uncovering of power-fantasy. The author has long been a good traveller over the landscape of America's huge secrets. This time he went farther, went deeper: *Underworld* is a novel with a uniquely warm glow at its centre – the colour of a life's experience, the noble gleam of decent inquiry properly met. DeLillo unwinds some of the more dark and mysterious configurations at the heart of American life during the Cold War. He takes us toward an understanding of how popular culture, across the century, has played into our dreams and our yearnings and our deepest fears, and he makes newly explicit the ties that bind art and ruin.

TWO: *Falling Man*

Let us take an ordinary man from that terrible day. His name is Kevin Michael Cosgrove. If you put his name into Google it takes exactly 0.12 seconds to discover he was born on January 6, 1955. It takes no longer than it is taking you to read this sentence to discover Mr Cosgrove lived in West Islip, New York, and worked as Claims Vice President of the Aon Corporation, based on the 105th floor of the South Tower. From the Wikipedia encyclopedia, you will find that he is buried in St Patrick's Cemetery in Huntington. If you have another 10 seconds to spare, you will be able to click to an image of the South Tower moments before its collapse, and hear a recording of Mr Cosgrove speaking his last words to an operator. 'I got young kids,' he says. 'We're not ready to die.' 'Please hurry.' 'We're young men.' And at the building's collapse, he says 'Oh God.'

Dying in full public view has been a theme of Don DeLillo's since 9/11 was a nothing day in the average American calendar, a zone of post-vacation humdrum two days before the beginning of Ramadan and one week after Grandparents' Day. In *Libra*, we find the image of a king mown down in his Lincoln in broad daylight, his death fixed in the gaze of his courtiers and his subjects. It was a scene to play forever in the public mind, and the exact moment of impact, as filmed on an 8 mm home movie camera by Abraham Zapruder, is understood in that book to act like an eye from the future, a place where the very worst of our dreams could be downloaded in 0.12 seconds. In a relatively recent Introduction to *Libra*, DeLillo outlines something he calls 'Assassination Aura', giving a notion of how the events of history might come to find themselves in the weave of fiction. 'Some stories never end,' he writes. 'Even in our time, in the sightlines of living history, in the retrieved instancy of film and videotape, there are stories waiting to be finished, open to the thrust of reasoned analysis and haunted speculation. These stories, some of them, also undergo a kind of condensation, seeping into the texture of everyday life, barely separable from the ten thousand little excitations that define a routine day of visual and aural static processed by the case-hardened consumer brain.'

It is the conjunction of visual technology and terrorism that really sets DeLillo's mentality apart – a setting apart which also put him on the road to having 9/11 as his subject long before it happened. *Players* features Pammy and Lyle, a Wall Street couple who get tangled up with a bunch of terrorists. (When DeLillo was writing that novel, a nine-year-old boy called Mohamed Atta was studying English in the bedroom of his parents' house in Giza outside Cairo.) That novel begins with a group of people on a plane watching an in-flight movie about a terrorist operation. It then moves to a scene inside the World Trade Center in which two women stand by the elevators and discuss their fear of being 'torn asunder'. Pammy works in the North Tower for a company called Grief Management ('Where else would you stack all this grief?'). She feels that 'the towers didn't seem permanent. They remained concepts, no less transient for all their bulk than some routine distortion of light.' And later on, when a group of friends are having a drink on the roof of their building and looking across at the WTC, someone remarks, 'That plane looks like it's going to hit.'

Many of DeLillo's novels are propelled by an acute sense of communal dread – of crowds, of surveillance, of the desperate 'creativity' of the terrorist, of an 'airborne toxic event' – and long before living history affirmed a number of his paranoid presumptions, his novels were making the case for America as a place where nothing very much was reliably innocent or safe. Here's Jack Gladney in *White Noise*, head of Hitler studies at the College-on-the-Hill:

> The discussion moved to plots in general. I found myself saying to the assembled heads, 'All plots tend to move deathward. This is the nature of plots. Political plots, terrorist plots, lovers' plots, narrative

plots, plots that are part of children's games. We edge nearer death every time we plot. It is like a contract that all must sign, the plotters as well as those who are the targets of the plot.'

Later, we find Gladney trying to have a conversation with one of his colleagues, Alfonse Stompanato, chairman of the department of American environments. DeLillo wrote those lines in the year Mohamed Atta turned fifteen – though at that time Atta may have called himself Mohamed El Sayed and his telegenic flight into the World Trade Center was half a life away.

'Why is it, Alfonse, that decent, well-meaning and responsible people find themselves intrigued by catastrophe when they see it on television?'

I told him about the recent evening of lava, mud and raging water that the children and I had found so entertaining.

'We wanted more, more.'

'It's natural, it's normal,' he said, with a reassuring nod. 'It happens to everybody.'

'Why?'

'Because we're suffering from brain fade. We need an occasional catastrophe to break up the incessant bombardment of information ... The cameras are right there. They're standing by. Nothing terrible escapes their scrutiny.'

'You're saying it's more or less universal, to be fascinated by TV disasters?'

'For most people there are only two places in the world. Where they live and their TV set. If a thing happens on television, we have every right to find it fascinating, whatever it is.'

'I don't know whether to feel good or bad about learning that my experience is widely shared.'

'Feel bad,' he said.

That was a key flavour in DeLillo's earlier work, that we were all waiting for something terrible to happen, something that might blow us apart but which might also bring us together. It might be shopping or marketing. It might be a toxic gas in the subway. But likely it would be something that partook of the energies of each of these things: American capitalism and the toxic waste residing at the other end of it. In 1997, when the novelist wrote the following wonderful passage in *Underworld*, Mohamed Atta was living in Germany and had just been recruited by Al Qaeda. As mentioned before, *Underworld*'s Brian Glassic works at Waste Containment, and he is standing next to a mountain of trash at the Fresh Kills landfill site on Staten Island:

> He imagined he was watching the construction of the Great Pyramid at Giza – only this was twenty-five times bigger, with tanker trucks spraying perfumed water on the approach roads. He found the sight inspiring. All this ingenuity and labor, this delicate effort to fit maximum waste into diminishing space. The towers of the World Trade Center were visible in the distance and he sensed a poetic balance between that idea and this one . . . He looked at all that soaring garbage and knew for the first time what his job was all about . . . He dealt in human behavior, people's habits and impulses, their uncontrollable needs and innocent wishes, maybe their passions, certainly their excesses and indulgences but their kindness too, their generosity, and the question was how to keep this mass metabolism from overwhelming us.

Don DeLillo is a writer who has become less funny as he gets older, perhaps more serious as he moves towards the presentation of his darker purpose. Not that he was ever *light*, mind you. In any event, it is part of his genius to have truly engaged with the discomfiting strangeness of our times, and by the time he published *The Body Artist*, in 2001, DeLillo's writing had entered a style of passionate numbness. The prose was cautious and drained and none of it seemed funny any more. Meanwhile, Mohamed Atta, the man of many aliases, had developed a hatred of American habits that bordered on the messianic. As DeLillo pressed the keys (and returned the carriage) to create the following passage, Atta was on American soil and in daily contact with his fellow conspirators whilst training on flight simulators at a rented house in Florida:

> His future is not under construction. It is already there, susceptible to entry.

She had it on tape.

She did not want to believe this was the case. It was her future too. It is her future too.

She played the tape a dozen times.

It means your life and death are set in place, just waiting for you to keep the appointments.

All these passages, written over the course of a career, could be understood to evoke something very like a terrorist's trajectory towards an encounter with the Twin Towers, but they also describe very well the journey made by a singular American novelist towards what might be considered the day of days for his preoccupations as an artist and his brio as a stylist. If the Twin Towers could be said to have stood in wait for the Mohamed Attas of the world, then the Mohamed Attas of the world were standing in wait for Don DeLillo. To have something to be your subject before it happens is not unprecedented in the world of literature – consider Kafka and the Nazis, Scott Fitzgerald and the Jazz Age – but the meeting of 9/11 and Don DeLillo is not so very much a conjunction as a point of arrival, and a connection so powerful in imaginative terms that it instantly blows DeLillo's lamps out.

'In a repressive society,' the novelist said in an interview published around the time of *Mao II*, 'a writer can be deeply influential, but in a society that's filled with glut and repetition and endless consumption, the act of terror may be the only meaningful act ... people who are powerless make an open theatre of violence. True terror is a language and a vision. There is a deep narrative structure to terrorist acts and they infiltrate and alter consciousness in ways that writers used to aspire to.'

And so it feels like something of a consummation when a person called Mohamed Mohamed el-Amir el-sayed Atta appears on page 80 of DeLillo's latest novel, *Falling Man*. The novelist seems to recognise Atta's impulses as if they were old friends: 'This was Amir,' he writes, 'his mind was in the upper skies, making sense of things, drawing things together.' But Atta has little narrative reality in DeLillo's book. He is the ghost in the machine, flying so fast he is barely separable from the surrounding ether, and the reader indeed will find himself knowing Atta only as a distinguished absence, present everywhere but visible nowhere, like Flaubert's idea of the perfect novelist.

The other main character in *Falling Man* is a youngish lawyer called Keith Neudecker, whom we meet at the book's opening as he walks north in lower Manhattan on the morning of 11 September 2001, his face covered in ash and blood and his hair full of glass splinters. He carries somebody else's briefcase and for reasons he might never fathom he heads directly from the rubble of Ground Zero to the apartment of his estranged wife Lianne and their son Justin. Keith and Lianne had been together for eight years before 'the eventual extended grimness called their marriage' ended in a well-educated state of suspended resignation. Lianne's mother, Nina Bartos, is an aged, recently retired professor – 'the So-and-So Professor of Such-and-Such,' says Keith, in a burst of the old DeLillo humour – and she has a lover called Martin. The women scrutinise each other as mothers and daughters often do, harbouring special, harsh feelings about the other's motivations and choices. To Nina, Lianne only married Keith to feel dangerously alive, but Lianne knows her mother would forgive Keith all his faults if he happened to be a raging artist.

The child Justin has two friends whom they call the Siblings and they live ten blocks away. The children talk in code and they are always standing at the window of the Siblings' apartment, looking at the sky through binoculars and whispering about a man called 'Bill Lawton'. Like children in a science fiction movie, the Siblings and Justin seem connected in some unspoken way to a much bigger picture, but we don't really get to hear a great deal from the children. (DeLillo is not good on children; they always exist as runes foretelling the bad weather of adulthood, and *Falling Man* is, to say the least, a book in pursuit of adult vexations on an international scale.) Keith survives the planes owing to a piece of luck, so he spends much of the novel embroiled in poker, the game that is a dramatisation of luck. Before the planes, he used to play it on Wednesdays with six men at his apartment: 'the one anticipation,' DeLillo writes, 'that was not marked by the bloodguilt tracings of severed connections.' The poker evenings ended when the towers came down, but he thinks about the game a lot. He is interested in the meaning of luck and we find in time that he is also a cheat, whatever that means. In the course of the novel he goes to see another survivor, Florence Givens, the owner of the briefcase he took from the North Tower; he visits her more than once, and he goes to look at his old, frozen apartment, the one he took up when he split up with his wife. Apart from this, there is only recovery, if that is what you'd call it. Keith does a little homework duty with his son and walks the boy to school, 'going slow, easing inward ... drifting into spells of reflection'.

Lianne is doing some work for a university press, editing a book about ancient alphabets. Her hobby survives the attacks: it involves conducting 'storyline sessions' in East Harlem, which take place in the company of half a dozen or so people with Alzheimer's. Apart from some calmness it perhaps brings to her – and aside from some kind of Manhattan mid-life ennui – it is not clear why Lianne spends so much time with these forgetful narrative-makers in East Harlem. They write about the planes. We also know that Jack, her father, had the beginning of senile dementia; not able to face it, he killed himself with a sporting rifle. Lianne is therefore a victim of violence, with a mother now messing around with an art dealer. Though DeLillo keeps it pretty spare, we feel we understand Lianne as one of his types. At some level she is surrounded by death – even her husband, when finally he comes home, walks in from the most famous American death-trap in history – and she is ripe for some kind of urban epiphany to set her heart in motion. The closest she comes is to see a performance artist known as Falling Man – he dangles upside down from a structure in Pershing Square, reminding people of the jumpers who chose air over fire on 9/11. 'It held the gaze of the world, she thought. There was the awful openness of it, something we'd not seen, the single falling figure that trails a collective dread, body come down among us all. And now, she thought, this little theater piece, disturbing enough to stop traffic.'

Don DeLillo has always been very good at male dissociation, especially the kind that can thrive in certain domestic environments, and he can be as good as Saul Bellow when it comes to showing the way married couples might go about dismantling one another's powers and confidence. On this occasion, he treats Keith like a male archetype. 'This was the period, not long before the separation,' he writes, 'when he took the simplest question as a form of hostile interrogation. He seemed to walk in the door waiting for her questions . . . she understood by this time that it wasn't the drinking, or not that alone, and probably not some sport with a woman. He'd hide it better, she told herself. It was who he was, his native face, without the leveling element, the claims of social code. Those nights, sometimes, he seemed on the verge of saying something, a sentence fragment, that was all, and it would end everything between them, all discourse, every form of stated arrangement, whatever drifts of love still lingered.' These descriptions are the best things in the book: they have the force of felt life, and through them we begin purely to understand what estrangement really means with this Manhattan couple. They each have known a little hate. But how can they relate to each other now that hatred means something else, now that it means flying planes into buildings? How are their own feelings changed now that hatred means terrorists and victims shouting in their final moments to different gods?

Yet such enquiries, however acute, however felt, cannot make

up for DeLillo's failure in *Falling Man* to imagine 9/11. The
hallmark of those novelists who have tried to write about the
attacks is a sort of austere plangency – or a quivering bathos –
that has been in evidence almost from the moment the planes
hit. Those authors who published journalism immediately after
the event failed to see how their metaphors fell dead from their
mouths before the astonishing pictures on television. It did not
help us to be told by imaginative writers that the second plane
was like someone posting an envelope. No, it wasn't. It was like
a passenger jet crashing into an office block. It gave us nothing
to be told that the South Tower came down like an elevator at
speed. No, it didn't. It collapsed like a building that could no
longer hold itself up. Metaphor failed that day to do anything
but make one feel that those struggling to deploy it had not
been watching enough television. After the 'non-fiction novel',
after New Journalism, after several decades in which some of
America's most vivid writing was seen to be in thrall to the
techniques of novelists, September 11 offered a few hours when
American novelists could only sit at home while journalism
taught them fierce lessons in multivocality, point of view, the
structure of plot, interior monologue, the pressure of history,
the force of silence, and the uncanny. Actuality showed its own
naked art that day.

DeLillo the novelist prepared us for 9/11, but he did not pre-
pare himself for how such an episode might, in the way of de-
nouements, instantly fly beyond the reach of his own powers.
In a moment, the reality of the occasion seems to have desic-
cated the ripeness of his style, and he truly flounders in this
book to say anything that doesn't sound in a small way like a
warning that comes too late. Reading *Falling Man*, one feels that
9/11 is an event that is suddenly far ahead of him, far beyond
what he knows, and so an air of tentative rehearsal resounds in
an empty hall. What is a prophet once his fiery word becomes
deed? What does he have to say? What is left of the paranoid

style when all its suspicions come true? Of course, a first-rate literary intelligence can eventually meet a world where reality acknowledges the properties of his style by turning them into parody, and in these circumstances, which are DeLillo's with this particular novel, the original novelist may be said to be a person quietened by his own genius. This is another American story – the story of Ernest Hemingway and Orson Welles – and it gives us a clue to the weakness of *Falling Man*.

But the novel itself is packed with clues, the first and most obvious being the author's inability to conjure his usual exciting prose. In his best novels, DeLillo is pretty much incapable of writing unexcitingly – but 9/11 busts his sentences before he can make them linger. Good prose in a novel depends on its ability to exhale a secret knowledge, to have the exact weight of magic in relation to the material, the true moral rhythm. DeLillo had all of that before 11 September – so much magic, indeed, that it was initially difficult to absorb the events of that day without thinking of his writing. On 11 September, however, novelists of his sort ceded all secret knowledge to the four winds: to CNN, to the website of the *New York Times*, to CCTV, and to the widespread availability of video cameras in Manhattan, each of which captured the event in real time.

Reading *Falling Man*, one often feels that DeLillo's formerly superlative intuition has become a form of ignorance: he dangles uncertainly between what he knows of that day from pictures and what of it he predicted in his novels. But the latest book is merely blank with shock, as if his sense of awe and disbelief may only express itself in a fetish with the obvious:

> She was awake, middle of the night, eyes closed, mind running, and she felt time pressing in, and threat, a kind of beat in her head.
>
> She read everything they wrote about the attacks.
>
> She thought of her father. She saw him coming down an escalator, in an airport maybe.
>
> Keith stopped shaving for a time, whatever that means. Everything

seemed to mean something. Their lives were in transition and she
looked for signs. Even when she was barely aware of an incident it
came to mind later, with meaning attached, in sleepless episodes that
lasted minutes or hours, she wasn't sure . . .

But things were ordinary as well. They were ordinary in all the ways
they were always ordinary.

This most assuredly is not the DeLillo of *Libra* or *Underworld*.
In the first of those novels, the author enacted wonders the
Warren Commission could never have imagined. He had readers in the corner of that room at the Book Depository, practically squeezing the trigger with Oswald. But *Falling Man* is a
distillation of awe and grief over real-life drama next to which
the 9/11 Commission Report reads serenely and beautifully.
Open that report at any page and you will find a breathtaking
second-by-second account of that morning, and of the hijackers' backgrounds, that will make DeLillo's novel seem merely
incapacitated.

DeLillo might know the nature of his trouble. He might see
it. At one point, we hear of a book written by someone called
the Unaflyer that predicted all the events: 'A book that's so
enormously immersed, going back on it, leading up to it . . . it
seems to predict what happened . . . It's badly written.' People
still speak of the anxiety of influence, but what of a novelist's
anxiety about his past work's influence on himself? *Falling Man*,
it seems to me, is about a brilliant writer's free-falling anxiety
of that sort, and most of it comes to be expressed in this novel
through ruminations on art and terror. This is old DeLillo stuff:
we've already met Klara Sax from *Underworld*, the lady who
once studied the Twin Towers as they were being built, later to
find fame as an artist who paints B52 bombers, the kind that
once carried nuclear weapons. She displays these *objets d'art* in
the desert with their innards ripped out and their shells coated
in beautiful colour. ('This is an art object,' she says, 'not a peace
project. This is a landscape painting in which we use the land-

scape itself.') Later in that novel, we discover that Klara and her contemporaries had been fascinated by the nearness of art to violence, hooked on a near-invisible graffiti kid called Moon-man 157 who paints subway trains. DeLillo has always favoured using the art world as a place where cultural anxieties are made compact and fashionable, but his repeat of this ploy in *Falling Man* pushes the book towards silliness.

Keith's mother-in-law has a boyfriend called Martin. He is an art dealer – apartment in Berlin, liking for the unreadable – whom we learn was once a member of a 1960s anti-fascist collective called Kommune One. Martin, it seems, was a kind of terrorist, living with people whose faces would one day end up on posters. 'We're all sick of America and Americans,' he says at one point. 'The subject nauseates us.' But Martin is a nullity: who could care about him and his little European pieties on the state of the world and the mysteries of art? Is he a terrorist? Who cares, he's a goon. Meanwhile, people are holding hands and jumping from the 102nd floor of the North Tower, the nov-elist's imagination nowhere in attendance. When Martin speaks we sometimes imagine he could be speaking for DeLillo. 'Noth-ing seems exaggerated any more,' he says. 'Nothing amazes me.' In this book, the events aren't enough, or they are too much, which amounts to the same thing for a novelist. There appear to be few novelists in America now who could bring us to know what might have been going through the minds of those people as they fell from the building – or going through the minds of the hijackers as they met their targets – but there is no short-age of those who would do what DeLillo does, and show us an anxious, educated woman watching a performance artist hang-ing upside down from a metal beam in Pershing square. It is a form of intellectual escapism. The oddity of the art world can easily be made to stand in for the profundity of life and death, but none of us who lived through the morning of 11 September 2001 could easily believe that the antics of a performance artist, no matter how uncanny, would suffice to denote the scale and depth of our encounter with dread. The Falling Man, the artist, can do no better than constitute some figurative account of the author himself, suspended in freefall, frozen in time, subject both to the threat of gravity and the indwelling disbelief of the spectators below.

3 J. M. Coetzee, *Disgrace*

TESSA HADLEY

When *Disgrace* came out in 1999 it made a stir outside the circle of those who already knew and admired Coetzee's work. For a while it was urgently talked about, recommended, lent around; passed from hand to hand, mind to mind, it left its trace of a thrill of excitement, disturbance, even danger, whether readers loved or hated it. In itself, that's nothing very remarkable, plenty of novels have their day in the sun, not all of them endure. But it's a curiosity for this vogueishness to befall a novelist so determinedly difficult, so uncompromising in not courting the popular kind of success. Coetzee had won amply, by this time, the passionate appreciation of an initiated readership (and, for that matter, prizes too: this was to be his second Booker, his Nobel was to come in 2003). *Disgrace,* though, seemed to mark a point in his *oeuvre* when his own pressing preoccupations intersected with a public mood, here in the UK at least (at home in South Africa its reception was more troubled). Something naked in the expression and the material of this novel cuts through all its complexities, reaches out of them to command attention.

It isn't cheapening that success to suggest that part of what commands attention is the novel's theme, announced in its first sentence: 'For a man of his age, fifty-two, divorced, he has, to his mind, solved the problem of sex rather well.' The sex by itself wouldn't detain us, these days: in that opening what's intriguing is the unvarnished statement, its tone not yet wholly decipherable, not mystification but not quite dirty joke either, though it's bleak with the irony that promises humiliations to come.

The story of the whole novel, unfolded in just this spirit of forensic, painful precision, is of a man caught in the crisis of his
transition from youth into age, agonised by the oncoming loss
of his gift of sexual attraction which has been his way of relat-
ing to the world. He has to re-make himself as best he can in the
light of that change: a light Coetzee holds up unflinchingly in
a dark place. David Lurie when we first meet him is an English
teacher at a university in Cape Town, passionate about Wordsworth, Byron, Faust, and formed in a tradition of Europeanised
high intellectualism; he has mostly to teach Communications
Skills. Outside his work, he seems chronically unsocialised,
unsociable: his two marriages have failed, there are no friends
who figure, his relations with his colleagues are cool at best, his
only strong attachment is to his daughter Lucy. Making love to
women – and the elusive signification of the word 'love' in that
context is part of what the novel explores – has been the adventure, the life-source, the joy, of this difficult man otherwise
locked away inside his defended privacy, inside his values which
may, he is sometimes afraid, have no point of contact with the
Africa outside his mind. Is joy over, now that he's fifty-two?

Inside the language of the novel, the value of the erotic is
continually asserted and continually ironised, without any resolution being offered between these two ways of seeing it. Lurie
has a brief affair with one of his students, a beautiful girl called
Melanie Isaacs; he calls it an 'affair', although, as with all the
value-words in this writing, we're made uneasily aware that 'affair' doesn't quite fit what it tries to describe, to circumscribe.
It's quite clear, Lurie knows perfectly well, that Melanie is only
ever half consenting, certainly doesn't return the strength of
his feelings. She 'intoxicates' him; he's 'astonished by the feeling
she evokes'; this very power of his response, he thinks, must
in some sense authorise his desire, make it a truth that ought
to be served: mustn't it? 'Strange love! yet from the quiver of
Aphrodite, goddess of the foaming waves, no doubt about that'.

Lurie more than once suggests it's sinful to ignore the authority of sex desire; he quotes from Blake ('sooner murder an infant in its cradle than nurse unacted desires'). The affair is what precipitates in the external world the 'disgrace' of the novel's title (although the idea of disgrace drags ever deeper as the novel develops): Lurie is brought in front of a tribunal of his peers and, refusing to go through the forms of apology they demand of him, loses his job. (He says, exasperating them, 'I was not myself. I was no longer a fifty-year-old divorcé at a loose end. I was a servant of Eros.')

It would have been possible to write a novel in which the actual experience of the 'affair' was vindicated against some diminished account of it given afterwards to a tribunal in thrall to a narrowly conceived correctness, but Coetzee hasn't done that. Leaving Melanie's flat, Lurie knows it was 'not rape, not quite that, but undesired nevertheless, undesired to the core'; he imagines her washing to cleanse herself of him. Yet the novel doesn't allow us either to dismiss the importance Lurie claims for his desire. It erupts into the writing as passionate language, transfiguring the grey prose of a diminished daily existence into poetry ('a last leap of the flame of sense before it goes out'), invoking the great archetypes that haunt his imagination: Aphrodite, Eros, Shakespeare's sonnets, Byron. The 'true value' of what went on between Lurie and the girl is held in the novel between possible readings, it remains equivocal. In the light of the rape that comes later, at the heart of the novel (Lucy, Lurie's daughter, is raped by intruders), the equivocation becomes even more uncomfortable; we aren't allowed to elide the two events – one act born out of 'love', one out of 'hate' – but we are scrupulously reminded of their resemblance to one another.

Love-making is sublime or grotesque, depending on how you look, where you look from: and perhaps what's splendid in youth becomes grotesque in the same man in his fifties, following the same impulse (at what point exactly, then, do the gods

withdraw their sanction from desire?). Lurie's ex-wife Rosalind
thinks it does: 'Am I allowed to tell you how stupid it looks?', she
says about the trouble he's got into with Melanie. 'Do you think
she finds it good to watch you in the middle of your ... ? ... You
are too old to be meddling with other people's children.' Much
later, watching Melanie in a play, Lurie has an epiphanic vision
of all the women he's made love to: they form in his mind for a
few moments an almost mystical company, and seem to constitute the most meaningful, transfiguring, contact he's ever had
with other lives. He risks again, to himself, a way of describing
these relationships that had at the time of his scandal been de-
rided in the newspapers: he imagines that 'by each of them he
was enriched'. The old-fashioned formality of the word is essential: again, at this point, there's that audacious change in the
register of Lurie's language, towards the archetypal, almost the
Petrarchan: 'like a flower blooming in his breast, his heart floods
with thankfulness'. His consoling vision, however, is cut short
when he's hissed at the next moment, and pelted with screwed
up bits of paper, by Melanie's lover (all we need to know about
him is that he's young, arrogant, aggressive – the perfunctorily
given goatee, leather jacket, earring, stand for these). He embar-
rasses Lurie, forces him to get up and leave the theatre; Lurie's
consoling memory becomes in a different perspective only his
absurdity, his comic predicament ('Find yourself another life,
prof, believe me.'). Driving home from the theatre, shaken, Lurie stops and buys the services of a young prostitute, 'younger
even than Melanie', who's too drunk or high even to be aware
properly who he is or what she's doing. So much for enrich-
ment (the word flips over into meaning some exchange quite
other, brutally transactional).

One of the ways in which the novel startles and grips readers is in these exposing explorations of a male erotic ideal (it's
almost Updike territory, although it would be hard to think of
any writer temperamentally and stylistically less like Updike).

The Byron-figure is strongly significant in Lurie's imagination. Lucy teases him for what she calls his determination to be
'mad bad and dangerous to know'; he is absorbed by the idea of
Byron in Italy, involved in the last love affair with Teresa Guiccioli, writing valedictory poems (in his mid thirties!) on the
end of his sensual life, his life as a lover of women, and dreaming of a heroic death in Greece. 'My days are in the yellow leaf; /
The flowers and fruits of Love are gone; / The worm, the canker,
and the grief / Are mine alone!' Unmistakeably there's a connection between this Byronic language with its spare symbol-
ising signification, only weakly denoting 'real' things, and the
way Lurie's language intensifies, in relation to the erotic subject,
opening up onto heavily laden signs – flower, fruit, flame, dove,
breast, ravishment – out of the precisely specifying realism that
is a more usual register in the novel (they eat, he and Melanie,
'anchovies on tagliatelle with a mushroom sauce', they talk of
her 'career plans' in stagecraft and design). Lurie wants to write
something about Byron, but not the kind of critical writing
he has done before, in his life as an academic. Characteristically quixotically, he chooses to work out his obsession as an
opera, which he knows almost before he begins will never be
performed, can't operate in any public context as a redemption from his disgrace, or recovery of his cultural authority. The
idea of the opera, which he first conceives of as describing the
lovers trapped poignantly together in Teresa's husband's house,
evolves into something more absurd and strange, in relation to
Lurie's developing awareness of his own absurd position. The
middle-aged Teresa, fat and wheezy, nursing her sick father,
yearns for her dead lover, who is reluctant to be dragged back
from his non-being among the shades. Her laments are to be
accompanied on a child's toy mandolin.

Byron in the novel stands archetypally for that theme recurrent in European culture from the troubadours onwards: the
male realising himself through sexual adventure and pleas-

ure. In this tradition the female is the love object, transfigured through a male fantasising poetic language (for as long as she's in favour, unattained, or at least not tired of) into transcendent beauty. *Disgrace* in some sense tests out this old tradition in a new world. Modernity has seen through the machinery of that erotic ideal to its predication upon female subordination, its dependence on a male connoisseurship prone to disallowing any separate female centre of subjectivity. Might we nonetheless, in repudiating the ideal, have too carelessly discounted forms of imagining which were worth keeping open? Wasn't that tradition, on reconsideration, one way after all of doing honour to women? Or, if not that, then perhaps its forms offered at least intensifications of experience; without those forms, perhaps the language in which we imagine love and sex runs the risk of losing its power to move us and change us out of ourselves, becoming blandly functional and banal. Coetzee does not innocently make Lurie think – for instance – that 'he does not like women who make no effort to be attractive', or 'sapphic love: an excuse for putting on weight': he knows (and Lurie knows too) that such thoughts are problematic for a liberal modernity. It's not that in the new world male desire has been made meekly obedient, or safe (Lucy's rape, at the extreme, is clear enough evidence to the contrary); it's only that in liberal discourse the male pursuit has become something to dissimulate or apologise for. Defiantly, knowing himself out of joint with the times, Lurie insists upon it; the novel through his insistence tests out the ideal, in its poetry and its absurdity. The idea of testing, of a way of thinking or a man being tested, comes up more than once: when the intruders break in on Lucy's farm Lurie thinks 'so it has come, the day of testing'. Postponing sitting down to begin his opera, he dreads 'the moment when he must face the blank page, strike the first note, see what he is worth'.

Lurie, setting himself these tests, in some sense always fails them. '*Out of the poets I learned to love,*' his Byron sings, '*but*

life, I found, is another story.' It might be possible to read Lurie
as tragic-heroic mind-adventurer, a man born too late, struggling to keep the old cultural values alive in a fallen world; but
this version of the story would be open to a hostile scepticism,
impatient with the difficulties he brings down on himself, his
social ineptitude, his inability to relax, unwind, join in. Who is
he, to pronounce on modernity, on Africa, whose only efforts
to reach out and establish contact with it are these fumblings
with an unwilling girl? A more nuanced and more interesting
reading of the Lurie persona is possible if we imagine the author's attittude towards his character in *Disgrace* as belonging
in a continuum in Coetzee's *oeuvre* with *Boyhood,* whose publication precedes it, and *Youth,* which comes straight afterwards.
Both these other books read as more or less autobiographical
(although the use throughout of the third person 'he' for the
protagonist holds us off from making that identification too
straightforwardly); *Disgrace* certainly isn't that, we presume
that none of the events of the story in any ordinary sense 'belong' to Coetzee's own life. But the voice that Coetzee found
for telling his story in *Boyhood* feels continuous with the narration of *Disgrace:* its stark sequence of events, its continuous
sceptical interrogations, its thin and mostly uncomfortable
representation of social interaction, its beautiful private flights
of imagination. The adult predicament described in *Disgrace*
could, imaginably even if not 'really', have its origins in the early
experiences and the temperament defined in those other books.
The tone of Coetzee's treatment of the boy and the young man
can help us toward a reading of Lurie in *Disgrace* which doesn't
have to be entirely earnest about his seriousness; which watches
him from an ironising, comical, distance.

Lurie in the opening pages of *Disgrace* thinks about temperament at length. 'That is his temperament. His temperament is
not going to change, he is too old for that. His temperament
is fixed, set. The skull, followed by the temperament: the two

hardest parts of the body.' To some extent the novel sets about dissolving Lurie's certainty: elements of what he takes at the beginning to be his temperament – the mocking urbanity; the immunity he imagines for his privacy – will crumble under the assault of events and humiliations, the testing of his disgrace. But a persisting truth of temperament is also something the novel asserts, implicitly against a more optimistic view of character as open to renovation and rehabilitation. Lurie often experiments with self-definition, as a form of self-knowledge: 'Even when I burn I don't sing,' he says. 'He thinks of himself as obscure and growing obscurer. A figure from the margins of history.' The word temperament might even be included among the rather old-fashioned terminology – beauty, soul, heart, disgrace – which it is part of the novel's quest to recuperate, or at least to try out for possible recuperation. What the reader has to judge is what distance there is between Lurie's temperament – difficult, bookish, furiously intelligent, passionately imaginative, serious, clumsy in intimacy, suspicious, easily hostile – and the author's own. Is this temperament something Coetzee simply unknowingly inhabits; or is this third person subjective narrative radically unreliable, so that we are meant to read around it, ironising its take on things?

This is where the narrative positioning of the more autobiographical books helps out. In them, the reiterative 'he' that begins so many of the sentences draws attention to itself, it's insistent beyond the usual invisibility of the third person, almost suggesting the fixed forensic scrutiny of a surveillance report, the spy sticking to his subject, reporting every twist and turn of action, awareness, conscience, writing always in the present tense. The see-er who notates perches at a very precise small distance from the do-er who performs: almost, but crucially not quite, as near as makes no difference. The see-er sits on the do-er's shoulder; or observes, notebook in hand, inside his mind. This gives these two autobiographical books their odd fine distinctive comedy:

the adult mind notates the inner life of the boy who is but is not him. The boy's peculiarity is available to the adult, he can scrutinise it, but he can't be irresponsibly completely free of it, he has to claim it, own up to it. Or he watches the 'youth' at large in London, profoundly lonely, cooking fish fingers in his bedsit, dreaming of impossible women imagined out of novels, painfully incapable of expressing to any of the real girls he persuades into his bed the pent-up longing he has been storing against their arrival. It's not a comedy in which the narrative securely, comfortably, knows better than the protagonist, or only laughs at him; it's isn't an option not to engage with these protagonists as significant agents. In the writing, they are co-extensive with the world, they are our only way into seeing it; but this doesn't mean that what they are isn't consciously included in what we're made able to see. Temperament is both a given, a perspective the author can't help – it's how he is – and something the author is separately able to get behind, achieve a perspective on. He can't help being himself, but he is also able to define and represent himself; and in fact that effort of self-transcendence, that move a small distance apart from the acting self, is crucial to any attempt at self-knowledge. In an important critical essay on Tolstoy, Rousseau and Dostoevsky, Coetzee has shown himself deeply interested in the problem of self-knowledge in writing: 'how to know the truth about the self without being self-deceived'.[1] He responds in particular to the layerings of acting and consciousness and consciousness-of-acting in Dostoevsky. Perhaps it is partly in response to the problem of inauthenticity-in-confession that he sets out in that essay, that Coetzee has evolved the third-person-at-one-remove sceptical scrutiny that serves his effort to write the truth in *Boyhood* and *Youth* (the titles must derive from Tolstoy's autobiographical writing).

In *Disgrace*, obviously, the relation between the author and the protagonist doesn't have the same ostensible frame as in

It isn't only in the dramatised responses of the other characters that the narrative preserves its crucial sceptical distance
from Lurie, transcends the given of his temperament; the scepticism is also there in how Lurie presents himself, so to speak,
to his own awareness. Progressively his initial position, inside
the self-contained tidy life of a man who 'thought he had solved
the problem of sex rather well', is eroded; he's forced into a hu-
miliating limelight, exposed even to the flashing cameras of
the press, to having his private, subtly chosen vocabulary for
his own discriminations (the women 'enriched' his life) stolen
and blurted in grotesque headlines. When the crucial second
disaster of the novel unrolls – he and Lucy are attacked in her
farmhouse – he is helpless to save her or even to try to fight the
intruders off; they lock him in the lavatory, like the old maids in
the song (he makes the comparison himself). After the attack,
he has to go around with his head in an absurd white bandage which he calls his skull-cap, because the attackers poured
petrol over him and set light to it. Something in Lurie – something one might not have suspected in the secretive, superior
man of the beginning of the novel – embraces the emblems
of his humiliation. He seems almost to relish how his bandage
makes him ridiculous, makes him a clown; how it undercuts
whatever comments he delivers, makes his utmost seriousness
somehow helplessly comical: all this paralleled by the crisis in
his sexual life, where without warning the eros he has counted
on has transformed into farce. Everything conspires – the novel
conspires – to take the authority and dignity of the man to bits:
this is the disgrace of the title. He lives out in a sense the role of
the holy fool (again, reminding us of the Dostoevsky who matters to Coetzee so much): adrift, wise and absurd inseparably,
making difficulties for others, unsettling them not from a position of imperturbable truth, but out of instability, because his
frame of interpretation can't be made to fit the reality he moves
through. The scene where Lurie kneels to ask forgiveness of

Melanie's embarrassed mother is particularly, uncomfortably, Dostoevskian: we can't know whether to admire the gesture or be appalled by it.

While he's staying with Lucy in the Eastern Cape, Lurie's house in Cape Town is broken into, his books at the university are packed away in boxes by his successor: there's no place for him in his old life any more, its categories and habits have closed against him. He moves to rented rooms in Grahamstown to be near Lucy, who is pregnant, carrying the baby of one of the men who raped her; he spends his days at Bev Shaw's veterinary surgery, helping her put unwanted animals to sleep, or working on the opera that will never be performed. Characteristically Coetzee makes it impossible to read any grandly resonant redemptive schema into this new, reduced life of Lurie's; its accommodations are minimal and provisional. It is impossible for him to romanticise, writing his opera in Bev's yard, his 'nest of sorts', where little boys peer over the wall, seeing 'a mad old man who sits among the dogs singing to himself'. He knows he could never explain to them, 'or to their parents, to D Village, what Teresa and her lover have done to deserve being brought back to this world'. In his subject, 'it is not the erotic that is calling to him after all, nor the elegiac, but the comic'. Teresa suffers from her time of the month, she plays her mandolin: '*plink-plunk,* squawks the banjo in the desolate yard in Africa'. Again, there's something almost triumphant in how Lurie situates himself at the position of maximum absurdity, refusing either to deceive himself over the value of the work he's doing, or to give it up. Sex with plain Bev on the surgery floor is a comic counterpoint to the passion and rapturous agonies he suffered over Melanie; he resigns himself to it, and then, after a while, to no sex at all.

After he and Bev have put the animals to sleep, Lurie takes it upon himself to see that their corpses are disposed of with dignity at the hospital incinerator (the men who work there break their rigid limbs with shovels to make them fit). He knows that the idea of dignity is absurd, in such a context, and that what he does makes no difference to anyone, least of all the dead dogs; but he persists in the absurdity (as with the opera) because it's a sort of minimum rehearsal of what he is, of what's left, after the succession of his humiliations and unravellings. He does it, he thinks, 'for his idea of the world, a world in which men do not use shovels to beat corpses into a more convenient shape for processing'; although, in the novel's perpetual restless movement through assertion into doubt, by the end of the page the confidence of that has resolved into his merely saving the honour of corpses 'because there is no one else stupid enough to do it'. That diminished restatement doesn't slyly nudge us to think otherwise, to think well of him: we've been made too sharply aware that in the context of this South Africa with its third-world poverty, its bloody and divisive history, its deep cultural damage, his concern for the dogs' dignity is compromised before it begins.

This is part of the novel's ruthless shearing away of the successive layers and versions of what Lurie thinks he is, and how he thinks he can live: all his awareness, including the age-old lament for the loss of his youth, is acted out against a background of politics and history that strips it of consoling meaning. The attack on the house and Lucy's rape are paralysing for Lucy and Lurie. The attackers can't be read into any schema in which they appear from beyond the boundaries of the world of the book to wreak their havoc and are then re-absorbed into the darkness, allowing meaning to be re-made behind them. These attackers don't, to begin with, disappear: it is peculiarly horrifying that one of the three returns to haunt them, not as a nightmarish vision but as a mundane, daily, domesticated presence, hanging around the farm. He's a peculiar, angry boy, related through unfathomable networks to Petrus, who works for Lucy and who has ambitions for his farm that borders on and

begins to absorb and overtake hers. The boy even has a name
– Pollux; he peers through the bathroom window at Lucy, and
threatens that he'll kill them all when Lurie catches him and
attacks him. What are they to do, about his persisting, exasperating, threatening presence; about the violent act that can't be
borne and yet remains unaddressed, undealt with? In the South
African context the question can't but resonate beyond itself,
open up bewilderingly and disablingly onto a whole history
of violence unaddressed. Angrily Lurie insists that there must
still be an ethical context in which to condemn the crime; stubbornly Lucy carries the rapists' baby, submits herself more or
less to whatever Petrus advises, submits even to the continuing
presence of the boy. Lurie wants her to leave and go to live with
her mother in Holland; even though a sustainable future for
her on the farm is almost – almost – unimaginable, Lucy insists
on staying, amidst all her sorrows (she's profoundly troubled
and damaged, naturally, by the rape – 'I am a dead person and I
do not know yet what will bring me back to life'). It's as if such
a future could only be lived into, in the body that stubbornly
and against common sense persists – weeding, planting things,
growing; it's not available to Lurie's intellectual processing.

Again, Coetzee doesn't cast Lurie as the wise interpreter of this
tangled nexus of violence and race history. He's meant rather to
blunder through it, sometimes eloquent, sometimes clumsy, but
never actually effecting any resolution, or even achieving any
clear understanding of what happened. Lucy isn't set up as more
'right' than him, either; simply, her arguments have the same
weight in the writing as his (and Bev Shaw's have their weight,
too, and Lurie's second wife's). In one of their discussions Lucy
suggests a continuum between the violence of rape and all male
sex desire (solitary now, she has been in a lesbian partnership);
the writing doesn't offer that as all-explaining, but in the context of Lurie's relationship with Melanie it can't be entirely dis-
missed either. Like other explanations, it's crucially present in

the novel without actually underwriting all its contents. Lurie becomes deeply suspicious of Petrus, even imagining at times a scenario in which Petrus conspired with the attackers, to try to drive Lucy off the farm, or at least to make her acknowledge her need to come in under his protection. There's no satisfactory denouement offered in the novel, where this scenario is confirmed one way or another, or where questions of responsibility, or punishment, or reparation are seized or sorted out. Every time Lurie talks to Petrus, we hear both men deploying frames of reference that are all but impenetrable to one another. Actually we can read round Lurie's suspicion and hostility to hear that Petrus's version of events, too, has its own cohesion and its own ethic – the rapist-boy belongs in somebody's family ('I also look after my child'), there are other ways of controlling violence than bringing in the police ('I also say it is bad. It is bad. But it is finish.'). Lucy, Petrus implies, must learn anyway that it's impossible for her to survive on the farm as a woman alone, in the circumstances of the new South Africa; she needs to come in under the protection of a man, of a family, yield to a different way of doing things. Lurie, burning with the shame of his failure to protect his daughter, feels that Petrus is trying to replace him in his role as father; then he's appalled, derisory, when Petrus offers himself as Lucy's husband, cutting Lurie out doubly, consigning him to impotent irrelevance. Lucy negotiates warily, tentatively, with what she can manage of Petrus's version of the future, but Lurie can't and won't hear any truth in the words the other man speaks.

The novel doesn't make it possible for us to know 'who's right': the truth isn't so easily available inside it. Lucy insists that her father can't grasp what the experience of the rape has meant to her. 'There are things you just don't understand.' Bev Shaw reiterates: 'you don't understand, you weren't there.' Lurie insists: he could imagine it, couldn't he? He makes up a version of the rape for himself: he can imagine horror, he's 'never been afraid of following a thought down its winding track'. The novel can imagine anything, that's the whole point, isn't it? And yet this novel insists equally on the importance of what it can't know: preserves as inviolable the space, for instance, in which the actual rape happens, which Lucy insists that we can't ever enter. In one of his literature classes in Capetown, Lurie reads just this argument about the interaction of imagination and actual witness into passages from Wordsworth's *Prelude*.[3] He reads Wordsworth as suggesting that revelation depends upon a balance between sense-perception and ideas: 'the sense-image . . . as a means toward stirring or activating the idea that lies buried more deeply in the soil of memory . . . we climb [mountains] in the wake of the poets, hoping for one of those revelatory Wordsworthian moments we have all heard about . . . But moments like that will not come unless the eye is half turned towards the great archetypes of the imagination we carry within us.' This is relevant, in its place in the novel, to Lurie's obsession with Melanie, where the passionately desired real sensual contact fuses with poetic archetypes (flower, flame, goddess). But the idea is larger than that, too: it becomes the problem of truth and knowledge in the whole novel, it becomes even the method of the novel, in its perpetual movement to speculative thought and imaginative interpretation through the precisely specifying realism of the story.

If anything, the balance in the novel between the two elements of thought swings, as Lurie's disgrace deepens, towards the power of witness, of the unanswerable sense experience: 'you don't understand, you weren't there'. Lurie's imagination, the language in which he reads and interprets, is often overwhelmed by the reality surrounding him, forcing itself upon him; under its pressure, for example, the original elegiac conception for his opera reshapes into comedy. How could he, really, persuade 'the inhabitants of D Village' that Teresa Guiccioli's love for Byron mattered as an idea; this fragment left over from a lost romantic Europe, absurd, extravagant, indefensible in the face of poverty, sickness, violence? And yet it doesn't stop mattering, to him; rehearsing it in some sense he practises what he is, he can't do anything else. The novel itself will test the value of the idea, haltingly and incompletely, trying out the intimations of dream and desire against its witness to real things, not arriving finally at any place that pretends to finalise the experience inside it. The case this novel argues for its art isn't, in the end, a transcendent one: the novel can't surpass the opacity of the mysterious life that surrounds it. Its aspiration isn't to that kind of mastery, anyway: rather, to submit to becoming the music in which the conjunction of the dream and the real expresses itself. 'So this is art!' Lurie thinks, at work on his opera, 'and this is how it does its work! How strange! How fascinating!' 'He is held in the music itself, in the flat tinny slap of the banjo strings, the voice that strains to soar away from the ludicrous instrument but is continually reined back, like a fish on a line.'

In the early 90s, in the book of his essays *Doubling the Point*, Coetzee talked about the 'pathos' of the postmodernist narrative position and its scepticism about the possibilities of representation; its writers, he suggests, are 'like children shut in the playroom, the room of textual play, looking out wistfully through the bars at the enticing world of the grownups, one that we have been instructed to think of as the mere phantasmal world of *realism* but that we stubbornly can't help thinking of as the *real*.'⁴ Through the years of his extraordinary narrative experiments – *Heart of the Country, Foe, Age of Iron* and all the others – he has written himself out of the playroom into a grown-up new realism that perhaps has its culmination in *Disgrace* (and in *Boyhood* and *Youth);* a complex realism that doesn't discount the experiments that came before but depends on them.⁵ Every signifying gesture in this novel, every sentence, is sprung in a tension between witness and awareness of itself as witness.⁶ The effect of this pressure, which might have been disabling, is instead a stark simplification, a new nakedness; it's perhaps somehow this nakedness that made it possible for *Disgrace* to step, as it were, outside of its own temperament – erudite, intellectual, difficult of approach – and cross over to reach so many readers. The achievement is of the order of what Lurie, writing his opera, allows himself to hope for (and in superbly Byronic language): 'that somewhere from amidst the welter of sound there will dart up, like a bird, a single authentic note of immortal longing'.

Notes

1 Coetzee, *Doubling the Point,* ed. David Attwell (Harvard University Press, 1992), p.252.

2 Of course Coetzee has in all his novel writing preserved careful narrative distances from his protagonists; we don't expect from him comfortable authorial identifications with a protagonist-narrator transparently interpreting events. What's newly striking in *Disgrace* isn't the sceptical distance: it's actually the confessional closeness.

3 Even before Lurie's life is disrupted, there's an element of comic absurdity in these classes where his students sit blank, unmoved, before his eloquence. The mockery isn't all one way, Lurie isn't an inspiring teacher, he hasn't adapted at all – that temperamental fatality – to the new cultural contexts his students come out of; he persists in offering them closed authoritative readings of the texts, rather than trying to open up any dialogue with it, or encouraging them to find their own ways in.

4 *Doubling the Point,* p.63.

5 And the writer's next move, into the strange textures of *Elizabeth Costello* and *Slow Man,* confirms that the 'realism' of *Disgrace* was not in any sense a lapse back upon a representational default position, only a significant moment in a writing career driven by restless doubt in its search for truthful ways to tell the contemporary story.

6 The same tension, although expressing itself so differently, is there in every sentence in the late James.

4 Arundhati Roy, *The God of Small Things*

AMIT CHAUDHURI

Reading is not about love at first sight; it has to do, more often, with evolution and chance. The fact that we evolve and change as readers – that a book which seems incomprehensible and dull at one point in our lives might, should we encounter it again, be deeply pleasurable (the process I've described is equally true the other way around) – implicitly informs the critical act. Not only is there no such thing as an instantly recognisable 'good book'; we possess no reliable faculty for instant recognition. Whatever instinct we have in this regard can't be coerced or even trained into existence; it's dependent upon a curious form of openness whose operations we can't predict or control. This is where chance comes into play. Chance makes the whole matter of literary history mysterious. The poet Arun Kolatkar addressed this mysteriousness in words he scribbled on a piece of paper, and which remained unpublished until after his death:

> I may register/ receive/ read some of Mandelstam's poems
>   in translation
> 40 years after he died
> or 60 years after he wrote them/ went nova
> It may take Mandelstam's light 40 years
> to reach me
> and then I may add his name to my star chart/ map/ catalogue
> and a dot may appear on my mental picture
> and a dot may appear where there was only
> darkness on the photographic plate of my consciousness

It may take 300 years for a Tukaram or a Villon or a Kabir
to be part of my consciousness
simply because I was born that much later
1300 years for Tu Fu to find a good translator a publisher
before he registers on my mind.

If I were to construct a life-history of my own reading, I'd
have to do so, in retrospect, in the terms of two distinct move-
ments. The first dates back to my early twenties, and involves
my discovery, as a young writer, of the importance to me of
the mundane; the supremacy of space, light, and objects rather
than what are called 'story' and 'character'; and the difficulty of
bringing this submerged preoccupation to the surface of my
mind. Around this time, I began to become aware of writers, or
works, or even passages or lines in those works, which had approached the ordinary or the particular from different perspectives. I can't now say whether I first discovered the ordinary in
those passages or in the world; in what order the discovery occurred – of the allure of phenomena, as well as the importance
of a literary and artistic tradition – has never been clear. But
to gradually piece together the latter – the tradition in question – was not only to experience pleasure, but to realise slowly
that there was a moral weight ascribed to this discovery; that
the particular had a lineage and a role in literature – beyond
story, beyond psychology. This, I remember, was a great relief
to me. Many of the lines and passages I refer to in general terms,
and which, in my early twenties, went into the construction of
this almost personal lineage, came to me by chance: I found
poets and writers quoted in other people's work, often in critics' writings, which I might be consulting to read up on figures
who were well known and whom I may or may not be entirely
interested in. Thus, I encountered Elizabeth Bishop first in Ian
Hamilton's biography of Robert Lowell; Naipaul's *A House
for Mr Biswas* in a handbook on 'Commonwealth' writing, in
the form of a paragraph on painting a shop sign; a dissonant

argument in *The Man Who Loved Children* (a book I've never got round to reading) in an essay by Randall Jarrell, a piece of such sustained, well-judged, and inspired advocacy that those sentences by Christina Stead have stayed with me and have almost seemed all I need to know of her work.

After years of promiscuous reading around (the years of curiosity and fantasy about reading) and serving an apprenticeship as a writer (the curiosity to do with using words), my first, most intense discoveries of what my temperament was about as a reader and writer came to me through the quotation, and it brought with it its own lessons: that the fragment was enough, and the overarching narrative and story were, in a sense, dispensable; that immersion in, sampling, and re-reading the quotation offered so much pleasure that the book itself became a tertiary entity; that compression and the shape of the unsaid were indispensable to the shape of the quotation; that craft determined the compression as well as the outline of the unsaid; that craft, in that it sought the essentials (making the paragraph or sentence quotable, free-standing, and re-readable), was at once moral and instinctual; that the quotation represented an inversion of orthodox notions of what was essential and what was superfluous.

With the experience of fundamental modes of delight comes a clearer sense of oppositionality. Now I had a more defined idea than ever before of the sort of writing, or artwork, I wanted to avoid, or keep clear of. No amount of emotion in the work could compensate for the moral and pleasure-giving value of the sentence: the pedestrian adjective or adverb was not only a minor violation on the level of language; it represented a failure of the imagination. One had to imagine the world one wrote about in every word, every sentence one used. And, no sooner had I arrived at this aesthetic, which would govern my artistic decisions from now on, than I began to resist it. This led to the second 'movement' in my reading that I mentioned earlier, the

a sympathy for the early work of Satyajit Ray, for its treatment of the improvised commonplace, I also developed a more clearly formulated animosity towards Ray's contemporary and alterself, Ritwik Ghatak: to Ghatak's epic and operatic predilections, his love of the over-the-top, the final, the melodramatic. It was only later, when, by chance, I saw Ghatak's work again, that I found the grand luminosity, the exaggerated, expressionist, living detail in his cinema that I would grow to admire. After that, not only did my resistance to Ghatak's *oeuvre* break down, but also the dichotomy on which the resistance had been created. The artist, arriving at what he thinks is self-knowledge, begins busily to make affiliations, largely on the principle of family resemblances; and then, over the years, gradually finds the principle subverted – pleasure and sustenance begin to come to him from sources outside of the family he's elected to belong to. One more example, this time of a single author: D. H. Lawrence. There was *Sons and Lovers*, with its quest for perfectability, its transformative version of the mundane; and there was the work that followed, where the border between good and bad writing was blurred, where there was a new, almost predetermined lack of exactness, and which still contained recurrent glimpses of the true and radiant – radically shifting, thus, the inner alignment of the work. *Sons and Lovers* had been crucial to me: I had read it and uncovered my own aesthetic through it; it was a moment of sudden but complete recognition. The later work, initially somewhat repellent, slowly revealed its compelling features. Here (with the later work), it was a matter of getting habituated to, and then inhabiting, the alien; learning to view the aesthetic from a radically different point of view, a point of view essentially antagonistic to the position one had arrived at, after much self-examination, as a writer; and to read, understand, and derive pleasure within that alien space wasn't possible unless, as Lawrence might have said, one 'killed' a part of one's identity and self-definition. Roy's novel itself is a constant enactment of this struggle for radical, agonistic extinction and departure.

The problem with *The God of Small Things* was that it was given a reception where it was either exalted or condemned on the grounds of the 'literary'. No one clarified what the 'literary' was; it was a given. Publishers and agents used the novel as a model and justification for a covertly Thatcherite world-view of the arts: that the 'literary' could (really should) also be 'popular'. It was praised (and condemned) as a modernist work might have been in the early twenties: for its 'new' language – though no one repeated what Pound had declared in his own capital letters to Harriet Monroe in connection with 'The Love Song of J. Alfred Prufrock': 'PRAY THAT IT NOT BE AN IMMEDIATE AND UNQUALIFIED SUCCESS'. It was compared, among other canonical moderns, to Faulkner. These references and positions were problematic. When, on an impulse, I finally borrowed the novel from someone, I found the text did not bear them out. My lender had 'loved' the book; distractingly, she, in her involvement, had underlined phrases, metaphors, and similes. So, in a novel in which words and sentences were anyway emphasised by a variety of devices (and underlined in a manner of speaking), I had to contend with steady pencil markings reappearing on the pages. Consulting that copy again (re-borrowing it for the purposes of this piece), I find the first four pages full of those marks. On the first page, in the first paragraph (which I mentioned earlier), 'still, dustgreen trees' and 'fruity air' have been singled out. Then there is a sentence I quite like: 'Boundaries blur as tapioca fences take root and bloom.' Two other sentences in the same paragraph, descriptive of the chaos of Ayemenem in early June, and as obviously, almost cheaply, alliterative as the underlined one, are ignored: 'Pepper vines snake up electric poles'; 'Boats ply in the bazaars'. Both appeal to me on a second reading for their mixture of almost-fake local colour and deeply accurate small-town tawdriness. On page 2, my large-hearted hostess has dragged her pencil beneath 'when life was full of Beginnings and no Ends, and Everything was For Ever'; on page 3, 'a viable die-able age'; on page 4, the simile (which teeters slightly): 'Her face was pale and wrinkled as a dhobi's thumb from being in water for too long' – the author means the dhobi's thumb spends a lot of time in the water, not the face in question. Underlining these sentences and images isolates them from the story – to which they belong in a curious but unquestionable way – and offers them up as fragments; but they don't bear being read in this fragmented, or fragmentary, incarnation, as, say, the opening sentence of Edna O'Brien's *The Country Girls* can: 'I wakened quickly and sat up in bed abruptly.' Roy's phrases are part of a tone, a polemic, and a polemic cannot be broken up and read in parts as, say, a work of poetry can. Encountered singly, they are too demonstrative, they exhibit signs of what that great New Critic Holden Caulfield would have called 'phoneyness'.

I persisted; it wasn't easy. But much depends on chance. The novel itself, whose narrator instructs us that 'things can change in a day', enshrines the fact almost too often. 'Things can change in a day' is at the core of the modernist aesthetic: the simultaneously constricted and inexhaustible frame of twelve or twenty-four hours; the transfiguration of the quotidian, of 'little events, ordinary things'. And yet it pushes, this prophecy, towards realms the modernists, with their adoration of the phenomenal world, averted their gaze from, and which the surrealists embraced: of destiny and of coincidence; of the equal significance and momentousness of the spontaneous and the manufactured. It's towards these realms, I think, that Roy's peculiar sensibility veers.

On page 92, I finally found the passage that unlocked this book to me. Rahel and Estha, twins, are back in Ayemenem, where much happened once that made their lives both extraordinary and miserable. Grown into a sort of adult orphanhood, they are back desultorily together, and it is Rahel who probably first registers and acknowledges the desire that silently characterises their relationship. She chances, and spies, upon her brother in the bathroom, naked, washing his own clothes with what appears to be a bar of cheap detergent soap:

> Rahel searched her brother's nakedness for signs of herself. In the shape of his knees. The arch of his instep. The slope of his shoulders. The angle at which the rest of his arm met his elbow. The way his toenails tipped upwards at the ends. The sculpted hollows on either side of his taut, beautiful buns. Tight plums. Men's bums never grow up. Like school satchels, they evoke in an instant memories of childhood. Two vaccination marks on his arms gleamed like coins. Hers were on the thigh.

The reference to men's bums might have been cheesy; but there's a genuine melancholy in the observation that they never grow up. The comparison of bums with satchels – funny and apt – was, for me, the first simile in the novel that provided me with access to its world. It's a curiously boyish comparison, tapping into the latent androgyny of Rahel's name, with its seemingly deliberate phonetic proximity to the masculine 'Rahul'. It's difficult to write tenderly and suggestively of the male body, as Roy does here, except, probably, in homoerotic terms, as in Allen Ginsberg's Whitmanesque homage to his infrequently bisexual (and, sadly, largely heterosexual) friend Neil Cassady in the poem 'Many Loves': 'I put my hand down to feel his great back for the first time, jaws and pectorals of steel at my fingers, / Closer and stiller, down the silken iron back to his waist . . . / I first touched the smooth mount of his rock buttocks, silken in power, rounded in animal fucking and bodily nights over nurses and schoolgirls, / O arse of long solitudes in stolen cars . . .' In contrast to the frank voyeurism, supplicating admiration, and dominance of the male gaze in relationship to the female nude, the homoerotic gaze is partly narcissistic, self-discovering, and implicated in what it sees; and this sense of self-absorption, primeval self-recognition, and tremulous implicatedness finds its counterpart, in the novel, in the way the twins relate to, reassess, and remake each other.

Rahel and her twin brother Estha have made their way back to her birthplace, the Keralan small town Ayemenem, on a visit. Their present-day lives are marked by a deceptive lack of distinction, and seem to be ignored by destiny – Rahel has worked in a disorganised way in America, Estha doesn't seem to do very much; drifters, they gravitate towards each other. Within this lightly sketched, wavering frame is contained the story of a family, of a day of childhood tragedy ('things can change in a day'), and another narrative of taboo love. Rahel and Estha, in this other tale, are seven years old; they live with their mother, Ammu, an impulsive, progressive, and (as mothers are) unique woman, who once made the mistake of marrying a seemingly sophisticated Bengali tea-estate official who turned out to be a completely immoral alcoholic. Ammu, having left this man, has brought up their children more or less alone. There are other people in the house: the twin's grand aunt, the vicious and oddly human spinster Baby Kochamma, the grandmother, Mammachi, and the Oxford-returned Chacko, who is divorced from the Englishwoman Margaret and is the doting father of Sophie Mol, and is the owner, in Ayemenem, of Paradise Pickles. At once comprador and Marxist, Chacko, with the rest of the family, is expectant – of a visit to Ayemenem by Sophie Mol and her mother (who seems to have parted ways with Chacko on relatively friendly terms) from England. Two unusual and entirely unpredictable events unfold during this banal small-town visit, and translate what's a deeply intelligent study of class, caste, politics, and development into the domain of the mythopoeic and the folklorish: Sophie and the twins decide to run away from home, to steal away on a boat ride, using a boat made by Velutha, the strong, much-beloved (of the children) *Paravan* untouchable, a worker in Chacko's factory. The boat capsizes in the current; the twins survive, but their cousin drowns. The other story that emerges at this point concerns Ammu's and Velutha's bizarre attraction for each other, a physical and emotional magnetism that has been unrecognised and then unarticulated, and is finally acted upon by Ammu with the moral conviction that only one such as she could possess. These liaisons are noticed with horror by Velutha's father Vellya Papen, and reported by him in the end to Mammachi, the grandmother, and Baby Kochamma; Ammu is locked away in a room, separated from her children; Velutha, 'the god of small things' (for his deftness with his hands, his skills in carpentry), is accused of rape, tortured and beaten up by the local police, and killed.

The river runs through the book, at once replete with industrial effluents and the children's and the narrator's longing for freedom and redemption. When the novel appeared, I was told by one of its admirers that it was, in many ways, a reworking of *To Kill A Mockingbird*. Certainly, there are elements in the earlier novel that seem to flow into the second one – the two children in the small town; the perilous house that belongs to the invisible 'Boo' Radley, reappearing in the *God of Small Things* as the History House; the trial of the black man accused of rape. But, to me, Roy's novel's counterpart and precursor lies in another work that precedes both Harper Lee's story and the Robert Mulligan film, Charles Laughton's disturbing and revelatory 1955 film noir, *Night of the Hunter*. Here are the two children again, the girl and the boy, but this time without the axis, the mooring, of Harper Lee's universe – the father. Instead, the mother, a hanged criminal's widow, is seduced by a malefic preacher who's after the dead man's money; seduced, murdered, locked in a car that's pushed into a lake. (A strangely serene underwater scene is filmed in a way that's remarkably akin to Roy's narrator's reimagining of the drowned Sophie: 'Green weed and river grime were woven into her beautiful red-brown hair. Her sunken eyelids were raw, nibbled at by fish.') The preacher's provenance, however, is uncertain; to prove his creed, he has tattooed on the knuckles of his right hand the letters LOVE, and on the knuckles of the left the letters HATE; both hands are deployed in one scene to demonstrate to the children the epic struggle between the two. The children escape with the money after the mother is killed, and much of the 'night of the hunter' follows their plight past a river, through the nocturnal wonders of nature clearly, and paradoxically, recreated upon a set. (This knowing paradox – the natural world as strategic setting; the translation of phenomena into theatre – too is echoed by the mordant cartoonish-poetic way in which Roy makes 'nature' participate in the boat ride and drowning episode: 'The deep-swimming fish covered their mouths with their fins and laughed sideways at the spectacle . . . A white boat-spider floated up with the river in the boat, struggled briefly and drowned.') Finally, the children arrive at the sanctuary of the brave but ageing Rachel Cooper's home: Cooper will hold off the preacher with a shotgun, returning the story from nightmare into deep, reassuring, child-like promise.

The father vanishes from Roy's novel early on, but never entirely. His absence, and then his covert, shadowy pursuit of the children, gives the tale its particular disquiet. The father returns in various troubling and cunning and unflagging guises: as the LemondrinkOrangedrink seller, who sexually abuses Estha in the cinema hall; as EMS Namboodiripad, the ur-Marxist; as the local Marxist functionary, Pillai; as the police, the state itself. Finally, the father is the law; and the law is opaque. The father, as law, enters the language, making it, occasionally, bombastic and directive-like, and sometimes incoherent. When the comedy is at its most obvious, the capital letters take on their own life and significance, as in the sign on 'the red and blue board':

P olitness
O bedience
L oyalty
I ntelligence
C ourtesy
E fficiency

At other times, words are truncated into syllables and fragments, made meaningless but still portentous; thus, the loaded
term 'later', broken up into 'lay' and 'ter', not a Joycean incanta-
tion, but a disconcerting and minatory message. Here, the law –
the father – operates insidiously through language, and Rahel's
phonetic imagination both echoes and records it as an obscure
childish anxiety. In the brilliantly composed chapter 'Work is
struggle', where, between themselves, Chacko and Comrade Pillai (his social inferior but his lordly petitionee) discuss, among
other things, the untouchable Velutha's fate, the children who
are being fashioned by law and its language are brought literally
centre-stage. Latha, a 'combative-looking young girl of about
twelve or thirteen', Comrade Pillai's niece, who won the 'First
Prize for Elocution at the youth Festival in Trivandrum last
week', is ordered to recite 'Lochinvar'.

> It was rendered at remarkable speed.
> > 'O, young Lochin varhas scum out of the vest,
> > Through wall the vide Border his teed was the bes;
> > Tand savissgood broadsod heweapon sadnun,
> > Nhe rod all unarmed, and he rod all lalone.'

This is language as law: irrefutable, near-incomprehensible. It
and the other instances I've mentioned have greater affinities
with the LOVE and HATE inscribed on the preacher's knuckles,
letters that separately cease to mean what they add up to but are
eerily united in a message of power, an admonition, than with
the wordplay of modernism, or with Rushdie's hybrid melange,
or even Foster's comic 'Esmiss Esmoor'.
   There is something else I'm reminded of in this profusion

of capital letters, full stops, and half-sentences. It is a mode of dissenting criticism. I am thinking, specifically, of D. H. Lawrence and Ezra Pound, of especially Lawrence's hectoring style in his essays, a vehicle, often, for the most acute analysis, coming out of, Tom Paulin suggests, a vernacular tradition of protest – namely, Protestant oratory. One can't view this language without, at once, admiration and ambivalence. Here are the opening sentences of Lawrence's celebratory 'Whitman', where he begins, however, by taking apart the American poet:

> Post-mortem effects?
> But what of Walt Whitman?
> The 'good grey poet'.
> Was he a ghost, with all his physicality?
> Post-mortem effects. Ghosts.

Then, moving swiftly, mocking Whitman:

> DEMOCRACY! THESE STATES! EIDOLONS! LOVERS, ENDLESS LOVERS!
> ONE IDENTITY!
> ONE IDENTITY!

Lawrence is poking fun at Whitman's optimistic humanism here. The other influential poet-critic who resorts to bullying, urgent, telegraphic critical language, largely in order to advance the cause of the avant-garde, is Pound; Lawrence and Pound are in many respects different, but they're both deriders of humanism – for Pound, as we know, this had disastrous consequences. Roy's politics are irreproachably liberal and humane; but her style at once critiques power – among other things, through spectacle and self-indulgent typography – and mimics some of its tonal characteristics, especially in the essays, with their mixture of orphan-like exhibitionism (a survival skill) and lofty prophetic rage and unappeasability. As an activist, she's a humanist; but, in the novel, she's constantly flouting (as Lawrence does) the humanist, Flaubertian bases of the crystalline artwork – by being over the top, unsettled and unsettling, demonstrative. The language of the novel represents a curious, petulant, critical – even competitive – relationship with the law.

The clearest metaphors for dissent and freedom running through the novel are, surprisingly, tropes from Indian devotional poetry: the river; drowning; and taboo love. Two anecdotes come to mind concerning the late nineteenth-century Bengali mystic Ramakrishna Paramahansa, who, through his bourgeois devotee and mediator, Swami Vivekananda, became an object of profound interest for the rationality-worshipping Calcutta middle class. One is probably apocryphal, and is about his rather cruel tutelage of a pupil who asked Ramakrishna if he too could see the goddess Kali, as the mystic claimed to have; they were standing on the banks of the Ganga when this conversation occurred, and, suddenly dunking the questioner's head into water by force, Ramakrishna held it there, releasing it only when the interlocutor had begun to thrash around desperately. 'When you long to see Kali with the intensity with which you longed for air, you will be able to see her,' Ramakrishna is reported to have said. The other anecdote is a homily, but an odd and telling one: 'You must pine for God as a woman pines for her paramour' – not for her husband, mind you. We know that almost all of *bhakti* or Hindu devotional poetry is constructed around an illegitimate relationship: the married Radha's obsessive trysts with Krishna. Ramakrishna's advice is, syntactically, frankly scandalous; he sets up an analogy in which the two halves come together poetically, but are also separated and then juxtaposed in an unnerving, discomfiting proximity – 'you must pine for God'/ 'a woman pines for her paramour'.

Let me add to these a third episode, to do with Vivekananda – still, then, the philosophy graduate Narendranath Datta – and his first meeting with Ramakrishna. Upon seeing Narendranath, Ramakrishna apparently went into a *samadhi*: a sort of spiritual *rigor mortis*, a divinely ordained epileptic fit. Vivekananda's first response was the normal *bhadralok* middle-class one:

embarrassment. (Nirad C. Chaudhuri, a far more inflexible and faithful product of the enlightenment than Vivekananda, also records, in his autobiography, the embarrassment he'd feel upon witnessing the religious ecstasies of Vaishnav devotees.)

During the rapid advance of capitalism in the late nineteenth and early twentieth centuries, it was popular culture that, besides religious extremity, at once embarrassed, offended, and challenged the middle class – especially sentimentality and melodrama. None of these discomfitures and registers (as well as, conversely, passionate endorsements) are inapposite to the reception of Roy's success, her style, her novel's radical language.

This is not to say that Roy has little sense of, or love for, literary language; indeed, she has a gift for it. The buoyant, joyous preamble to the boat ride, when the children march up to Velutha's hut; the dour, oppressive meeting between Chacko and Comrade Pillai in the latter's house; the final passages, at once retrospective and premonitory, about Ammu's and Velutha's passion – all these are among the most perfectly captured and rendered, the most fiercely yet slyly observed, moments in contemporary Indian writing. But it's in the tension between these almost self-contained pages and the author's unspoken but palpable compulsions – to do with form, convention, experience, ambition, desire (both spiritual and material) – that the power of the novel lies. Here is a language that's on the cusp, at the crossroads, of the declamatory and the personal, the public and the imaginary, the popular, the ecstatic, and the fake on the one hand, and the unillusioned, disabused, and authentic on the other. This cusp – between the law and its transgression; the father and the errant children – is resistant, narrow, and dangerous, and it pulses with life.

MARY HAWTHORNE

The Life of Sisyphus

Like a misunderstood child, who cries and cries but whose
source of distress cannot be fathomed and is thus curtly dis-
missed by the doctor with palliatives, Anita Brookner's books
are often shunted aside in exasperation, sometimes even by
those who are kindly disposed to them: the characters are tiresome and redundant in their relentless isolation, their neurotic
obsession with the minutiae of their lives and elusive love objects, their maddening inability to act: we've heard it all before.
Every year or so, since 1981, when Brookner published her first
novel, the autobiographical *A Start in Life*, at the age of fifty-
three, like Sisyphus, her soulmate, she has shouldered one stone
after another to the top of the hill and watched it descend again,
as shortly she begins contemplating her next battle against in-
exorable fate – which is to say, the cruel indifference of the gods
toward the dutiful, the good, and the well-behaved. But in this
struggle, as Camus tells us, we must imagine Sisyphus happy.
As, indeed, Brookner proclaims herself to be, continuing to
polish off volume after volume since her first, nearly all of them
devoted to the solitary's quest for simple love, which, of course,
is never simple, never quite the same, and never lasting, if such
a thing is ever to be found at all.

Brookner has been compared to Barbara Pym and Jane
Austen and Henry James and Jean Rhys, but she actually has
little in common with any of them. If anything, she is more a
blend of something like P. L. Travers, by way of the touching
primness, the hauteur, the otherworldly remove, and above all

the hidden pangs of longing of Travers's famous Mary Poppins; Benjamin Constant, by way of *Adolphe*, his masterly dissection of the bondage of love and the speciousness of freedom; and Philip Larkin, in his spinsterish craving for sexual intimacy and his lyrical grief over having found himself largely on the wrong side of it.

At the center of Brookner's books is nearly always a female protagonist, living in a state of solitariness which she both thrives on and abhors. In thrall first and foremost to her own strict notion of the manly ideal, she yearns for an actual man who can meet it. Like Travers, Brookner challenges us to embrace a heroine with whom it is difficult to sympathise, let alone love, despite the strangely fascinating hold of her various eccentric incarnations: student, librarian, flâneuse; first dowdily, then beautifully, clothed, expensively scented, preoccupied with coiffure and toilette. Clothes and impeccable grooming, we learn, are not just forms of feminine allure but, more important, a means to worldly protection. Randomly, we need only examine Ingres's stunning portrait of Mademoiselle Rivière, when she was fifteen, in her extravagant tan suede gloves, white mink stole, and perfect helmet of hair, to understand the truth of this idea (although her allure has just as much if not more to do with her own palpable confidence in her innate beauty and desirability; furthermore, as Brookner witheringly demonstrates in her novel *Providence*, even exquisite clothes are capable of ruthless betrayal). But in the end, after years of testimony, one is all but compelled to embrace the Brookner protagonist, so convincing is the record of suffering in the face of rectitude and sincerity, so insistent the author's refrains of foul play at the hands of fate. This, finally, is the Brooknerian triumph, a triumph born of long struggle: what emerges is a point of view, one with profound existentialist underpinnings.

You can read one Brookner novel without considering the lot (or most of it), but it misses the point not to, intricately interrelated thematically as all her books are. Like a diamond cutter carefully examining his facets through a loupe, Brookner has considered her heroines' predicaments from every conceivable angle, and in the minutest increments she has revealed a little more of her authorial self over the years as well, along with her own lessons learned, which are slightly different, from book to book. Brookner has chosen the Schopenhauerian route: 'Fundamentally it is only our own basic thoughts that possess truth and life, for only these do we really understand through and through.' (Which isn't to say that the truth of another Schopenhauer observation does not sometimes apply: 'There are very many thoughts for him who thinks them, but only a few of them have the power of engaging the interest of a reader after they have been written down.') In the process, though, like a difficult friend with whom you dine but twice a year, you suddenly realise that she's grown more interesting, over time, through her very repetitions; you begin to examine the fixations differently, understanding that they are, finally, the point.

For it is only over the course of time that the reader truly grasps the essential fact that the Brookner heroine (and perhaps the author herself) has actually spent a life sentence in emotional jail – in true solitary confinement – from which, by dint of complexities of temperament or moral upbringing or psychological limitation or the simple decrees of fate – or just plain faithfulness to the starkness of her own perceptions – she does not have the wherewithal to escape, try as she might. She has become devoted to this harsh sentence, by dint of having lived it out, as if it were religion itself (though she is always atheistic), because everything in her experience harkens back to the burden of isolated state, because it is the bone her mind won't stop gnawing on. Like Freud, Brookner believes that everything begins, and to all intents and purposes ends, in childhood experience. In her 2001 novel *Bay of Angels*, which chronicles the death of a youngish woman's mother, Brookner vividly evokes

the kind of claustrophobia and attendant anxiety that such a
life of constraint gives rise to. (Not that a life of so-called freedom, Brookner will have us know, gives rise to anything different.) After a night of troubled dreams featuring the inevitable
non sequitur, in this case a flap of aberrant wallpaper covering
over an opening in the wall of her dilapidated little rented room
in Nice – an opening too small to enter through or exit from –
the narrator, Zoë, has a revelation:

> My business was and always had been, my mother; however much I
> repudiated the idea it refused to go away . . . My life had become a
> stasis I was unable to alter in any direction; that was why every other
> enterprise seemed beyond me, beyond even my eventual possibilities.
> My timid affections remained timid for that very reason; they were
> prevented from moving forward, for I was a prisoner in that room, and
> until the gap widened I could not proceed . . . My life was that poor
> room, with its enigmatic opening, the purpose of which was not to let
> me out but to have me contemplate it for so long that I could no longer
> relate to the rest of life, even though that life was my own.

And so, like hardened criminals, Brookner's heroines are the
leopards that prove unable to change their spots. (The difference
between 'unable to' and 'don't really want to' is an interesting
one to contemplate, though impossible to unravel; some would
say that they are one and the same.) Eager to get their days over
with, they look forward to what, eventually, becomes the almost
comic ritual (though it is in truth anything but) of the evening
bath and as early a bedtime as can be respectably managed. The
bath represents both a cleansing, a cancelling out, of the day's
insult and injury and a preparation for descent into the unconscious; the early bedtime both a testament to the day's unhappiness and disappointment and also a hopeful jump-start on the
day ahead, when the sun will shine again, when the Sisyphean
struggle will begin anew. The point is to get through the night
with as much psychic pleasure and enlightenment and as little
torment as possible. We all know something of this.

Brookner's protagonists are at once uniquely her own – that is, a mirror of her own particular consciousness – and also a mirror of today's Odd Women, an unglamorous yet increasingly numerous breed, to judge by the continued interest in her books, which are read chiefly by women, and by the ongoing erosion of social mores. One reads Brookner as one reads a murder mystery (as opposed to a romance novel), obscurely titillated by the terrifying fate that befalls her characters – relegated to the margins for their failures, which are always born of their innocence as opposed to their guilt (for which they inevitably feel guilty all the same), of their 'blamenessness,' a favorite Brookner word – and anxious, too, for clues as to ways to avoid this fate oneself. Sometimes the dreaded conclusion already has befallen us as well, sometimes we are swimming to keep our own heads above water, and mistakenly look to Brookner for solace or solutions, which are never forthcoming; in this regard, she must always disappoint. (It comes as something of a surprise to discover that Brookner can be quite scornful on the page – she writes to console no one except herself, and womanly worth, refreshingly, is far from an absolute.) Some of her readers give up on her after the third or fourth novel, unable to take any more. (One beautiful, well-educated, solitary Egyptian woman who lives in New York told me recently, shuddering, that her own mother had made it to nine.) But Brookner's message is calm and matter-of-fact: her characters are *destined* to become what they become, even though they do not necessarily glean this until the action is complete, when the tables have already been turned, when it's too late to fight; this fact must be accepted with dignity and stoicism and moral valor. Obsessed with time and with time running out, her protagonist becomes highly attuned, finally, to the price of every sexual foray and every social alliance, able to tabulate the results of the minutest demographic disparities, in class and age and ethnicity. At the same time, she is frequently baffled as to how to use up her days, especially when long-awaited freedom from responsibility, usually filial, finally arrives. Often we find her walking the streets for hours, without a destination. This is the Brookner conundrum. The constant awareness of time, devotion to the hours, accompanied by limitless and often baffled waiting, is one of the most resonant elements in her books. It serves to confront the reader with the realisation that her time, too, is fast running out. How to live out one's days, especially all alone? This, finally, is Brookner's great question, touching, uncomfortably, on the essential eternal concern of one's own mortality, however impossible that may seem. ('I have never understood how men can so lightly cast it out of their minds,' Constant's Adolphe remarks, recalling the death of an older woman with whom he once discussed the subject endlessly, a woman whose 'remarkable and highly original mind' had had a great influence on him. 'But she did not understand the ways of the world and, again like so many others, through failing to adapt herself to an artificial but necessary code of behaviour, she had lived to see her hopes disappointed and her youth pass joylessly away, until at last old age had overtaken but not subdued her.') *But not subdued her.* What gets the Brookner heroine up and out of bed each morning is what gets every prisoner up. Aside from the *duty* to live, an emotion perhaps more irrational, more absurd, even than love: hope; or, rather, hope against hope. And therein lies remarkable valiance.

Edith Hope, the narrator of Brookner's best-known novel, her fourth, *Hotel du Lac*, published in 1984, is a writer of romance novels, of the satisfyingly resolved Harlequin or Barbara Cartland or even Brontë sort (Brookner herself is a writer of anti-romance novels of the fraught, doomed sort). At one point in the novel, Edith recalls a luncheon with her publisher in London, just before her arrival at the exclusive Swiss hotel on Lake Geneva to which she has recently been banished for significant social misconduct (which is to say, something so bad that mental instability is suspected). The publisher gently tries to suggest that she consider a new tack, today's readers being more interested in sex than in romance. Edith demurs. As for her readers, 'they want to believe that they are going to be discovered, looking their best, behind closed doors, just when they thought that all was lost, by a man who has battled across continents . . . to reclaim them. Ah! If only it were true.' (A century before, Rhoda Nunn, in George Gissing's *The Odd Women*, blames the spell of such mythologies for a young girl's recent elopement: 'All her spare time was given to novel-reading . . . Love – love – love; a sickening sameness of vulgarity. What is more vulgar than the ideal of novelists. They won't represent the actual world; it would be too dull for their readers. In real life, how many men and women *fall in love*? Not one in every ten thousand, I am convinced . . . There is the sexual instinct, of course, but that is quite a different thing; the novelists daren't talk about that.') Edith herself is well aware of being a proponent of the vulgar ideal, and even dimly, shamefully aware, in spite of herself, of being in its grip. For Edith, the most potent myth of all for her readers is Aesop's fable of the tortoise and the hare, a myth she consciously exploits herself. In her books, she explains, 'It is the mouse-like unassuming girl who gets the hero, while the scornful temptress with whom he has had a stormy affair retreats baffled from the fray, never to return. The tortoise wins every time. This is a lie, of course,' she goes on, 'In real life . . . it is the hare who wins . . . The propaganda goes all the other way, but only because it is the tortoise who is in need of consolation. Like the meek who are going to inherit the earth.' This is the suspense, such as it is, at the center of nearly every Brookner novel: Will the tortoise finally win? Will the tortoise even make headway? Will the tortoise perhaps demonstrate that her own nuanced qualities, not shared by the hare, are redeeming in their own right? Finally, will the tortoise ever be seen as an object of desire? (In *The Rules of Engagement*, Brookner's 2003 novel, one of two competing tortoises does 'win', but only briefly, and only in secret ephemeral intimacy. Passion actually counts for very little in the world, we are not altogether surprised to learn, even though it is the most real thing we know. Naturally, things end badly, as they must.) What actually and consistently does win is power or money or strength or beauty or tallness or boldness or ascendant class – or, preferably, a heady cocktail of all these things. Love plus love equals zed, let's face it. And yet: it is what we crave, all of us. (Aesop features in Brookner's meditations, but where is Darwin?)

This is the Brookner lament: her heroines subscribe to the myths – not just those of Aesop but of the King James Bible, the Western canon, all of it – they honor their parents, consider their neighbors, are faultless in their worldly dealings, make the most of their personal attractiveness, and yet they still go unrewarded. They've been lied to, Brookner would have us know, robbed in the church, and she is at first bewildered, then furious about it. (As are many of her readers.) The cunning and successful – the 'plausible,' or the 'bold,' Brookner calls them – never abided by such rules in the first place. (And when, we may ask, have they ever, in the history of mankind?) But the worst of it, the final humiliation, is that the honorable are now held in contempt. Further, there appears to be scant refuge: Religion? Please! For Brookner, the only God is the sun. One is still obliged to make one's way through the world as a kind of orphan saint, bereft of the comforts of a father, and in accordance with one's own moral imperatives. ('Only that possesses value which you have thought in the first instance *for your own instruction*,' Schopenhauer reminds us. There is no other way.) Though there is almost unbearable sorrow in this dim view, there is also great relief, just as there is in, finally, giving oneself over to the sun, a God with no face. For as Brookner magically demonstrates, there is in fact enormous solace to be found in the divinity of simple light. The great painters understood this, too. The sun rising and setting in the sky every day, its subtle casts of gold and silver that mark our days, the glittering chartreuse of new trees that we remember from spring to spring. There is the anxiousness to be done with it all, certainly, and then again no. It is the light that gives one pause. The beautiful Brookner clothes are a strangely fitting counterpart to the porcelain-blue skies, devoid of duplicity, with their promise of heaven. Perhaps dress is also a way to honor the beauty of the world. And so – what? A return to paganism of sorts; a pagan book of hours. This must suffice.

To the relaxed and amoral, the new (or neo-new) order of greed and implacable striving comes easily; there is no thought of any need to oppose it. To the chaste and circumspect and punctilious, this is a dismaying thing, for we are speaking of the rare flowers, which bloom for only days at a time in February. In truth, the chaste and the circumspect have always been on the wrong side of things, as Brookner sees it, or half sees it (she is, after all, one of the rare February blossoms). Their blame lies in their refusal (or inability) to see things as they are, to acknowledge wickedness, vainglory, Versace. Ignorance of the real is no excuse, nor is innocence. The world has changed – once again – for the worse. Yet another noir is born.

Edith herself, behaving in accordance with the tenets of Harlequinism, has recently left a seemingly kind and unobjectionable prospective husband (a man who, like herself, has been faithful to the rules) at the altar simply because she doesn't love him, finding herself unable at the last minute to renounce an unpromising but presumably sexually fulfilling relationship with a married man (Brookner is austerely unspecific as to this critical point, perhaps by reason of Edith's innate delicacy, though the author herself becomes more expansive in successive novels). A horrified friend has sent her off to the mysterious hotel on the lake, to regain her senses (implied penance being a part of the process). On arriving, ensconced in her hotel room, whose most notable feature, despite its bright immaculateness, is 'its air of deadly calm', with its 'veal-colored' carpet and curtains and counterpane (even though you may never have been in such a room, you know its austere and faintly disturbing elegance instantly), Edith contemplates the view:

> From the window all that could be seen was a receding area of grey. It was to be supposed that beyond the grey garden, which seemed to sprout nothing but the stiffish leaves of some unfamiliar plant, lay the vast grey lake, spreading like an anaesthetic towards the invisible further shore, and beyond that, in imagination only, yet verified by the brochure, the peak of the Dent d'Oche, on which snow might already be slightly and silently falling. For it was late September, out of season; the tourists had gone, the rates were reduced, and there were few inducements for visitors in this small town at the water's edge, whose inhabitants, uncommunicative to begin with, were frequently rendered taciturn by the dense cloud that descended for days at a time and then vanished without warning to reveal a new landscape, full of colour and incident: boats skimming the lake, passengers at the landing stage, an open air market, the outline of the gaunt remains of a thirteenth-century castle, seams of white on the far mountains, and on the cheerful uplands to the south a rising backdrop of apple trees, the fruit sparkling with emblematic significance. For this was a land of prudently harvested plenty, a land which had conquered human accidents, leaving only the weather distressingly beyond control.

This is the true magic of Brookner – her ability, through cadenced classical sentences, to conjure up an atmosphere that is not quite of this world, one that is balanced between a slightly hyperreal landscape – also the terrain of great painters – and dreamscape, which together summon up a rich emotional backdrop for her drama (or anti-drama; you choose). The paragraph might describe a painting of Caspar David Friedrich's; indeed, Edith herself might be the *Wanderer Above a Sea of Fog*, which might in turn be a title from one of her books, *Beneath the Visiting Moon* and *The Sun at Midnight* being two of them. The book's first paragraph's metaphorical voyage from dreary,

unsettling wintery opacity to bright, sunlit paradise also charts
the pilgrim's progress of the novel of romance. Brookner must
inevitably suffuse this perfect scene of order with the disorder
of conscious or unconscious human volition.

Brookner, an art historian by training, has a practiced eye
and an exquisite sensitivity to the nuances and associations of
color and light, and also a rich allegorical vocabulary. Nearly
everything in her book has emblematic significance. The lake,
the garden, the peak, the reduced rates, Switzerland itself, are
all the material of vivid dreams, to which Edith succumbs each
night, clad in her virginal 'long white nightgown'. In the evening
after dinner that first day, walking along the lake's shore, Edith
is reminded of 'nothing so much as those silent walks one takes
in dreams, and in which unreason and inevitability go hand in
hand. As in dreams she felt both despair and a sort of doomed
curiosity . . .' And the vast lake is of course the great symbolic repository of the unconscious, both alluring and terrifying
in its associations of sex and death by drowning and voyages
to uncertain, distant shores. In Brookner's most recent novel,
Leaving Home, the narrator Emma Roberts observes, 'It was not
wakefulness that disturbed me; it was sleep itself, that descent
into the unfathomable, the unknown, the element that threatens us all.'

The hotel itself is a kind of emblem, in off season resembling
more a sanatorium, with its handful of guests, nearly all of
them wealthy women in various states of exile. (A 'gyneceum,'
as Edith refers to it, with dry distaste, it is also something of
an orphanage, a nunnery, or even a women's correctional facil-
ity, all homes to the marginal.) There is a taciturn elderly deaf
countess who dresses in black and wears anachronistic veils with
tiny velvet bows; the hotel is where she lives half the year, banished from her ancestral home by her son's venal, flamboyant
second wife, who has no use for the old woman, whose life in
turn has been reduced to stoical waiting for her son's monthly

Sunday visits. There is a cynical, fierce, and beautiful young woman with an eating disorder and a small noisy dog; her despised husband is in need of an heir, and has sent her off to the hotel in order that she may optimise her health. And there is a fabulously rich mother and daughter whose devotional bond is cemented seemingly by nothing more than extravagant shopping sprees (the mother's quirky, vividly described nightly dinner costumes seem straight out of the pages of *Élegance*, though we are now situated in the early stages of brand psychosis, and so maybe not). The only male on hand is an attractive middle-aged Englishman who dresses in grey and wears a deerstalker hat and whose wife has left him a few years earlier for a much younger man. A collector of antique *famille rose* dishes, he fancies himself a connoisseur of women as well and is prospecting among the hotel's exiles, this mostly purposeless set rendered poignant by their collective abandonment – they are like lost change on the beach.

Edith little by little comes to know the hotel's guests and something of their histories. She writes dull, rambling, self-abasing letters (mercifully unsent) to her lover, David, back home, in a painful attempt to amuse him – her writerly dog's trick – and finds herself distressed upon rereading them to note that her narrative has somehow 'accumulated elements of introspection, of criticism, even of bitterness'. (The reader suspects the truth about this man at once: at a Sunday noon drinks party, moments before Edith actually makes his acquaintance, examining his back she detects from his impatient movements 'a burning desire to get away'. Later, on the day she's failed to show up at her own wedding, she calls for him at the auction house where he works. His assistant says, 'doing a sale outside Worcester. Anyone could have done it. I don't know why he went.' Such are the moments when the mind's reason crosses swords with passion's paranoia; we all know which one wins out. This ghostly, treacherous, yet divine man makes countless appearances, in various guises, in Brookner's books.) When the beautiful worldly woman with the dog takes Edith into her confidence and gives her the lowdown about the guests, Edith sheepishly realises that while she is capable of making up characters, she's unable to read those of real life. 'For the conduct of life she required an interpreter.' Edith is the odd woman out in this crowd, of course. All of the women present know the rules of the game, which are duly explained to her by the mysterious gentleman in grey, Mr Neville. To him, she reveals, flushing, that there are two kinds of writers: 'Those who are preternaturally wise, and those who are preternaturally naïve, as if they had no experience to go on. I belong in the latter category.' This is a great confession for a writer, any writer, to make.

'Edith, you are a romantic,' he declares one brilliant, mellow day over lunch at a trellised restaurant at a nearby village, delivering the deadly blow. The devil's advocate – there is very often one in Brookner – he argues for a personal selfishness that rather uncomfortably recalls the tenets of Ayn Rand: 'You have no idea how promising the world begins to look once you have decided to have it all for yourself. And how much healthier your decisions are once they become entirely selfish . . . To assume your own centrality may mean an entirely new life.' Thoughtful, Mephistophelian Mr Neville would like to persuade Edith of the puerility of love, which she is naturally loath to accept. 'I cannot live without it,' she declares. 'I cannot think or act or speak or write or even dream with any kind of energy in the absence of love. I feel excluded from the living world.' To which he counters, 'You do not need more love. You need less. Love has not done you much good, Edith. Love has made you secretive, self-effacing, perhaps dishonest?' To which she can only nod in tacit agreement. The idea of putting herself first, for once, is an appealing one, which she seriously considers. Mr Neville proposes that what Edith needs instead is the social protection of marriage, but one without the bourgeois restrictions of faithfulness, and this he offers himself, aboard a boat, as it crosses the lake.

Inevitably, given Edith's companions at the gyneceum, her musings turn to mothers and their children, particularly to mothers and their daughters, to Mrs Pusey and her apparently devoted daughter, Jennifer, and to Edith and her own mother. She is drawn into stinging remembrance of an experience with her mother that pales in the face of the Puseys' apparently easy relationship (easy, too, to make a typo here). What is the greatest shame of a child? Not having felt – or, indeed, been – properly loved, with abandon: as a child, for simply being a child, a discrete individual, the joyful product of her parents' joyful union. Another shame: perhaps, too, a feeling that one's parents are not quite like those of the others around one – financially insecure, withdrawn, excessively reliant on their own child for protection, rather than the other way around. Nearly every one of Brookner's heroines suffers from some sort of variation of this crippling handicap, having made itself felt in earliest childhood. When Mrs Pusey celebrates her seventy-ninth birthday with a gigantic perfect Swiss cake, Edith is reminded of her own paltry birthdays, on which it fell to her to make her own cake and serve it. These sorts of memories make Brookner's characters withdrawn, nervous, unduly watchful as to their own conduct, searching for errors that might explain their fall from grace. Edith, because she is doomed to conscientiousness, is forced into a meditation on her own mother's bitter disappointment with life, which summons up the inevitable pity. Her failure to realise her own ideal being foremost in her mother's mind, she largely ignored Edith. No one's fault, you could say, but the effect has been grievous. Edith, being intelligent and hypersensitive and eager to compensate for any inadequacy of her own, has always strived for something her father taught her in times of distress: strength through character. 'This is when character shows,' he explains, whenever poor Edith is reduced to tears.

('Good women always think it is their fault when someone else is being offensive. Bad women never take the blame for anything,' Mr Neville shrewdly observes on his outing with Edith; the prospective value to himself of Edith's tragic empathy and conscience is not lost on him.) Still, at the hotel Edith finds herself mulling over not her own vulnerability but her mother's:

> I never knew my poor mother to do much more than bark with derision. And yet I think of her as my poor mother. As I grow older myself I perceive her sadness, her bewilderment that life had taken such a turn, her loneliness. She bequeathed to me her own cloud of unknowing. She comforted herself, that harsh disappointed woman, by reading love stories, simple romances with happy endings. Perhaps that is why I write them.

When Mr Neville's offer comes, Edith must refuse it, as the dictates of Brookner's novel insist. For just as she's about to send off a letter to David, renouncing their relationship, once and for all, she spies Mr Neville at dawn, post-in flagrante delicto, as he is leaving the bedroom of Mrs Pusey's daughter, and the mortification is too great. Mr Neville is no Mr Rochester. But what is Edith's David back home? The closest thing she's known to love. Or to the fundamental satisfactions of the flesh, body for body. 'My life,' she refers to her lover, as her father had done her mother. Such succumbing in the absence of reciprocation (David has made no effort to contact her, of course, though he knows where she is) can be fatal for a sincere young woman with little experience to go on, with ruinous implications, lasting for years, or even a lifetime. When Edith writes, and finally sends, a note containing the simple word 'Returning' to her lover, our hearts sink. Returning to what? He's gone.

I have often wondered why it is that I have continued reading Brookner year after year, when she has so often disappointed me. I, too, have been annoyed at her characters who can't seem to struggle out of their straitjackets. (I am also unpleasantly reminded of private ones of my own that I can't seem to wriggle out of, either.) But the dilemma of what to make of one's life, of how to become oneself, of how to reconcile the conflicting obligations toward oneself and others, especially toward one's parents, and, most essentially, of how to live in the world in the absence of having achieved one's heart's desire is eternal, and Brookner sounds it again and again, for this is her Sisyphean burden.

At one point in *Leaving Home*, Emma Roberts comes upon the son of a possible compromise companion, a somewhat older doctor who is separated from his wife, as she's searching for a bathroom upstairs in his house. The son, a beautiful young man, is naked – asleep in a bedroom she accidentally enters, and she can't refrain from stealing into the room to look more closely at him. 'For a moment I contemplated him, as Psyche once contemplated Cupid, raising her lamp, willing him not to wake and witness her transgression. At the sight of his surrendered nakedness I saw what had been missing from my life. It was another *coup de foudre*, information received, though not knowingly given.' This is a breathless moment, a summoning up of an indelible image – the Delaistre sculpture come to life. And yet the realisation itself is strangely marvellous, too, for it captures the essence of life, the essence of beauty, the essence of time: it is the captured moment of revelation. Such moments of consciousness are Brookner's gift to us. The myth of Psyche and Cupid is just another myth, of course. We know that Edith's Cupid will never come to reclaim her. Still, she has known his caresses, and that in itself is some kind of victory.

JASON COWLEY

In 1992 Martin Amis published an amusing short story about male narcissism and rivalry called 'Career Move'. Its turbo-charged engines were, for Amis, the familiar ones of ironic inversion and paradox: two writers, a poet and a screenwriter, experience a remarkable reversal in fortune when the poet finds himself being flown first-class to Hollywood, where he is feted by agents and directors competing extravagantly to make a major movie of one of his poems, 'Sonnet'; meanwhile, the screenwriter is condemned, as most poets usually are, to submitting his work, wearily and with increasing desperation, to an impecunious, low-circulation arts magazine as he seeks publication in any format, anywhere. The two writers, once friends, become ever more anguished rivals, especially when the movie of *Sonnet* opens in 437 theatres and 'does seventeen million in its first weekend'.

Male rivalry – especially between writers – is a recurrent theme in Amis's fiction. 'All writers,' he once said, 'if they mean business, if they're ambitious, have got to think they're the best. You haven't got a chance of being the best unless you think you're best.'

As the son of a famous novelist, the late Kingsley Amis, and an ardent reader of Saul Bellow, with whom he became close friends, as well as Nabokov, Amis was from the beginning unusually interested in style, in what it means to write fiction in a style that is ostentatiously your own. 'I don't want to write a sentence that any guy could have written,' he told an interviewer, staking out territory, issuing a challenge. No, he wasn't here to make up the numbers and, like his father, he would write comedy, but with a twist of nastiness.

His first novel, *The Rachel Papers*, published in 1973 when he was twenty-four, was a work of aggressive exhibitionism. The fancily-writing, smart-talking narrator, Charles Highway, is a kind of amalgam of Holden Caulfield and Patrick Bateman, the nihilistic anti-hero of Brett Easton Ellis's *American Psycho*. Highway, who is nineteen, and preparing to go up to Oxford, is willfully cruel in the way he seduces and then spurns young women. He keeps fastidious records – his papers – of his conquests and couplings. He is an auditor of the carnal. The novel has a young man's dread of and disgust for the middle-aged, for what time does to us all. 'The skin had shrunken over her skull,' Highway writes of his mother, 'to accentuate her jaw and commodious collerage for the gloomy pools that were her eyes; her breasts had long forsaken their natural home and now flanked her navel; and her buttocks, when she wore stretch slacks, would dance behind her knees, like punch balls.'

This much-quoted sentence – so showy yet funny and inventive, too – was like a declaration. Everything that would define Amis as a novelist and stylist was here in microcosm: the grotesque humour and revolt against pulchritude ('her breasts had long forsaken their natural home'), the cruelty (who really would talk of their mother in this way?), the ironic knowingness and allusions ('the ... pools that were her eyes' – Shakespeare, innit?), the baroque phrase-making. Young Martin was on his way; if he stayed fit, away from the booze and off the drugs, if he kept reading and writing, there would be little to stop him, because he had talent (a key word in the Amis lexicon) as well as the required tenacity, and evidently knew exactly what he wanted to say and how to go about saying it.

In *The Moronic Inferno and other visits to America*, a collection of his journalism and essays published in 1986, Amis argued that Saul Bellow wrote in a style fit for heroes, the High Style. 'To evolve an exalted voice appropriate to the twentieth century has been the self-imposed challenge of his work . . . The High Style attempts to speak for the whole of mankind . . . to remind us of what we once knew and have since forgotten.'

Amis, too, wanted to write in the High Style, to develop his own exalted voice, and, on the whole, he achieved just that: working both as a novelist and literary journalist he continued to publish prolifically throughout his twenties and thirties, his novels all the time deepening and hardening in their preoccupation with decay and disaster. He wrote comic novels but without the usual consolations of comedy. He was drawn again and again to the defining crises of our modernity – to the corruptions of capitalism and Thatcherite excess (*Money*, 1984), to the nuclear threat (*Einstein's Monsters*, 1987, a book of stories about the uneasy tensions of the Cold War), to the anxieties of millenarianism and visions of apocalypse (*London Fields*, 1989), to the Nazi catastrophe and the Holocaust of the Jews (*Time's Arrow*, 1991), to the loneliness of a godless world (*The Information*, 1995).

Amis is, wrote John Updike, an 'atrocity-minded author who demands we look directly at things we would rather overlook'. It was as if in his restlessness and ambition he were seeking subjects worthy of the grandeur of his exalted style and of the seriousness of his intent, the big subjects of our time: genocide, nuclear war, environmental degradation. He wanted to write about the whole of society, not only a small part of it. 'The 19th-century British novel was, if you like, a superpower novel,' he told the *New York Times* in 1990. 'It was 800 pages long, about the whole of society. With [British] decline, the novel has shrunk in confidence, in scope. In its current form, the typical English novel is 225 sanitized pages about the middle classes. You know, "well-made" with the nice color scheme and decor, and matching imagery. I almost try and avoid form. What I'm interested in is trying to get more truthful about what it's like to be alive now.'

Whether or not he was succeeding in this, he was being read. People were listening. His 'stuff', as he likes to refer to his work, was news. He was becoming a literary celebrity in the American model: watched, gossiped about, well rewarded, admired. His mastery of different registers and modes of address, his blokeish banter and sardonic fascination with the tawdry excesses of contemporary popular and street culture – with porn, and booze, and drugs, and easy women – soon meant that, for better or worse, he became the novelist most widely imitated in style and voice by any number of younger British writers, from Richard Raynor to D. J.Taylor to Will Self to Tibor Fischer. Even now you can detect the influence of Amis's urgent, rhetorical, insistently comic style, his riffs and repetitions, his improbable reversals and playful paradoxes, his inner-city locations, in the first two novels of the Booker-shortlisted author Zadie Smith.

Yet in the early 90s something happened to Martin Amis. It was as if he had made a wrong turn. Attitudes hardened against him; reviewers traduced him; diarists and columnists eviscerated him. He was still the most influential writer of his generation, in the argot, but this influence was perceived increasingly as baleful. How did this happen? The answer can be given in two words: *The Information*. This was no ordinary novel. This was his superpower novel. Five years in the writing, it was marketed as The Amis Novel, a work of the highest verbal ambition, comparable in reach and achievement to the very best of Bellow or Updike or Philip Roth, something that would show us the truth of how it was to be alive in Britain at the end of empire and of the most violent century in human history. Amis certainly gave the impression, before publication, that he had produced something very fine indeed. His best novel?

He had long been preoccupied by how good he was and by his place in the literary scheme of things. 'People kept saying that I was the most influential novelist of my generation or whatever, and so I wanted to see what I was worth,' he said at the time. So he instructed his agent Pat Kavanagh, the now sadly deceased wife of his long-time friend and fellow novelist Julian Barnes, to extract an advance of £500,000 from Jonathan Cape, the once-independent imprint that had published him for more than twenty years. The amount was considered unreasonable even for an author as esteemed as Amis; though widely admired, his books were never bestsellers and he was seldom a contender for the main literary prizes, such as the Booker, which have an exponential impact on sales. Following much anguish and vilification, Amis found himself a new agent, and a new publisher prepared to pay the desired advance, HarperCollins, part of the Rupert Murdoch media empire. By the time it was published, in April 1995, *The Information* was as much a journalistic as a literary event – and was received as such; Amis, perhaps unfairly, found himself under review both as a man and as a writer. His moral character became part of the wider discourse; this was literary criticism as hatchet biography. The book was a commercial and critical failure; Amis would soon afterwards return to Jonathan Cape, his reputation diminished.

I read *The Information* shortly after publication, and recall being exhilarated and frustrated in about equal measure. I had long admired Amis as a writer, especially the journalism. His profiles of American writers collected in *The Moronic Inferno* were one of the main reasons why, in my early twenties, I had wanted to be a journalist; those essays delighted me with their disciplined intelligence, their empathy, reach and invention, as much as if not more so than his fiction. I always thought something important was missing from the fiction, especially the early novels: heart, love, fellow feeling. I enjoyed some of the phrase-making, as well as the manic comedy, but seldom felt the urge to return to these books. It was the journalism that mattered most to me, when Amis was writing well to deadline, and within strict word limits, and about any number of subjects from literature to sport to pornography to celebrity. It is not that he has no hierarchy of taste: he is an unashamed elitist, dedicated to the great works of the Western canon. Rather, what made him such a good journalist is his curiosity and ability to consider all things, not of equal value, but of equal interest. He is no relativist. But he is open to all possibilities.

The Information was about a mid-life crisis; Amis, who was forty-five in 1995, certainly seemed to be living through some kind of existential crisis of his own: his long-time marriage had ended; he was having expensive and painful surgery on his troublesome teeth, which had turned him into a figure of fun; and the details of his pursuit of a talent-affirming advance was being reported in the newspapers as if it were a story of national significance, like sudden severe shifts in the weather or the fall of a government minister. The media frenzy seems, in retrospect, absurd but for Amis *The Information* proved to be a terminus. After its publication, he was taken far less seriously and ceased to be the most influential novelist of his generation. Instead, in the following years, writers close to him, such as Ian McEwan and Kazuo Ishiguro, achieved the kind of career-defining commercial and critical success that he, above all literary novelists of that time, had once seemed destined to enjoy. He has written nothing notable since *The Information*, turning away from grand, 500-page state-of-the-nation-style novels as he experiments instead with other forms: noirish crime (*Night Train*, 1997), memoir (*Experience*, 2000), political narrative (*Koba the Dread*, 2002, a book about the crimes of Stalin and why the left for too long stayed silent about communist oppression), the novella (*The House of Meetings*, 2006) and the autobiographical novel (*The Pregnant Widow*, 2009). There was one shortish, hypercharacteristic novel, *Yellow Dog* (2003), which has the usual desolate inner-London setting; the usual comic cast of preposterously named grotesques, such as a tabloid-reporter called Clint Smoker (Amis evidently likes the name – a character called Smoker appears in *The Information* as well); the usual supercharged prose style, mixing the vernacular of the street with a more refined literariness. Unfortunately, *Yellow Dog*, as Michiko Kakutani, a longstanding admirer of Amis, wrote in the *New York Times*, 'reads like a sendup of a Martin Amis novel written by someone intent on sabotaging his reputation'. It need not detain us here.

So what of *The Information*? It certainly reads as if it were the culmination of an entire fictional project. All the old obsessions are here: male rivalry, inevitably; literary envy; the allure of dirty money; the unknowability and mystery of women; the impossibility of love; the fear of time's irreversibility; metaphysical terror. *The Information* is a comedy of cosmic humiliation; the strivings of two writers, who both live in west London and turn forty as the novel begins, are set in the context of a godless and pitilessly indifferent universe. Throughout the book the omniscient narrator stands apart, mocking and commenting on the small struggles of his characters as he reminds us of the futility of artistic ambition, indeed of all ambition, and of the absence of larger meaning in our lives. We are hard-wired, he seems to be saying, to seek meaning in a universe in which there is none. This is the real information that comes in the night, that comes to us when we least expect and want to think about it.

The Information begins well, with Richard Tull at home in west London and in bed with his wife, Gina; it is the middle of the night and he is weeping. The first sentence is rather lovely – 'Cities at night, I feel, contain men who cry in their sleep and then say Nothing.'

Who is the speaker here? Is this to be another first-person confession, in the style of *Money*, which was narrated by the junk-food-addicted, coke-addled John Self, or *London Fields*, narrated by Samson Young, an American in London who is dying from an unnamed wasting disease, possibly Aids? Not quite. The 'I' of this first sentence turns out to be the omniscient narrator, a distinct, self-conscious character all his own. His initials are MA, as you would expect, and he directly enters the narrative when he meets Richard in a park, just as John Self in one of *Money*'s best set-pieces meets a writer called Martin Amis in a pub, observing how the writer is 'small, compact, wears his rug fairly long'. This time, the role of Amis-as-narrator is much more directly controlling and interpretative. He is at once complicit in his characters' miseries and at an ironic remove from them. Again and again he interrupts the story to apostrophise and pontificate, like a puppet master breaking the spell of performance directly to address his audience, which serves merely to remind us of the artificiality of the entire exercise and of the visibility of the strings through which he exerts control.

Once Richard is up and about the next morning we discover what it is he has to cry about. He is a novelist who no longer publishes novels. He is a father of disruptive twin boys, from whom he seeks to escape even as they turn the family home into a battleground. He is impotent, naturally. His marriage is moribund – Gina was once his 'sexual obsession', which was why he married her, but that was a long time ago. He has no money. He has just turned forty, and has a cyst on the back of his neck, which he disguises by growing long what is left of his hair. Worst of all, his closest friend, Gwyn Barry, is a successful novelist: a bestseller, a prize-winner.

The writers are in continuous competition. They compete in the snooker hall, over the chess board and on the tennis court – as well as, naturally, in the shower, where Richard furtively watches Gwyn 'toweling his humid bush' while speculating on how 'nice' it would be 'to have had a big one'. Richard beats Gwyn at chess, at snooker, at tennis. None of this matters to him because, when it comes to writing, to the literary high stakes, Gwyn is winning. Gwyn has everything that Richard wants: wealth, a readership, Hollywood interest in his work and a beautiful young aristocratic wife he adores and fucks as often as he can. As if this weren't enough, as the novel opens, Gwyn discovers that he is on the shortlist for a prize, the nicely named Profundity Requital – which, if he wins, will provide him with a considerable income for the rest of his life. Good work if you can get it.

Amis enjoys taking us through the routine of Richard's days, contrasting his calamities and woes with Gwyn's successes. Richard dresses ridiculously in bright waistcoats, reviews literary biographies, edits the arts pages of *The Little Magazine*, sells scraps of literary gossip and moves without purpose through the degraded streets and sordid parks of west London, the familiar Amis territory of Holland Park, Notting Hill and Ladbroke Grove, his fictional patch, his manor.

At night, Richard retreats to his study to work on his latest novel, Untitled, a novel so opaque and experimental that it induces a migraine in whoever tries to read it. We have been here before in the company of Amis, most obviously in the early novel *Success* (1981), an engaging caper in which two foster brothers are set against each other in perpetual competition, especially over women, with one more successful than the other, until their fortunes are reversed, as in the story about the poet and the screenwriter, 'Career Move'. The rivalry between the writers in *The Information* is darker and far more treacherous than in these earlier fictions, at one with the unremitting bleakness of the urban setting – and there is to be no dramatic reversal for Richard. If anything, his luck is destined to run out altogether, especially once he decides that he can escape the prison of his envy only through destroying Barry, through 'fucking him up' once and for all. This becomes his consuming mission. What sustains him in his unhappiness and envy, what keeps him going as he trips and stumbles in his various attempts to topple Barry, is the knowledge that his rival's novels are worthless and

shall have no afterlife. 'Gwyn's success was rather amusingly –
no, in fact completely hilariously – accidental,' he tells himself.
'And transitory. Above all transitory. If not in real time then,
failing that, certainly in literary time. Enthusiasm for Gwyn's
work, Richard felt sure, would cool quicker than his corpse. Or
else the universe was a joke. And a contemptible joke.'

To smooth his mission Richard enlists the help of a street
thug he meets one afternoon by chance. He is Steven Cousins
(aka Scozzy) and, together with his two black sidekicks, a driving instructor called – wait for it – Crash, and 13, a man who answers not to a name but a number, and an unlucky one at that,
certainly for Richard, as it turns out. Amis, like Bellow before
him, invariably introduces criminals into the mix with writers
and aristocrats. He likes the comic possibilities of this cross-
cultural slippage and he likes experimenting with different
modes of speech. Here is 13, complaining about the enhanced
powers of the police in Thatcher's Britain:

> 'The titheads . . . is like a gang. The Old Bill is like a gang. Hired by the
> government. When did it happen? It happened when they upped the
> pay. 1980 or whatever. They saying: It's gonna get rough. Unemploy-
> ment is it. Riots or whatever. You keep a lid on it and we pay you extra.
> Where's the money come from? No worries. We'll fine the fuckers.'

This amusing passage is evidence of Amis's fine gift for listening
and then for replicating the multiracial patois of the inner city.
The trouble is: he is seldom prepared to loosen the reins of narrative control; he is always insistently and tiresomely present,
pre-empting the reader. So 13's riff about the police is prefaced
thus: '13 drew breath: he was about to give voice – and in the
high style. His intention, plainly, was to speak not just for himself but for all men and all women, in all places, in all times – to
remind the human heart of what it had once known and had
now long forgotten.'

Haven't we heard something like this before? 'The High

Style,' wrote Amis of Bellow, 'attempts to speak for the whole of mankind . . . to remind us of what we once knew and have since forgotten . . .'

Because this is an Amis novel it must necessarily follow that Cousins – and 13 and Crash – shall be a comic grotesque, rather than a comic surprise. It follows that he must conform to (stereo)type, even though he introduces himself to Richard as 'an autodidact', in a way that is against type. This interests Richard and, for once, he stops thinking about himself and thinks instead about Cousins. 'Autodidact – that's a tough call,' he says. 'You're always playing catch-up, and it's never wholly that you love learning. It's always for yourself.'

This is one of the most poignant observations in the book, because true, but Amis never takes it anywhere. He never attempts to develop Cousins as a character or explore the possibilities of his quest for knowledge as, say, Forster did with the character of the yearning suburban clerk Leonard Bast in *Howard's End* or Zadie smith did in the character of a young black American rapper in *On Beauty,* her homage to *Howard's End.*

This is, above all, a failure of imaginative empathy, a failure that extends most problematically to Richard's wife, Gina. We are told often that Richard is impotent. Indeed, Amis repeatedly riffs around the theme of impotence. Richard, he writes, was 'impotent with her [Gina] every other night and, at weekends, in the mornings too . . . Nor did the bedroom mark the boundary of their erotic play. In the last month alone, he had been impotent with her on the stairs, on the sofa in the sitting room and on the kitchen table.'

Later, he returns to the subject:

After each display, after each proof of his impotence, it was into his excuses that Richard poured his creative powers . . . In the early weeks they explored the themes of tiredness; and then re-explored it . . . There they lay together, yawning and rubbing their eyes, night after night, working their way through the thesaurus of fatigue: bushed,

whacked, shattered, knackered, zonked, zapped, pooped . . . As excuses
went, tiredness was clearly a goer, amazingly versatile and athletic; but
tiredness couldn't be expected to soldier on indefinitely. Before very
long, tiredness made a natural transition to the sister theme of over-
work, and then struck out for the light and space of pressure, stress
and anxiety.

All of this is tolerably amusing, if only as adolescent dormitory
humour, but it is also unbelievable, especially in the context of
the marriage as depicted in the novel. Amis insists on telling
rather than showing the details of Richard and Gina's sexual
difficulties. When on the few occasions they are shown together, fretting over unpaid bills or discussing Richard's chances of
finding a publisher for Untitled, their encounters are brief and
rather fraught. This marriage is ashen and deathly. Richard and
Gina are emphatically not portrayed as being a couple who,
when chance would have it, are attempting to make out on the
stairs or kitchen table, heady and reckless with mutual intoxica-
tion. Nor does Richard and, by implication, his puppet master
Amis pause to reflect on how all this rejection may be affecting
Gina. This would be to cross a border into altogether unfamil-
iar terrain. So instead of pathos, we have pontification; instead
of empathy, we have stylised effect.

To Martin Amis prose style is not mere decoration; it reveals
moral character. 'When I read someone's prose I reckon to get
a sense of their moral life,' he wrote, preposterously, in *Koba the
Dread*. So what of his own moral life? If you read Amis's prose
against itself, seeking meaning in the ellipses and omissions of
his style, you find an empty space where once the consolations
of faith and belief might have been for the nineteenth-century
novelist, where for later writers, perhaps, a political programme
would have been, and where now love ought to be, however
tangentially expressed. Many of Amis's best non-fiction pieces
are enriched by love – the love he feels for his father and siblings

and children and for the writers and books that mean most to him. There is no love in his fiction, certainly for or between characters. There is only a love of style, something that precedes and is anterior to the fiction. So the very act of writing for Amis must be an act of love, even if he is repeatedly drawn to what is most morbid and debased in the human story, even if in his land of the make-believe the word itself catches amen-like in his throat. It cannot be spoken or expressed.

Amis inhabits a resolutely post-religious world, in which everything is perishable and there is no redemption. The universe, he keeps telling us in *The Information* is not, emphatically, about us. He returned to this theme in his next work, the novella *Night Train*, narrated by a tough, lonely Irish-American female cop with a man's name (Mike Hoolihan). *Night Train* is, like *The Information, un livre sur rien* – a book about nothing. Or, rather, about nothingness. Hoolihan is investigating the death of a young woman, the well-named Jennifer Rockwell, who has been shot in the head. But this is a detective novel without a murderer and it soon becomes apparent that Jennifer, a family friend of Hoolihan's, was not murdered. She committed suicide as she sat one day alone in her apartment – but why? We learn much about Jennifer during the course of Hoolihan's sad investigation, most pressingly, and oddly, that she was happy enough and largely fulfilled in her life.

So why did she do it? There is a clue to the mystery of her death in the work she did. Jennifer Rockwell was an astronomer; it was her professional duty to study emptiness and voids, to be paid to think about being and nothingness. Pascal wrote that 'man is equally incapable of seeing the nothingness from which he emerges and the infinity in which he is engulfed'. Not so with Jennifer Rockwell. She, Amis suggests – and the reader must accept, because nothing else in her fine bright life of achievement and opportunity indicates that she would have killed herself – evidently saw into the nothingness of Pascal's 'immensity of

spaces which I know not and which know not me'. This knowledge, this terror of the infinite void, destroyed her.

A terror of the void is also what keeps disturbing Richard
Tull in his sleep, awakening him to the reality of his earthly failures. When Amis is not pushing these fears on to the hapless
Richard, he stands apart from the narrative, taking time out,
as it were, to talk about time – and space. Long passages of the
novel are given over to astronomical equations and calcula-
tions. 'Out there, in the universe, the kilometer definitively has
it over the mile. If the universe likes roundness. Which it seems
to do. The speed of light is 186,282 mps, but it is very close to
300,000 kps. One light hour is 670,000,000 miles but it is very
close to 1,000,000,000 kilometres . . .'

Even the characters think of themselves in cosmological
terms. If people were planets, Richard thinks, he would be Pluto, and Charon his art. Pluto was the smallest of the planets, so
far away from the sun. How would he feel now, all these years
later, to discover that Pluto is no longer even a planet; that in
2006 it was downgraded to the status of 'dwarf planet'?

The universe's first appearance as a major character in an
Amis novel was in *London Fields*, published in 1989 but set a
decade later, on the eve of the new millennium. Despite the
title, this is an anti-pastoral, a study in urban psychosis and
alienation. The sense of crisis is once more acute: time is out
of joint, London's streets are polluted, crowded and violent; the
weather has gone wrong (in 1989, Amis knew all about the heat
waves ahead) and the threat of nuclear and environmental catastrophe is omnipresent. Samson Young, the narrator, alone in
his flat, and dying, writes, 'We have all known days of sun and
storm that make us feel what it is to live on a planet. But the
recent convulsions have taken this further. They make us feel
what it is to live in a solar system, a galaxy. They make us feel –
and I'm on the edge of nausea as I write these words – what it is
to live in a universe. Particularly the winds. They tear through

the city, they tear through the island, as if softening it up for exponentially greater violence.'

Many scenes take place in a west London pub called the Black Cross, where a promiscuous and jaded woman of thirty-four called Nicola Six (or should that be Sex!) is searching for a murderer – her own. She ends up meeting Keith Talent, a wife-beating, small-time crook and darts player, and perhaps Amis's most energetic low-life creation. (Keith – he has no talent at all, of course. Ha ha.) *London Fields* is sprawling and fragmentary, a novel about writing, full of intertextual jokes and self-references – Samsom Young is staying in the flat of an absent writer, one Mark Asprey, who may or may not be the same 'MA' who, in Nicola's diary, is referenced as her most accomplished lover. MA – get it? The plot, such as it is, is incoherent. Nicola knows that she is to be murdered and when, on her next birthday – when she will be thirty-five, such a resonant age in literature – but not by whom. How she comes to know this is never properly explained, as Amis is no major realist, with minors in psychology, motivation and agency. The suspense turns on who is to be the murderer. Is it to be low-lifer Keith Talent, over whom Nicola exerts considerable sexual control, or high-born Guy Clinch, the naive and gullible posh boy with the demanding wife and demented child, who Nicola gleefully teases and torments?

It doesn't really matter in the end who the murderer is, though the murder takes place all the same as we knew it would, because Nicola, Keith and Guy have all the garish unreality of cartoon characters. We are encouraged to care little or nothing for them. What we are encouraged to care for, instead, is the big picture: the language, the artifice, the art. To read *London Fields* is, in many ways, to encounter a writer with too much talent. He wants to try everything – anything – because he can, and more often than not it comes off. Look at me, he seems to be saying, I can juggle with all the balls in the air.

*

Shortly after the publication of *London Fields*, Amis was interviewed in the *New York Times*. At the age of forty, he had begun
to feel old. 'It's a little death, middle age. Romantic possibility ...
changes. It's calmer waters now, windless seas – if not the doldrums. You always thought it was a hilarious secret that while
everyone else got old, you weren't. But children redefine everything for you. A lot of the self is lost, thank God; the internal
gibber of wants and need dies down.'

Ah, calm seas, the doldrums ... as it turned out, Amis could
not have been more wrong, because he would soon find himself adrift in very turbulent waters indeed. If *The Information*
is a book about a mid-life crisis it was written, as Amis told me
when I interviewed him at home one evening in the summer
of 1997, at the end of what he called his own 'cataclysmic mid-
life crisis'. In retrospect, the entire book reads like an extended
crisis – of ambition, of confidence, of over-reach. In the last instance, it is an exercise in heroic decline, the monumental work
towards which Amis had long been moving as each novel became more complicated and multilayered, as each novel strove
to be truly novel: new, urgent. A superpower novel!

Yet approaching the final 100-page stretch of *The Information*, once the two writers have returned from a protracted and
hysterically rendered book promotional tour of the US, the
structure begins to mimic that of its central character. It begins
to atrophy. It begins slowly to collapse in on itself. The strain becomes palpable. In the fourth and final part of the book, Amis
starts closing each discrete section with a ruled line, a technical-
ity introduced for no apparent reason. He begins to shift points
of view and, intermittently, we are inside Gwyn Barry's head.
The weather becomes more extreme ('All the rumours of the
wind now gathered themselves, in riptide') and the astronomical musings even more overwrought, as if it is not only Richard Tull who feels he is running out of time: 'The Man in the
Moon is getting younger every year. Your watch knows exactly

what time is doing to you: tsk, tsk, it says, every second of every day. Every morning we leave more in bed, more of ourselves, as our bodies make their own preparations for reunion with the cosmos . . . The planesaw whines, whining for its planesaw mummy. And then there is the information, which is nothing, and comes at night.'

During our meeting, I was baffled as to why the experience of ageing should have been so traumatic for Amis. The complacency of youth, no doubt. Now, having reread *The Information* all these years later, I understand how the real subject of the novel is not literary envy or male rivalry, the ordinary motors of comedy. It is the fear of death, a fear that can come upon some of us suddenly, nightmarishly, in early middle-age. 'During a mid-life crisis you feel stupefied,' Amis told me. 'You are living in a land you no longer recognise. You don't know the language anymore. You feel lost. Women have a biological change; men don't. It's a pity because the whole thing might be understood more if they did. A mid-life crisis is really about reaching an accommodation with death.'

For Amis, more than most, the passing of youth must have been especially painful. He had always achieved so much so young; he had always been the coming man, the writer with the youthful high-energy style and the cool, street-smart persona, the writer in search of the new rhythms. He always seemed to have so much promise, and he kept on improving: each new book seeemed at the time to be an advance on the one before – until, that was, he wrote *The Information*, and revealed how increasingly over-reliant he was on the same effects and satirical conceits, the same overheated tropes, how destined he was to repeat himself again and again, like poor Pincher Martin scrambling for survival on his blasted rock.

Like Woody Allen, Amis is a comedian who wants to be a catastrophist. This may explain why no matter how much he labours to import seriousness into his fiction – through writing about the nuclear threat, the Holocaust, Stalin's gulags or Islamism and the al-Qaeda attacks on New York and Washington of 11 September 2001 and the cultural wars that followed – his novels never really move or, I think, succeed in conveying the textures of felt experience. There is something powerfully ersatz about them. They never carry us to the heart of the human muddle in the way that his non-fiction can. Largely this is because his characters remain trapped within the matrix of his style. They are ghosts orbiting, forever lost in the monotonous sublime of caricature. You cannot believe in them because their creator does not bestow upon them the gift of autonomous life nor does he want you to believe in them, and if you cannot really believe in them, you cannot care.

'All writers,' Amis once said, as noted, 'if they mean business, if they're ambitious, have got to think they're the best. You haven't got a chance of being the best unless you think you're best.'

Does Amis still think he's the best?

Much of his writing is about artistic rivalries, even if his ambition is to write about very big issues, not just middle-class mores. Yet this preoccupation with artistic rivalry, and the possibility of defeat in such rivalry, is intensely personal and rather parochial, echoing his own experiences in the smart, young literary set in which he moved in the 1970s. As a subject, it isn't really the stuff of literature. It is too weak and flimsy, hence the need for all that additional heavy-duty intellectual support – for the scaffolding of astronomy.

As Amis enters his seventh decade – his seventh! – what has it cost him, all this striving and effort to be the best? How does it feel nowadays to be Martin Amis, a writer who, in critical mode, long ago declared war on cliché, a writer who, after all this time, remains a self-appointed warrior of words?

Early in *The Information*, as the narrator digresses to speculate on a future in which 'the polar icecaps have melted and Norway enjoys the climate of North Africa', he teasingly suggests future readers can 'check' the accuracy of 'these words against personal experience'. Yes, he expects his work – this novel – to have a glorious afterlife, to continue to be read long into the future. It's a nice joke. Will future generations, similarly, read Amis? Will his stuff last? The final cruelty, as Richard Tull and indeed Amis himself know only too well, is that 'only time shall tell, if not real time then, failing that, certainly literary time'. And Amis, like the rest of us, is skewered on time's arrow.

IAN SANSOM

And anyway, anyway, it's the first week of the semester, and I'm going with my 'What Is the Point of the Novel?' talk, part of the over-subscribed, and under-taught, and utterly intellectually bankrupt interdisciplinary Twentieth-Century Studies Honours degree Programme; it usually gets them going.

And I'm standing there, waving my arms around, Leavis-style open-necked shirt, Eagleton-style hip-hugging cords, talking. (The clothes, I think, when I was younger, were intended to suggest both cultural mastery and social ease: now they're not just what I wear, they're what I am; they have eaten into my flesh). When I was starting out I tried to model my lecturing style on A. J. P. Taylor – casual, but authoritative; I saw some old footage of him on the telly once, in black-and-white – but recently one of my students told me that everyone calls me Mister Sharofsky, out of the TV programme *Fame*; the repeats have been running on satellite and cable.

'What I want to do for the next twenty minutes', I say, 'is to offer some kind of answer to the question "What is the point of the novel?", and if we have time we'll move into some structured class discussion. Twenty minutes isn't really long enough to develop an argument, but it is long enough to offer an opinion, or to make a point. So what I want to do in answering the question "What is the point of novel?" is – simply – to make a point, to offer a point, which we can then discuss. Hmm.' Talk, talk, talk, and all the time I'm talking about The Point of the Novel, I'm thinking, What Is the Point of Talking about The Point of the

Novel? Of course, this way madness and long-term unemployment lies, so I plough on, focusing on a flickering strip-light at the back of the room so as not to meet the eyes of any of the poor sufferers being subjected to this guff and so to spare both me and them the shame of mutual acknowledgement of our shared fate: a long slow stifling by boredom. I wonder, did Lloyd George ever feel like this? Did Roosevelt? Churchill? Martin Luther King? The great orators of the twentieth century? Or even the not so great. Like, did Billy Graham? All those people on television? Does everyone really know when they're talking rubbish? I mean, deep down inside, down below? Do you?

I also put my hand to my mouth and surreptitiously blow into it for a quick moment, the hot breath rising to my nostrils, like a blast from blocked drains, checking for the tell-tale signs of nerves. I always get bad breath when I'm teaching. And toothache. I really need to go and see a dentist.

'Hmm. My point' – I say, my tongue exploring the entrance to a tender little pot-hole in a molar up on top – 'is simply this: the point of the novel – or *a* point of the novel – is that there is no point to the novel. This is not the same thing as saying that the novel is pointless.' Ouch. The pot-hole is getting more like a crevasse. What on earth am I saying? Do I really believe this? Hmm? How come I'm spouting this sort of horseshit? And while I'm thinking this, or rather – let's not flatter ourselves – while this thought is occurring to me, I stroke my beard and I find some pieces of croissant there, like little sugar-frosted flakes of dry scalp – another of my distinguishing features, as it happens – and I have to halt my flow and pause while I quickly brush the crumbs out and down onto my tank-top, which I notice is becoming a little ruched around the waist, and which I pull up and which in so doing drags up my shirt with it, leaving my untucked butter-gut and beer-belly exposed to the sight of the class for a moment before I can hurriedly retuck and rearrange myself and go on.

I think, for a moment: this is a disaster, I am useless at this, I can't go on.

I go on. That's life.

No, actually, that's Samuel Beckett.

'Hmm.' I don't know when I started the hmming. It's one of those academic affectations that just seems to have crept up on me, overpowered me, and beaten me senseless. It's awful. I hate it. But I can't seem to stop it. 'Some things might be said to have a point - a sharp stick, obviously, containing a mixture of graphite and clay, what we call a pencil might be said to have a point, in a number of senses.'

This usually gets a little laugh. And sure enough, there's a faint buzz of laughter, like flies round a rotting corpse. The first rule of lecturing: make 'em laugh, make 'em cry. Give them something juicy to get their teeth into, a nice bit of carrion, something soft, something easy. Even A. J. P. bloody Taylor told jokes. *'World War One? World War One? I'll tell you something about World War One, missus. World War One was started by the railway timetables!'* Oh yes, very funny guy, A.J.P. He was a real cheeky chappie. He was like Arthur Askey. He was practically vaudeville. He was music-hall. And you can understand why. I mean, you've got to say something to get them on your side, to get their attention. You need a catchphrase. It's all about riffs and tags and punch-lines. Because when it comes down to it, it's all about winning them over: it's rhetoric, the power of address. And you've either got it or you haven't got it, the right address, or the right of address, as it were.

And I haven't.

I live in the provinces, literally and metaphorically – not that it's a cause for regret. Not really. It's not that I once had it and then lost it, not as if I've moved from W1 out to the suburbs. I never had it, was never there. Never took up residence in the mental West End. Some people have it of course: the right of address. NW1, intellectually, a lot of people. SW11. But I started out in the suburbs, and now I'm in the provinces.

(Where do you live? London? New York? Edinburgh? Berlin? OK, well, let me explain where I live. We're not talking a backwater here, we're not talking Yonville, like in *Madame Bovary*; we're talking Nowheresville, Anywhere, in the Kingdom of the Back of Beyond. We're not talking *backwater*, we're talking *backwash*; the grey frothing spittle round the lips of the big bad gaping City. You don't live in a city? You live in the country? OK. Imagine a field. Good. Now imagine the ditch. That's where I live.)

And at the weekend we were at this party. And at this party I was eating stuffed mushrooms and drinking champagne, though not too much – I was the designated driver. But I figured one glass should be OK; I don't need to worry about just one glass of champagne. I'm wearing my best trousers and an ironed shirt. It's a fortieth birthday party – my demographic, my people, my constituency absolutely: middle-aged, lower middle-class, well-intentioned people with sensible cars and smart-casual clothes. The house is semi-detached. The kitchen is knocked through to a family room – toys, CDs, DVDs, prints of old film posters. The children are all crowded onto the sofa watching *Shrek 2*, which is a great film, us adults all agree, drifting through the kitchen and out into the garden. I like *Shrek 2*; everybody likes *Shrek 2*.

'It's one of those films, *Shrek 2*,' says a man whose name I have instantly forgotten, 'that's a sequel that's better than the original.'

'Like *Toy Story 2*,' says another man who I recognise vaguely from off the telly; I think he reads the local news.

Outside, the men are talking about going to the gym, about five-a-side football, about summer holidays, and about the nice Indian restaurant over in Stranmillis. The women are talking about their children, and about secondary schools, and a

good recipe for flapjack: 'Dried cranberries,' a woman wearing
sunglasses and a wrap-around dress is saying. 'Dried cranberries are the secret.' I make a mental note of the dried cranberries, and also of her wrap-around dress.

I'm talking to a man who works for Tearfund, and his wife,
who works for Barnado's. They are good people; there is no
doubt about it: they make eye contact when they're talking to
you; they laugh when you say something funny; they nod their
heads in agreement when you make an interesting point. We're
talking about Tearfund's plans for the commemoration of the
abolition of slavery, and government funding for after-school
clubs – it's an interesting conversation – and then they ask me
what I do for a living, which is always tricky, a no-win situation and embarrassing for everyone, but I guess the one glass
of champagne has loosened my tongue and anyway I like these
obviously good people and so I swallow my pride and admit
that I do a bit of teaching, but that really I'm a writer.

'Oh, really?' they say, and this is the bit that's always tricky.
'What's your name? Will we have heard of you?'

'No,' I say, laughing. 'You wouldn't have heard of me. But
that's fine. Even *I* haven't heard of me!'

They laugh. They're good people.

Anyway, they're in a reading group, these good people at the
party who I like a lot. They love the reading group. It's nice to
meet with other people and discuss literature. They enjoy listening to other people's ideas and opinions, although of course
these days there's always the Google problem, says the man.

'The what?' I say.

'Do you pretend your ideas about the books are your own,' explains the man, 'or do you admit that you got them off Google?'

I ask them what they've been reading recently in the reading
group. They have been reading Philip Roth's *American Pastoral*.

'Wow!' I say, genuinely impressed. 'What did you think?'

'Well . . .' they say, looking at each other.

They certainly haven't got their ideas about *American Pastoral* from Google. They absolutely hate *American Pastoral* – loathe it. Revile it. Despise it. They hate everything about it.

'A really miserable book,' says the lady.

'And the sentences are so long,' says the man.

They couldn't see the point of it at all. They're much happier now with *The Color Purple*.

On the way home in the car I say to my wife, 'Can you believe it! How can they not like *American Pastoral*?'

'I don't know,' says my wife.

'*American Pastoral*!' I say. 'Philip Roth!'

'Uh-huh,' says my wife.

'Honestly, though, what are they, stupid?' I say.

My wife, like the Tearfund man and his Barnado's wife, is a good person. Like the Tearfund man and his Barnado's wife, she works in the public sector. She gets up every morning and goes out and tries to make the world a better place.

'They are not stupid,' says my wife. 'I would have thought,' she says, 'that they're just coming at it from a different angle.'

'What angle?'

'Just a different angle,' she says.

'A reading-group angle,' I say.

'Maybe,' she says.

'The wrong angle,' I say.

I do not belong to a reading group. I think I'm not tempera-mentally suited to being a part of a reading group. I have a fear that reading groups might be secular versions of Bible-study groups – what churches call 'home groups'. In home groups the Bible, and literature, becomes reduced to a kind of moral top-up, like anti-freeze or echinacea: books as strengthening and as consolation and encouragement; literature as healthy exercise, a way of warding off infection. But personally I find reading the Bible, or books, usually has exactly the opposite effect on me: depletion, drainage, and weakening. And not just the rubbish books, all the dross you have to wade through to get to the good stuff. Even the classics get me down. Shakespeare. Totally depressing. George Eliot. Totally depressing. Chekhov. Kafka. Flaubert. Ditto. I know why. Do you want to know why? I think I know why. I think I've worked it out. Do you want to know what's my grand theory? My angle? Do you want to know what I think is the point of the novel, indeed of all great literature, including the Bible?

'Do you know what's the point? If there was a point?' I ask the class. They just look at me, obviously. 'People are bad,' I say.

That's it. People are bad; they're bad. I'm not telling them anything they don't already know, obviously. I mean, what are the figures? Four million men, women and children dead in the Congo civil war and seventy thousand dead in Darfur, and that's just one year, picked at random, 2007 – a year which also featured, by the way, around about five million children dead of hunger, three million dead of Aids, and tens of thousands slaughtered in the various little skirmishes, and civil wars and whatever it was America and her allies thought they were doing in Iraq and Afghanistan. Even in my home town last year – my useless, uninteresting, utterly insignificant scabby wee seaside town in the middle of the middle of nowhere – there were two murders, any number of assaults and beatings, one reported rape, and a family from Pakistan were burnt out of their house because they were from Pakistan. On a clear day when I look out of my front window I can see the swastikas spray-painted on the bandstand in the park opposite, and two weeks ago, on a Sunday night, a gang of people broke into the little pets' corner there in the park and killed all the birds, slitting their throats and stamping on them – dozens of them, including rare-breed chickens and canaries and two peacocks. The birds were all lying there broken and bloody the next morning as people walked their children to school. 'The fact of sin,' I say. 'What G. K. Chesterton calls "a fact as practical as potatoes".

'A fact as practical as potatoes,' I repeat. 'People are bad,' I repeat. 'That's the point. If there is a point.' I'm assuming they all know Roth's essay, 'Writing American Fiction', first published in *Commentary* in March 1961, where he muses that 'the American writer in the middle of the twentieth century has his hands full in trying to understand, describe, and then make credible much of American reality. It stupefies, it sickens, it infuriates, and finally it is even a kind of embarrassment to one's meagre imagination. The actuality is continually outdoing our talents, and the culture tosses up figures almost daily that are the envy of any novelist.' And in case they don't, I quote it.

And then I notice this one guy sitting towards the back of the class. He's called Paul. He's a third-year. He's always there, at the back, like the metaphorical and holy ghost at the sacral feast, or in this case, another beggar at our sad, long, mind-numbing intellectual fast. He obviously thinks he's a pretty cool customer: little round glasses, big coat. He looks a lot like I used to when I was a student. There's a particular way of wearing the clothes that never changes, I've noticed that, like they're too long in the arm and too broad in the shoulder, like they don't fit, even when they do fit. And he's leaning back on his chair, staring up at the ceiling, disinterestedly, and I think, how can I get this bloke's attention, this overcoated young man, this Paul, this notional and literal Student X, the very audience the University of Y is setting out to reach in its quest to bring higher education to the masses? (I'm paraphrasing our mission statement here.) And it reminds me of the time I gave my first public lecture, at the special open day, a couple of years back, just a few months after I'd been appointed.

I was so nervous, it was like I was Lucky Jim or something – stayed off the drink the night before as a precaution – and this smartly dressed elderly woman came up to me after the lecture, pearls and all, court shoes, hairspray, and she said, 'I only have one thing to say to you young man', and my heart was in my mouth, expecting some sort of disagreement over my interpretation of Empson on Milton or queries about possible variant readings based on other editions of the *Lyrical Ballads*, and then she said, 'and that's I noticed you were leaning back on your chair before you got up to speak and I had a friend once who leaned back on her chair, and she fell back and ended up in hospital being treated for spinal injuries, which eventually healed, thank God, but which cast her into a deep depression, which meant her husband left her, and she lost her home and her children, and I wouldn't want something like that to happen to you.'

Hmm.

I feel like going up to my Student X, this Paul, my paradigmatic ill-fitting young man in the back row, and kicking his chair away from under him, inflicting spinal injuries, and standing over him and wagging my finger and shouting this lesson to him. That'd get his attention.

But I don't, of course. I just go meandering on.

'Hmm', I say. 'A pencil clearly has a use as a writing implement. It has a function, or an application. But the novel is not a tool, and is not an applied art: it can't be said, in the same sense as a pencil might be said, to have a point. The novel, in this crucial sense, is not a pencil.'

I go on and on, quoting Dr Johnson, and quoting Milan Kundera, and George Eliot, and Henry James, and Kurt Vonnegut, and Bohumil Hrabal, and just about anyone else who comes to mind – Marilynne Robinson, I say, read Marilynne Robinson, and not just the novels, read the essays, I say, and Jean-Philippe Toussaint, and Roberto Bolaño, and Stefan Zweig, it's worth learning German just to be able to read Stefan Zweig, I say, and Haruki Murakami, Kerstin Ekman, and anyone, everyone, who's written anything and thought about anything for more than about five minutes, and in the end even I can't remember what my point was, and before launching into the discussion,

funny, but not in a funny ha-ha kind of a way: asked in an interview about the influence on his work of stand-up comics like Lenny Bruce, Roth, I say, Roth famously remarked that he was 'more strongly influenced by a sit-down comic called Franz Kafka.' 'That's funny,' I say – even though nobody laughs. 'That. Is. Funny.' And his clarity – I talk about his clarity, obviously – his rich, lyrical clarity. And his clear understanding – unlike, say, Saul Bellow – that you can't improve your style just by using inflated words. And his abundance, obviously: the cascades of wit, and the fountains of bile, the vast rolling similes. And the way he uses the novel as a means of moral demonstration – or at least the demonstration of moral contradiction, and contingency, and consequences, and conflict. And the fact that in *Sabbath's Theater* (1995), say, and certainly in *American Pastoral* (1997), and *I Married a Communist* (1998) and *The Human Stain* (2000), those three magnificent books bundled together by Roth and by his publishers and by the critics and often referred to as the American Trilogy, he has written what is pretty much the definitive statement on the emotional bankruptcy, the moral idiocy, and the intellectual dishonesty – the pure badness - which characterised the late twentieth century, same as any other century. And *Portnoy's Complaint* (1969), of course, that gets a look in, that big soiled Kleenex of a novel, which has the best pay-off line of any novel. Read it, I say. Read the novel. Read all the novels. 'But bear in mind,' I say, 'that these are not really novels. These things are bigger than novels,' I say. 'They are a moral reckoning. "What do novels do, then?" someone asked Roth in an interview, way way back, and he gave the best answer I've ever heard anyone give. "Novels," he says – and I'm paraphrasing here – "Novels provide readers with something to read. At their best writers change the way readers read." That's it,' I say. 'That's the right answer.' 'Read Philip Roth,' I say. 'And you'll end up hating Philip Roth.' 'I loathe him,' I say. 'He's left nothing for me.' And I quote from Kafka's famous letter to his father, quoted by Roth in his own essay on Kafka in *Reading Myself* (1975): 'Sometimes I imagine the map of the world spread out and you stretched diagonally across it. And I feel as if I could consider living only in those regions that are not covered by you or are not within your reach.' Philip Roth should create a rage in you, I say. He should make you ashamed. 'He makes me ashamed,' I say. 'He makes me ashamed to be human, and to pretend to call myself a writer, because in comparison to this sort of a writer, I am nothing: *you* are nothing.'

At which point we're way beyond the twenty-minute mark and almost up to the hour, and I can see them beginning to shuffle. 'Just read the books,' I say. 'At least read *American Pastoral*,' I say. 'This is a book,' I say, 'that begins with possibly the most unpromising sentence in English literary history: "The Swede." Or in fact, in my cheap English paperback edition – look! – it's all in capitals, "THE SWEDE", so it looks like it's going to be a book about a giant vegetable!' Cue laughter. 'But it's not,' I say. 'It's about a man, Seymour Irving Levov, who looks Swedish. But he's not Swedish. He's Jewish. He's not what he seems. Which is what the book is about – Seymour "The Swede" Levov, "a human platitude" – slowly waking up to the way the world is, and what he is. As the Swede's brother puts it, in one of those riffs which makes Roth one of the greats – let me read it to you. "You think you know what a man is? You have no *idea* what a man is. You think you know what a daughter is? You have no idea what a daughter is. You think you know what this country is? You have no *idea* what this country is. You have a false image of *everything*. All you know is what a fucking glove is. This country is *frightening*." *American Pastoral* is frightening, I say. 'The linguistic felicity. The inventiveness. And not just the inventiveness: the *reinventiveness*. The way he reinvents the cliché of the high-school reunion. The moral reckoning. And the stories – the torrents of story. If you take just one story, just one little incident,' I say, 'like when the Swede's brother, Jerry, is making a coat out of hamster skins. No, really. He's trying to impress a girl. He dries out the skins, sews them together, and finishes it off with a silk lining made from an old white parachute. And this is what Roth writes: "He was going to send it to the girl in a Bamberger's coat box of his mother's, wrapped in lavender tissue paper and tied with velvet ribbon. But when the coat was finished, it was so stiff – because of the idiotic way he'd dried the skins, his father would later explain – that he couldn't get it to fold up in the box.'" You could write a whole PhD on the Point of the Novel, based on these sentences, I say. Why? Because this little incident tells a great truth – a truth about disconsolation. 'And this,' I say, 'This I take to be the good of the novel.'

And the next class is tapping on the door and waiting to come in.

FRANCES WILSON

'You may as well call it a fish'

Separation is traumatic. It's horrible to think that people have to part. Not only that they have to part, but that they may even hate each other before they part. And when you hate someone, you maybe behave monstrously towards them, which is a disgusting thought. And they hate you as well . . . Writers happen to write it down, which makes them bad.

Hanif Kureishi, *Guardian*, 17 November 2003

'I have been reading an account by a contemporary author of his breakup with his partner. It is relentless, and, probably because it rings true, has been taken exception to.'

'Strangers when We Meet,' Hanif Kureishi

Every so often a popular author writes an unpopular book. This is not the same thing as a good author occasionally writing a bad book. A bad book is a temporary tumble, and after a suitable period of shame the writer will pick himself up, dust himself down and begin the business of wooing the reader back into his world. The unpopular book is not so easily forgiven. It appears less frequently than the bad book, but some significant examples stand out: neither Lytton Strachey's *Eminent Victorians*, Byron's *Don Juan*, nor Salman Rushdie's *The Satanic Verses* were welcomed on arrival. Strachey insulted our ancestors, Byron insulted everyone, including his wife, while Rushdie insulted Islam. The unpopular book is something whose existence the public does not want; it is received as a samurai attack, a biting of the hand that feeds.

Given that serious writers generally set out to question and

provoke rather than to gratify and sooth, it is surprising that as
many books are as popular as they are, and that so few writers
succeed in outraging their readers. Hanif Kureishi is a writer
whose value has been precisely his capacity to provoke. 'Each
piece of writing should be a risk,' he says, 'it would be worthless
otherwise,' and until his 1998 novel *Intimacy* his risks seemed
to pay off, increasing his value as a writer. He is celebrated
for his post-colonial tales of suburban aspiration, desire,
and transgression, for rescuing second- and third-generation
Asians from the image of 'premature middle-age', for giving them back their youthfulness. He was, at the time of his
Oscar-nominated screenplay, *My Beautiful Laundrette* (1984)
and his prize-winning novel, *The Buddha of Suburbia* (1990), 'a
talismanic figure for young Asians', wrote Sukhdev Sandhu in
an elegiac essay in the *London Review of Books*. 'We had previously been mocked for our deference and timidity. We were
too scared to look people in the eye when they spoke to us. We
weren't gobby or dissing . . . Kureishi's language was a revelation. It was neither meek nor subservient. It wasn't fake posh.
Instead it was playful and casually knowing . . . He seemed to
lack all fear.'

Because he 'didn't try to be liked', Hanif Kureishi used to be
a very popular author indeed. He was that unheard of thing:
a cool Paki, a dope-growing, cunty-fingered, rock'n'roll Asian
enfant terrible. With his mantra, 'If you think "I shouldn't say
that", it's always the thing you should say,' he was the Byron of
suburbia, a cocky upstart, on the make and on the move. He
didn't have coconut oil in his hair, he wore great clothes, he
was iconic: his image was so much a part of the writing that
his handsome face with its scrutinising gaze (he is one of those
authors whose photo graces the front cover, not the back flap,
of his books) became synonymous with the cultural moment
of the late 80s. When *Intimacy* was published, Kureishi was still
doing what he did best: saying the unsayable and making Brit-

ish Asian lives recognisable. Only now it was the very recognisability of the story he was telling that was the problem.

Intimacy is about a man's decision to leave a comfortable bourgeois family home in order to sleep on the floor of his friend's flat, which shows how far Kureishi has moved on: his first screenplays begin with characters being evicted from their squats. Because he is interested in conflict, the idea of home has been central to Kureishi's work. Homes – your country, your parent's country, the house where you live, the house where your mother lives – provide the complex political and personal roots of identity. They are what we must have in order to be free and what we must leave in order to become more free.

Kureishi's subject has been restlessness and mobility in a community which, as Sandhu writes, 'craves stillness'. He filled his earlier works with a picaresque range of characters – cheating businessmen, corseted mistresses, queers, skin-heads, con-men, adolescent entrepreneurs, wheelers, dealers and pushers – all snorting, licking, sucking, buggering or rutting as much as they could. His family hated what he did, but finding ways of pissing people off gives Kureishi inspiration: 'The film brings to light your total lack of loyalty, integrity and compassion,' wrote an aunt from India after the release of *My Beautiful Laundrette*, in which a white skinhead and an Asian boy fall in love: 'We didn't know you were a poofter.' When it was only the conservative values of Asian parents and grandparents – his own and other peoples' – that Kureishi was provoking, we were unconcerned. Until he extended the range of his 'total lack of loyalty, integrity and compassion', we didn't much mind how irritating he was.

In *Intimacy* Kureishi transformed himself from the chronicler of Anglo-Indian identity who kept dutifully to his patch, to a satanic Milord more at home in the subterranean world of Romantic introspection than the squats and semis of south London, and the book was received as a literary affront. It is a very brief novel to have caused such a stir, sparingly set during the final night that Jay, a restless, middle-aged, award-winning British Asian writer, spends with his partner, Susan, and their two small boys. 'It is the saddest night,' the novel begins, 'for I am leaving and not coming back.' But Jay is not especially, or not simply, sad. Those of his memories, thoughts, and philosophies we share as the night progresses express fear, relief, sentiment, desire, anger and, only on occasion, sadness. In a claustrophobic interior monologue we are given Jay's feelings about Susan ('I want to say the smell of mimosa reminds me of her. I want to say she will always be with me in some way. But it is gone, and she is an unmourned true love'), about his sons ('they are ebullient and fierce, and people say what happy and affectionate children they are . . . tomorrow I will do something which will damage and scar them'), about his mother ('Most of the day she sat, inert and obese, in her chair. she hardly spoke – except to dispute'), and about his two best friends, Asif and Victor. The former is happily married to a woman with whom, 'when they are not discussing their children or important questions of the day', he will read Christina Rossetti; the latter has left his wife and children in order to live out of suitcases, despite his son's subsequent suicide attempt. And there is Jay's idealised hippy girlfriend, Nina, who allows him to eat strawberries and cream off her buttocks.

Intimacy is a painful read, especially for women, particularly for any woman who has ever been left. 'Tomorrow we will kiss and part,' Kureishi says. 'Actually, forget the kiss.' But is it a *good* novel? Whether it is good or bad has been of little critical concern because Kureishi has been judged a Bad Man (he is 'the ambassador of the Bad Bloke,' wrote Cressida Connolly in the *Observer*). The aggressive ordinariness of his style and the artless transparency of his prose were not commented on by most of his critics, any more than the novel's wincingly awful opening line ('It is the saddest night, for I am leaving and not coming back'). It is either liked or disliked, but mainly disliked, regardless of its artistic merit, which at least makes it an *effective* novel. 'I wrote a book that was intentionally horrible . . . The book worked because people got furious,' Kureishi told Robert McCrum in an *Observer* interview, 'so I felt that I had written a book that was, on its own terms, successful.' If the strength of a text can be measured by the repetitions it inspires, by the way in which its central concerns – in this case, falling out of love – are re-enacted by the response of its readers, then *Intimacy* is a very strong text indeed. A novel about separation, it resulted in a violent separation between Kureishi and his once loyal public.

The contents and critical reception of *Intimacy* are themselves something of a repetition: we have heard this story several times before. Byron's own leaving-home poem, *Don Juan*, written in 1819 when he separated from his wife and went into exile, was likewise thought too aggressively personal to be literary, too honest to be readable, a manual of offensive thought and distasteful experience. 'So now all things are damned,' Byron wrote, 'one feels at ease.' *Don Juan* was, one reviewer said, the product of an 'unrepenting, unsoftened, smiling, sarcastic, joyous sinner'. The portrait of Lady Byron was vindictive ('But – oh ye lords of ladies intellectual! / Inform us truly, have they not hen-pecked you all?'), the picture of contemporary England was cynical, the descriptions of home-life and relationships were bitter and jaded. Byron's readers were appalled: this is not want they wanted at all. The poet should have stuck to the East for his subject matter and kept them satisfied with another round of formulaic tales about a melancholic hero. Byron, once the most popular poet in the country, was described as 'no longer a human being, even in his frailties; but a cool, unconcerned, fiend'. As for the descriptions of his abandoned wife, 'To offend [her] love . . . was wrong,' wrote a reviewer in *Blackwood's Magazine* – 'but it might have been forgiven; to desert her was unmanly – but he might have returned and wiped forever from her eyes the tears of her desertion; – but to injure and to desert, then to turn back and wound her widowed privacy with unhallowed strains of cold blooded mockery – was brutally, fiendishly, inexpiably mean.' Byron's response? 'I shall not be deterred by an outcry.'

Then there is the case of the American poet Robert Lowell, whose sonnet collection *For Lizzie and Harriet* described the breakdown of his marriage, while *The Dolphin* (1973) incorporated, verbatim, lines from letters written to him by his wife, Elizabeth Hardwick, during their separation and divorce. 'Art just isn't worth that much,' said Lowell's friend, Elizabeth Bishop, when she saw what he was doing. Adrienne Rich, describing *The Dolphin* as 'a cruel and shallow book', asked – in genuine perplexity – what could be said 'about a poet who, having left his wife and daughter for another marriage, then titles a book with their names and goes on to appropriate his ex-wife's letters written under the stress and pain of desertion, into a book of poems nominally addressed to the new wife'. Lowell had stretched the confessional form to snapping point, and *The Dolphin*, like *Don Juan*, was soon recognised as a masterpiece.

Intimacy did not, as Kureishi believes, create and infuriate its readers because 'the subject is infuriating'. There are two reasons for *Intimacy*'s unpopularity. Initially, its narrative form: it is told in the first person with an uncomfortable mixture of serene critical detachment and more intimacy – in the sense of more information – than the reader can bear. The sentences smart like slaps in the face: 'There are some fucks for which a person would have their partner and children drown in a freezing sea.' Secondly, the plot repeats intimate events in Kureishi's own recent history: he, like Jay, left the house he shared with his partner and two young sons because, he said, 'it was more interesting to go'. In Kureishi's writing it tends to be the fathers who work to preserve the culture of the home, and the sons who leave. For his fathers, having a home means adopting an identity, a home is something to which they aspire; for his sons, the opposite is the case. In *Intimacy*, home represents the erosion of paternal identity and Jay, the father, is given a Dante-esque meditation on being lost in the midst of life, or as he puts it 'lost in the middle of life and no way home'. 'Father, six years dead, would have been horrified by my skulking off,' he considers. 'He didn't approve of leaving.' It is fathers and not sons who now leave: the problem with *Intimacy* is that it is too close to home.

Certain stories offend our understandings of what it is acceptable to say, or even feel. *Intimacy* not only transgressed, as Kureishi put it in an interview in *Time Out*, 'the Koran of the middle classes', it also crossed the line of discretion and good taste, of what can and cannot be written down, and of the genre in which you are entitled, or not, to write it. 'Anyone even with a scrap of rectitude could not fail to find *Intimacy* a repugnant little book, not least in view of the open secret that Kureishi's own life is known to mirror the events he describes,' wrote Cressida Connolly in the *Observer*. The critical assumption is that Kureishi, being the same person as Jay, has produced not a novel but a barely disguised piece of autobiography. 'Let's believe this book is a work of fiction,' wrote Laura Cumming in the *Guardian*. 'Immediately we won't have to worry about the effect the rancorous tale of a writer who leaves his partner and two small children might have on the family he has recently left . . .' 'Kureishi left his family before writing this beastly little book,' Kate Kellaway wrote in the *Literary Review*. 'I hope that it is only a novel and that an autobiography would read differently.' (In many descriptions of *Intimacy*, its awfulness is yoked to its brevity, reminding one of that old joke, 'the food was dreadful, and so little of it'.) Tracey Scoffield, the mother of Kureishi's two small children and the long-term partner he left, joined in the debate. 'There are sections and sequences in that book which are intended for me only and only I can understand them,' she said. Of Faber, *Intimacy*'s publisher (who happened to be her former employer), she declared, 'They think it's called a novel, therefore it's fiction, therefore they are not responsible.' Of Kureishi, she went further: 'He says it's a novel, but that's an absolute abdication of responsibility . . . Nobody believes it's just pure fiction. You may as well call it a fish.'

There has always been something fishy about the value of autobiographical fiction. But at what point does a writer's fictional depiction of his own experience become an abdication of responsibility? 'I think it is the writer's job to be irresponsible,' Kureishi shrugged, and we used to like him for it. In the *fin de siècle* ennui of *Intimacy*, he does not tell us what we want to hear about either break-ups or grown-ups. He did not write the book we wanted him to write. Along with *Midnight All Day* and *Love in a Blue Time*, *Intimacy* represents for Sandhu 'the ongoing decline of a once vital writer . . . In his earlier writing he captured and defined a precise historical juncture. He changed the lives of many young Asians.' 'I want to be free to not only be an Asian writer,' Kureishi insists, but none of his readers, neither Asian nor White, want to grant him this freedom. Kureishi should continue to write about race rather than giving us grim tales of middle-age and falling out of love; or at least he should tell us how difficult it is to leave your family and how guilty the guilty party feels: 'People speak of the violence of separation,' Kureishi writes in *Midnight All Day*, 'but what of the delight?' 'I have been trying to convince myself,' says Jay, 'that leaving someone is not the worst thing you can do to them. Sombre it may be, but it doesn't have to be a tragedy. If you never left anything or anyone, there would be no room for the new.' We like his autobiographical fiction only when Kureishi is writing about being young, hip and Asian; when he stops telling us illuminating things about that and instead says something illuminating about the choices made by men as they grow older, we stop listening.

The vocabulary used by the *Intimacy*'s reviewers was peculiarly intimate: 'deeply irritating', 'odious', 'beastly', 'repugnant', 'verging on the psychotic'. Kureishi's 'right to write the book' at all was raised by Susie MacKenzie in the *Guardian*, while Randeep Ramesh in an *Independent on Sunday* profile described 'loathing' not the book but Kureishi himself, 'for his apparently confessional, mean-spirited, and at times hateful outbursts'. But *Intimacy* is also described, by those same reviewers, as being too *honest*: it is 'relentlessly honest', 'chillingly honest'. No wonder Maggie Gee asked, in her own review, 'what are we to make of this?' One of our most cherished assumptions about fiction – the assumption on which the whole edifice of literary criticism has been built – is that it reflects experience, that the source of a story can be located in the life of its writer. Universities churn out English Literature graduates by the thousand who have been taught to read *Sons and Lovers* as an account of D. H. Lawrence's childhood and *Villette* as a fictionalisation of Charlotte Bronte's unhappy love affair. And yet, when a story so blatantly reflects experience, so *unapologetically* describes the life of its writer, it loses its *value*. There is no room in a novel for honesty on this scale. Honesty of the 'irresponsible' sort is the preserve of autobiography.

So what are we then to make of the statements which appeared in the press by Kureishi's mother and sister at the time that *Intimacy* was being reviewed, denouncing as *far from honest* the picture he drew in the book of his run-down, impoverished and emotionally deprived childhood? Rather than revealing home truths, Kureishi gave an entirely 'false impression of family life', which his mother and sister regard as every bit as unacceptable in the novel form as the 'chilling' and 'relentless honesty' to which Tracey Scoffield objected. 'Does being famous mean you can devalue all those around you and rewrite history for even more personal gain?' asked Kureishi's sister; 'He has sold his family down the line.' 'Hanif has made us sound like the dregs just because it suits his image and career,' said his mother, who had been told by her daughter not to read the book. 'I suppose it is trendy and fashionable for an author to pretend they had a working-class background [Kureishi uses, in fact, the term 'lower-middle class'], but Hanif had everything he wanted as a child . . .' Kureishi responded to these comments with his usual sigh: it is inevitable to find different members of the same family interpreting facts and events – even their own social class – in differing ways.

For one half of his family, the problem with *Intimacy* is that Kureishi made up too little, for the other half it is that he made up too much. What is curious is the way in which his family squabbles, the comments of his ex-partner and sister, have been treated in the press as literary criticism, so that *Intimacy* has been evaluated not on the grounds of aesthetic merit (the way in which he deploys language, form, style, structure, tradition, and so forth), but entirely on grounds of *honesty* and *responsibility*, as though these moral categories constituted valid and useful critical terms.

Break-ups, like the children's stories that Jay reads to his sons at bedtime, tend to be cruel. Their peculiar unhappiness makes each break-up feel unique but part of their cruelty is the uniformity of the hurt, the predictability of the narrative, the fact that in the end every break-up amounts, like every birth and death, to more or less the same story. For Tracey Scoffield, what stung 'to the power of ten' in *Intimacy* were those aspects of Jay's and Susan's relationship that only she could understand, which were meant as a message from Kureishi to her. But the sting in the tale is actually that, in Kureishi's hands, there is nothing peculiar or specific to this particular break-up, there are no hidden codes or secret meanings. Jay's and Susan's separation involves nothing more than the boiling down of a shared language to a few tired lines. 'I am leaving because I cannot make her a cup of tea,' Jay realises.

The problem with *Intimacy* is not that Kureishi has moulded personal experience into novel form, the true worth of which can only be appreciated by Tracey Scoffield, but that he tells a general enough tale to describe the experience of more or less anyone who has ever broken up. This is where the vertiginous thrill of the novel lies and why it is so appallingly readable. By stopping the clock, by giving us nothing but Jay's consciousness over one night, Kureishi gives us the triumph of selfhood in all its egocentric monstrosity at the same time as revealing Jay's story to be everyone's story, and his revelations to be common-place. Separating couples are trapped in an airtight lexicon. The complexities of the relationship can be reduced to one or two sentences, gone over again and again like a Mobius knot. 'What puzzles me more than anything?' Jay ponders. 'The fact that I have struggled with the same questions and obsessions, and with the same dull and useless responses, for so long, for the past ten years, without experiencing any increase in knowledge, or any release from the need to know, like a rat on a wheel. How can I move beyond this? I am moving out. A breakdown is a breakthrough is a breakout.'

The novel's skill lies in what Sukhdev Sandhu criticised as its 'prim, medium-lengthed, stiffbacked, shorn of excess' prose. The flat, insolent drive of Kureishi's seemingly effortless sen-tences, his ironic refusal of sentiment, depth, and emotional grandeur, mimic the vertical plunges of self-reflection: 'I know love is dark work, you have to get your hands dirty', 'We begin in love and go to some trouble to remain in that condition for the rest of our lives', 'Victor says that once the lights on a love have dimmed, you can never illuminate them again, any more than you can reheat a soufflé', 'Naturally, to move on is an infi-delity – to others, to the past, to old notions of oneself', 'Sure-ly the ultimate freedom is to choose', 'After a certain age sex can never be casual', 'After a certain age there are only certain people, in certain circumstances, whom we allow to love one another.' This is the language of intimacy, and Kureishi tosses out his profundities like bones to a dog.

KEVIN JACKSON

'I write for those on whom the black ox hath trod' – Fulke Greville

Paul Auster has often spoken of how Fulke Greville's simple, monosyllable-heavy declaration has haunted him over the years, and come to serve as a tersely eloquent mission statement for his own work as a writer. Greville adapted his phrase from a common folk saying of his day: to be 'trodden on by the black ox' was to suffer ill-fortune: disease, poverty, dispossession, betrayal, defeat, imprisonment. So: to write 'for' the afflicted is to bear constantly in mind several kinds of possible relationship between the wounded and the would-be healer. It might, for instance, commit the writer to seek his audience mainly among those who are temperamentally given to sorrow: melancholics, misfits, recluses, self-haters. Or – a harsher, more demanding interpretation – it might mean trying to write on behalf of those who cannot themselves write, or even read: the prisoners, the murdered, and all of Fanon's 'wretched of the earth'.

Since it is in large part a novel about the pitiless demands of a radical social conscience, and the explosive violence that might come of those demands, *Leviathan* (1992) is much possessed by the latter implication of Fulke Greville's words. It ruminates uneasily on how fiction might perhaps, or might never, be able to serve the cause of elementary human justice, and on why a sufficiently anguished novelist might come to feel that all writing, however well-intentioned, is a poor or contemptible substitute for acts of force. And yet for all the darkness of its matter, the book remains, as all worthwhile novels must remain, a form of agreeable entertainment, too – a pleasure in easy times, a palliative for which we may one day, soon, be grateful in the endless insomniac nights of bereavement, illness or broken love.

Not all novelists have felt this tug-of-war between imperatives – some, plainly, have made careers out of mocking the afflicted – but there is a vital tradition in the European and American novel of balancing diversion with ethical and political concern (a tradition that updates classical injunctions to the effect that works of art must instruct as well as delight). The most accomplished writers in that vein, from Dickens to Henry James and beyond, have achieved ethical gravity as well as writerly grace. *Leviathan* is a valuable recent recruit to that tradition – a point insufficiently stressed by all those critics who have treated Auster's books mainly as dry metaphysical puzzles, or as cryptic utterances that stand in urgent need of decoding. Not very interesting in their own right, they seem to me to have slighted and impoverished a body of work that is often intensely pleasurable as well as sometimes disconcerting.

Literary criticism of this tiresome kind usually involves the deployment of (metaphorical) scalpel and forceps. At the end of the exercise, we have no doubt learned something about how a frog works, but there is a horrible mess on the table, seeping with vile juices and jellies, and the poor thing will never sit on a lily pad again. (Wordsworth: 'We murder to dissect.') There are better ways of doing the job. One of them requires, as it were, a bright lamp and a magnifying glass. At the end of the session, the gem remains glittering and intact and, if it has proved its carats, the jeweler makes a sale. *Leviathan* is a book with many wonderfully cut facets. I will try to hold ten of them up to the light, and hope not to do too much damage with clumsy handling.

1 Friendship

'When I came home from work on Wednesday afternoon, I immediately sat down and wrote him a letter. I told him that he had written
a great novel. Any time he wanted to share another bottle of bourbon
with me, I would be honored to match him glass for glass.'

One of the world's oldest stories is the story of male friendship:
Achilles and Patroclus, Hamlet and Horatio, Falstaff and Hal,
Don Quixote and Sancho Panza, Estragon and Vladimir. In this
respect, *Leviathan* takes a very old story and makes it new. It
tells of a fifteen-year friendship between two intelligent, decent,
white American men, both of them writers – a friendship at first
warm and mutually sustaining, then increasingly splintered and
vexed, and finally blighted by chance and ideology. The narrator,
Peter Aaron, looks back from early middle age on the time when
he was a youngish man, freshly back in New York after a stint
in Paris, gradually passing from spirit-crushing years of anxiety, genteel poverty and marital break-up to the nursery slopes
of recognition and success, and to private happiness. He recalls
how he came to meet an older writer, Benjamin Sachs, the author of a single large and ambitious novel, *The New Colossus*.
Sachs is remarkable, charming, troubled, hard to fathom.

Their friendship begins in traditional male-bonding style,
with an enjoyable, bourbon-soaked evening in a bar, and is
soon consolidated when Peter reads Benjamin's singleton book
and recognises a considerable talent, a man he can admire. They
grow closer, especially when Benjamin and his equally sympathetic wife Fanny nurse Peter through his painful divorce; but
there are already the beginnings of division in this quasi-pa-
ternal care for the younger man's well-being. By chance, Peter
and Fanny had known each other slightly some years ago, when
they had attended the same course of lectures on aesthetics, and
Peter had been smitten by her beauty.

When Benjamin goes off to Hollywood for a few weeks to

work on a screenplay version of *The New Colossus*, Peter and Fanny have a brief, intense affair, and Paul falls for her badly; so much so that he is willing to sacrifice his most important friendship to stay with her. When he finds that Benjamin knows all about the affair, and claims not to mind, Paul is enraged, almost horrified at such indifference. After some edgy exchanges, they pledge to remain friends despite it all. Plainly, though, things can never be quite the same again.

Peter recovers from his heartache, and within a matter of months finds sudden and wholly unexpected bliss; he meets the wondrous Iris. Soon they are married; it is from the comfort and safety of this ideal marriage that he either witnesses or learns about Benjamin's strange path. The transformation seems to begin with a near-fatal accident – during a boozy July 4th party, Benjamin falls from an upper storey while flirting with a sexy woman, and emerges from his convalescence a different man.

Benjamin distances himself from his wife, gives up writing as a futile activity. After a violent encounter on a back road – he kills a gunman who has just shot the innocent local who was giving Benjamin a ride – the quondam novelist and essayist gradually becomes a political activist. A terrorist, most people would call him, though a terrorist who is careful not to harm people, only symbolic objects: to be exact, replicas of the Statue of Liberty. In the course of one of his self-imposed bombing assignments, Benjamin accidentally blows himself up. The FBI find a paper among his remains which leads a couple of agents to come and interrogate Peter . . .

Which, roughly speaking, is how *Leviathan* both begins and ends. Its first sentence: 'Six days ago, a man blew himself up by the side of the road in northern Wisconsin.' Its last: 'We' – meaning the narrator and an FBI agent named Harris, who after two months of investigation has uncovered the identity of that dead man, and at least something of his links to Peter – 'walked up the stairs together, and once we were inside, I handed him the pages of this book.' So the main conceit of *Leviathan* is that it has been hastily assembled in the weeks between Benjamin's death and the FBI's successful sleuthing.

Among other things, then, *Leviathan* is a memorial volume, a work of mourning for a dead friend: a tale told against a ticking clock, swiftly, urgently, yet with as much human sympathy as the narrator can muster, so that its ethical complexities and nuances might have some chance of prevailing even when cruder versions of the same story – the 'official version' of solitary lunacy – come into circulation and become the received wisdom. And *Leviathan* was also the name, Peter tells us, that Benjamin had chosen for his uncompleted book. But things aren't quite that simple.

2 Imaginary friends

'Of all the tragedies my poor friend created for himself, leaving this book unfinished becomes the hardest one to bear. I don't mean to say that books are more important than life, but the fact is that everyone dies, everyone disappears in the end, and if Sachs had managed to finish his book, there's a chance it might have outlived him.'

Friendship is a rich field for any novel to plough, not only because of its centrality to our lives but because the experience of being caught up in a novel can sometimes feel like entering into a peculiarly intimate form of friendship. Auster/Aaron tips us the nod almost from the outset: '. . . They read your book, and something about it strikes a chord deep in their soul. All of a sudden, they imagine that you belong to them, that you're the only friend they have in the world.' Those readers who enjoy this contact of subjectivities a little too much are, we tend to feel, at best a shade naive, or perhaps mildly unhinged, like those notorious viewers of soap operas who confuse jobbing actors and the roles they play. In the worst instances, they may turn ugly, resorting to 'The unbalanced letters, the telephone

calls at three o'clock in the morning, the anonymous threats.'
Writing novels is hardly like mining coal, but even such a quiet
and sedentary profession has its occupational hazards.

To enter too thoroughly into imagined lives can be foolish,
even corrupting. (Flaubert wrote a novel about this: *Madame
Bovary*. So did Cervantes: *Don Quixote*.) Recall Coleridge in his
radical days, righteously angry at the thought of young ladies
weeping over sad lovers in pretty romances, while they carelessly sweetened their afternoon tea with 'the blood of Negroes'
– sugar imported from the slave-worked Caribbean planta-
tions. Coleridge gave up his radicalism, but two centuries on,
the remark has not lost its power to sting.

On the other hand, it can also feel as if the refusal to play the
part of cooperative reader is to be clenched, sour, boring; somehow less than fully human, or at any rate less than *homo ludens*.
Lots of children have imaginary friends; they usually grow out
of that phase. If they are lucky, though, they will discover the
joys of fiction and have imaginary friends of a different kind:
friends like 'Peter Aaron'. One reason why *Leviathan* can be a
page-turner is that we almost immediately like Peter, and soon
like him a lot more. It's largely a matter of the way he talks.
(One of Auster's gifts is a narrative style which creates the illusion of being spoken to our inner ear, even when it takes flight
from its plain, demotic diction and calculatedly easy-going
rhythms.) It's the voice of a decent, unpretentious, thoughtful,
sympathetic kind of guy; someone, we might hope, really quite
a lot like us, taken at our best.

Now, American fiction from Poe to Nabokov and onwards
notoriously teems with narrators who are con-men or seduc-
ers or lunatics, selling you their self-justifying take on reality,
entangling you in their chains and skeins of delusion, ambition
or obsessed horror. Peter Aaron explicitly denies any such skill:
'Generally speaking, I don't have much of a talent for deception,
and in spite of my efforts over the years, I've rarely fooled any-

one about anything.' In many other novels, this would be a big red warning sign. (Beware the travelling salesman who claims to have no bottles of snake oil, no designs on your wallet.)

In *Leviathan*, this is almost certainly not the case: the novel is shot through with moments of uncertainty and avowed ignorance, but not of the kind which snag the threads of narrative coherence, and so expose a fiction as a lie. We need to like Peter, and to feel that he is a good and thoughtful man, in order to carry out the much harder task of feeling measured sympathy for Benjamin Sachs. One of the main points of reading literature, the great critic William Empson often said, is that it is the best means – apart from actual friendships or love affairs – of understanding that other human beings, equivalent centres of self, can feel and think in entirely different ways. Novels are a kind of company: imaginary friends in their own right. They may also offer an account of the way we live now.

3 Politics

> 'The idea of writing disgusts me. It doesn't mean a goddamned thing to me anymore . . . I don't want to spend the rest of my life rolling pieces of paper into a typewriter. I want to stand up from my desk and do something. The days of being a shadow are over. I've got to step into the real world now and do something.'

Both the title and the epigraph of *Leviathan* announce it as a political novel. The title alludes to Thomas Hobbes, and his conception of the state. (*Leviathan, or the Matter, Forme and Power of a Commonwealth Ecclesiastical and Civil*, 1651); the epigraph, from Ralph Waldo Emerson, narrows the focus a little to American politics, and to a traditional Yankee suspicion of the state and its mechanisms: 'Every actual State is corrupt.' But Auster's book does not adumbrate; it mulls, ponders, broods. It addresses the ways in which the broader political climate of the time, from the Vietnam war to the fall of the Berlin Wall and the election of President Havel, can change the feeling of daily life, filling it with optimism or despair:

> The age of Ronald Regan began. Sachs went on doing what he had always done, but in the new American order of the 1980s, his position became increasingly marginalized. It wasn't that he had no audience, but it grew steadily smaller, and the magazines that published his work became steadily more obscure. Almost imperceptibly, Sachs came to be seen as a throwback, as someone out of step with the spirit of the time. The world had changed around him, and in the present climate of selfishness and intolerance, of moronic, chest-pounding American-ism, his opinions sounded curiously harsh and moralistic. It was bad enough that the Right was everywhere in the ascendant, but even more disturbing to him was the collapse of any effective opposition to it. The Democratic Party had caved in; the Left had all but disappeared; the press was mute. All the arguments had suddenly been appropriated by the other side, and to raise one's voice against it was considered bad manners.

Like most of Auster's other novels, *Leviathan* is in large meas-ure about writers and writing. It meanders around the topic of what writing can and cannot do to redeem the time, and ac-knowledges that – in a dark period – honest, uncompromising and even admirable souls may come to look on the business of stringing words together as futile and decadent. Reed Dimag-gio, the man killed by Sachs on a country road, is the writer in *Leviathan* about whom we know least. He is also, we suspect, the most politically extreme. His magnum opus is a study of a moderately obscure American anarchist. Sachs, of whom we know a good deal more, is at first a more conventionally literary writer, who comes to question the value of writing and launches an idiosyncratic form of terrorism. As noted, his two books are a novel, *The New Colossus* (the title is derived from Emma La-zarus), and an uncompleted sequel, *Leviathan*. Peter Aaron, our narrator, is the author of at least one successful novel (about which we know almost nothing save its title, *Luna*: probably, then, quite similar to *Moon Palace*; *Luna* was one of that book's earlier titles), and a few essays, notably one on Hugo Ball; and the book we are reading as he writes it over the course of two months, also called *Leviathan*.

As the mysteries unfold, we gather that Dimaggio appears to be an actual terrorist; hard to find any other explanation for his weapons, gun and big bag of money, though there is a possibility that he may all along have been an agent provocateur, funded by the government and playing a fatal double game. Sachs, who stubbornly sat out a period in prison during the Vietnam war, at first seems to be a disciple of Thoreau:

> Thoreau was his model, and without the example of 'Civil Disobedience', I doubt that Sachs would have turned out as he did. I'm not just talking about prison now, but a whole approach to life, an attitude of remorseless inner vigilance. Once, when *Walden* came up in conversation, Sachs confessed to me that he wore a beard 'because Henry David had worn one' – which gave me a sudden insight into how deep his admiration was . . ..

But Sachs renounces words, and he grows, or declines, into a symbolic terrorist – a prankster and underground folk hero, travelling from town to town blowing up local replicas of the Statue of Liberty, and gaining a certain cult following as the 'Phantom of Liberty'. (A nod to Buñuel's late film, and to surrealist mischief in general.)

And Aaron? Aaron does not seem to be an overtly political writer, though it is clear that he admires Sachs's self-lacerating spirit of perfectionism, as well as finding it dismaying:

> He accepted everyone else's frailties, but when it came to himself he demanded perfection, an almost superhuman rigor in even the smallest acts. The result was disappointment, a dumbfounding awareness of his own flawed humanity, which drove him to place ever more stringent demands on his conduct, which in turn led to ever more suffocating disappointments.

If a man is admirable, does this mean that we should strive to emulate him, no matter the cost?

4 Coincidence

'I didn't realise it at first, but I happened to be standing in the American fiction section, and right there at eye level, the first thing I saw when I started to look at the titles, was a copy of *The New Colossus*, my own little contribution to this graveyard. It was an astonishing coincidence, a thing that hit me so hard I felt it had to be an omen.'

Strange but true: coincidences, those staple embarrassments of Victorian fiction, are sometimes felt to number among the riches of Auster's fiction. There are many small examples of coincidence in *Leviathan*, and two overwhelming ones. Quite early in the book, Maria Turner, the conceptual artist, finds the notebook which eventually leads her to rediscover Lillian, an old friend who has made a steady career as a prostitute. Later in the book, Sachs is menaced by a gunman in a lonely place, and kills him in self-defence. The dead man proves to be Reed Dimaggio: Lillian's husband. Why do these brazen improbabilities not exasperate Auster's readers? One very simple answer is that we know, from *The Red Notebook* and other sources, that coincidences have played a significant part in Auster's own life, and that he is so fascinated by the subject that he collects them.

Ponder these subjects too long and you are in danger of heading down the roads previously trodden by the likes of Jung in his essays on 'synchronicity' and Arthur Koestler in *The Challenge of Chance*. I can think of two possible reasons why readers are beguiled rather than disgusted by coincidence in Auster. One: however realistic the surface details of the novel – and *Leviathan* was, on its publication, the closest Auster had so far come to writing a novel wholly founded on quotidian reality – the roots of his fiction have the appeal of wonder stories, fables, well-I-never yarns. Two: the book's narrator is engaged in a noble but necessarily futile attempt to explain an exceptional life. But there are moments when the plausible chains of cause and effect, influence and action, break down. The world remains mysterious, resistant to commentary and narrative. (There is a faint, sometimes more than faint, intimation of the mystic in Auster's writings.) And what we cannot speak about we must pass over in silence.

5 Families

Maria became his companion, his consolation prize, his indelible reward. He cooked breakfast for her every morning, he walked her to school, he picked her up in the afternoon, he brushed her hair, he gave her baths, he tucked her in at night. These were pleasures he couldn't have anticipated . . .

Despite what Mr Tolstoy said, not all happy families are alike. Some happy families, like the awkward triad of Sachs, Lillian and her daughter Maria, are not even real families, but improvised equivalents of that old institution, and yet they can offer unexpected solace as well as predictable torment. Most novels – all novels? – have at least something to do with families, and *Leviathan*, though it does not make much fuss about the fact, is no exception. Aaron's first attempt at creating a family quickly fails; Benjamin's marriage to Fanny, though childless, seems far stronger. Then Peter finds Iris, and from that point on we hear very little about his life save that he has another child and is entirely happy. After Sachs's marriage breaks up, he forms a potent if tentative bond with the wife and child of the man he killed. Had it worked out, there would have been no Phantom of Liberty, no explosive death . . . and no *Leviathan*. Nietzsche once quipped that there is no feast without cruelty. Perhaps there are no true novels without a due measure of discontent, loneliness, and failure to achieve a happy family life. Happiness writes white.

6 Toads and gardens

I can only speak about the things I know, the things I have seen with my own eyes and heard with my own ears.

The sweet cheat of fiction is to make us accept, at least for the duration of reading, that imagined things are true. One of the standard ways of pulling off this trick is to set, as the poem has it, imaginary toads (characters, events) in real gardens (New York, Vermont, California). The correspondences between Peter Aaron and Paul Auster could be guessed at by the most naive reader; and when you know just a little bit more about the author, they become almost insultingly obvious. PA and PA have both spent time in France, both come back to the USA in their late twenties or so, both undergo a painful divorce, both remarry (Auster to Siri Hustvedt; Aaron to the anagrammatical 'Iris'), and so on and on.

Unless we react with exasperation – for God's sake, at least make a bit of an effort at disguising yourself, Auster! – the apparent half-heartedness of the fictional disguise has the effect, not so much of making Sachs more real (in the old sense of 'a well-rounded character') as of making us uncertain of how we have stored our memories. Hang on a moment – did Auster really know someone like this? How about that mad novelist he mentions in one of his memoirs, the bloke who handed out money to strangers in the street? Maybe *Leviathan* is only very lightly fictionalised? Maybe Sachs is, was, real?

Quite a few modern novels nest their levels of reality one inside the other; *Leviathan* is unusual, and possibly even unique, in the complexity of its wanderings in and out of the garden of reality. On the preliminary page containing publication details, we read the line 'The author extends special thanks to Sophie Calle for permission to mingle fact and fiction.' As most Auster fans now know, the works of conceptual art and private rituals that Aaron ascribes to the character 'Maria Turner' were either actual projects by the artist Sophie Calle, or, in the wake of the novel's publication, became so. See Sophie Calle and Paul Auster, *Double Game* (1999) for further enlightenment.

Curiouser and curiouser: the character of 'Iris' is not only Siri

Hustvedt in semi-transparent disguise, but a character in her own novel *Blindfold* (published in 1994); Auster, she has told interviewers, asked her permission for the characters to marry. And in a later novel, *What I Loved* (2003), she draws on some of the same shared experience with Auster – the case of an apparently charming and honest adolescent boy who ultimately proved to be a sociopath – that provided him with some raw material for *Leviathan*.

And somewhere behind the characters of Sachs and Dimaggio stands the strange and ragged figure of Theodore Kaczynski, aka the Unabomber.

7 Terror

He didn't come right out and say it, but I could tell that he supported Berkman, that he believed there was a moral justification for certain forms of political violence. Terrorism had its place in the struggle, so to speak. If used correctly, it could be an effective tool for dramatising the issues at stake, for enlightening the public about the nature of institutionalised power.

Written almost exactly a decade before the killers flew across the sky and into Manhattan's highest buildings, *Leviathan* frets at thoughts of domestic rather than imported, Jihadist terrorism. Even so, the novel now seems at least modestly prophetic of the early twenty-first century and the mental climate of the War on Terror. The passing of a decade deepened rather than diminished its power. Ezra Pound's famous claim that artists are the antennae of the race now seems almost as dated and puffed-up as Shelley's contention that poets are our unacknowledged legislators. But isn't it one sign of a good novel that it should be sufficiently alert to new things in spirit of the age – its novelties, small and large – that it will come to seem newly pertinent when the seeds mature and the times suddenly, terribly, change?

There is a strong autobiographical component here. In *Hand to Mouth*, Auster recalls how, in the summer of 1969, he walked into a post office and idly looked at the FBI's list of ten most wanted men. He knew seven of them. From early 1968 until the summer of the following year, Auster's alma mater, Columbia, had become one of the most turbulent universities in the nation: sit-ins, demonstrations, occupations and riots were the order of the day. Auster himself, too much a solitary to submerge himself altogether in the self-styled 'revolution', was no more than a sympathetic onlooker throughout most of this, but he was none the less appalled by the plight of those who became 'casualties of their own righteousness and noble intentions'; 'the human loss', he says, 'was catastrophic', and he names three losses in particular.

Mark Rudd, one of his childhood friends, joined the Weather Underground and had to spend more than a decade in hiding from the law. Dave Gilbert, 'an SDS spokesman whose speeches had impressed me as models of insight and intelligence', was sentenced to seventy-five years in prison for his part in a politically motivated bank robbery. And, most pertinently for *Leviathan*, there was Ted Gold, who 'blew himself to smithereens in a West Village brownstone when the bomb he was building accidentally went off'. There but for the grace of . . . coincidence? *Leviathan* is an act of imaginative sympathy with those clever, ardent young men and others like them around the world.

At least one critic has pointed out that *Leviathan* may be read as a reply to Don DeLillo's *Mao II* – another book about writers and terrorists and their unelected affinities. Here is an angry remark by DeLillo's protagonist Bill Gray, an ageing writer who, in the Salinger/Pynchon tradition, has shunned all publicity for many years, and lives an anchorite life of perpetual tinkering with a novel he will never be able to release to the world:

> 'There's a curious knot that binds novelists and terrorists. In the West we become famous effigies as our books lose the power to shape and influence . . . Years ago I used to think that it was possible for a novelist to alter the inner life of the culture. Now bomb-makers and gunmen

have taken that territory. They make raids on human consciousness. What writers used to do before we were all incorporated.'

Other characters muse in similar vein: 'And isn't it the novelist, Bill, above all people, above all writers, who understands this rage, who knows in his soul what the terrorist thinks and feels?' asks one of them. 'Through history it's the novelist who has felt affinity for the violent man who lives in the dark. Where are your sympathies? With the colonial police, the occupier, the rich landlord, the corrupt government, the militaristic state? Or with the terrorist? And I don't abjure that word even if it has a hundred meanings. It's the only honest word to use.'

This is a character's outburst, not DeLillo's. One doubts that Miss Austen would have thought it a sensible view. Would Conrad? Dostovesky? Bely? Or any of the other novelists who embraced acts of terrorism in their novels if not in their hearts and minds? Surely, many of us would reply, it is the job of the novelist not to be partisan but to be myriad-minded – to take imaginative hold of the colonial policeman and the landlord as well as the desperate bomber? Can it really be true that, in our times, the law of the Black Ox should take priority over all other claims? Or is that just facile extremism, masochistic posturing . . . in a well-worn phrase, Radical Chic?

These are not cosy matters. And novels are not wholly about consolation and escape.

8   Name dropping

He was a great one for turning facts into metaphors, and since he always had an abundance of facts at his disposal, he could bombard you with a never-ending supply of strange historical connections, yoking together the most far-flung people and events. Once, for example, he told me that during Peter Kropotkin's first visit to the United States in the 1890s, Mrs Jefferson Davis, the wife of the Confederate president, requested a meeting with the famous anarchist prince. That was bizarre enough, Sachs said, but then, just minutes after Kropotkin arrived at Mrs Davis's house, who else should turn up but Booker T. Washington?

Only Sachs could have informed you that when the film actress Louise Brooks was growing up in a small town in Kansas at the beginning of the century, her next-door playmate was Vivian Vance, the same woman who later starred in the *I Love Lucy* show.

Leviathan is not a didactic novel; not, at any rate, in the sense that it 'teaches' any neatly paraphrasable doctrine or argues a party line. It does, however, fairly consistently instruct us about things, or at any rate suggest lines of future enquiry for the lively reader. (Anthony Burgess once pointed out that a very reasonable reason for reading novels is to educate oneself painlessly about the state of the world. Hundreds of tons of mass-market fiction are sold on the promise of telling people how the CIA works, or how autopsies are conducted, or how drug cartels operate.) So we are told, for instance, that Fanny had 'an abiding passion for such artists as Ryder, Church, Blakelock and Cole'. Ryder, we find out further down that page, was Albert Pinkham Ryder. (An almost identical list of painters appears in *Moon Palace*.) The doorway to further erudition has been opened for us, should we choose to enquire more deeply.

If you are curious, here are some of the other names scattered across its pages: Hugo Ball, Admiral Peary, Emma Lazarus, Sitting Bull, Ralph Waldo Emerson, Joseph Pulitzer, Buffalo Bill Cody, Auguste Bartholdi, Catherine Weldon, Rose Hawthorne, Nathaniel Hawthorne, Ellery Channing, Walt Whitman, William Tecumseh Sherman (Sachs quotes him: 'Grant stood by me when I was crazy, I stood by him when he was drunk, and now we stand by each other always'), Grand Duke Alexis, 'Moose' Skowron, Bakunin . . . and Alexander Berkman (Sachs takes Berkman's name when on the run). Less than thoroughly well-versed in the minutiae of American anarchism, I wondered whether the last of these names was a real person, and whether the brief biography of his life given in *Leviathan* is accurate. The facts checked out.

One final name-check: Sir Walter Raleigh. 'He was fond of saying that a poet was responsible for bringing his mother's family to Boston, but that was only a reference to Sir Walter Raleigh, the man who introduced the potato to Ireland and hence had caused the blight that occurred three hundred years later.'

All of Auster's major works include at least one allusion to Raleigh.

Not everyone knows that. As Sachs might have said.

9 The American Grain

'Too many years without baseball, I suppose. If you don't get your ration of double plays and home runs it can begin to dry up your spirit.'

So Aaron to Sachs, explaining on their first meeting why he felt it was time to return from France. This is not just guy stuff, male bonding between bookish chaps who want to seem like regular dudes. Like his friend Don DeLillo, Auster has had a lifelong passion for the holy American game. One day some one will no doubt write a thesis on Auster and baseball; there is certainly no shortage of material. His first completed work of fiction, published under the pseudonym Paul Benjamin, was a thriller set in the baseball world, *Squeeze Play*; in his years of poverty, he devised and tried to market a card came, Baseball Action; he has even suggested that he owes his vocation as a writer to a disappointment he experienced at the age of eight. At his first major-league game, the boy Auster approached Willy Mays and asked for his autograph. Alas, no one had a pen or pencil, and from that point on, Auster took always to carrying a pencil with him. Books became inevitable.

Baseball plays a relatively minor part in *Leviathan*, though one of its secondary characters is called Dimaggio, and he is killed – how pleasant it is to report that this does not feel like a cunningly planted 'symbol' – by a blow from a baseball bat. But the book teems with other types of Americana, from the Emerson quotation onwards: Aaron refers to Ichabod Crane, to John Brown, to 'Rip van Winkle', to Huckleberry Finn, to Ishmael, to Daniel Boone . . . and, again and again, to the Statue of Liberty. One of the other poisonous heritages of the Reagan (and, we can safely extrapolate, Bush Sr and Jr) ideology as Aaron and Sachs see it is that the forces of moronic, chest-pounding Americanism have taken out a monopoly on patriotism, and can see those who are compelled to dissent as treacherous scum. But Sachs, and Aaron, are tormented by their country precisely because of their passionate love for what it is and what it can be.

> For the past hundred years, it [the Statue of Liberty] has transcended politics and ideology, standing at the threshold of our country as an emblem of all that is good within us. It represents hope rather than reality, faith rather than facts, and one would be hard-pressed to find a single person willing to denounce the things it stands for: democracy, freedom, equality under the law. It is the best of what America has to offer the world, and however pained one might be by America's failure to live up to those ideals, the ideals themselves are not in question. They have given comfort to millions. They have instilled the hope in all of us that we might one day live in a better world.

Leviathan is a noble attempt to yank patriotism back out of the hands of the yahoos.

10 Secret dungeons

> If I'm wrong about this, then everything I've written so far is rubbish, a heap of irrelevant musings. Perhaps Ben's life did break in two that night, dividing into a distinct before and after – in which case everything from before can be struck from the record. But if that's true, it means that human behaviour makes no sense. It would mean that nothing can be understood about anything.

And perhaps everything I have written in this short attempt at detailed praise is also rubbish, a heap of irrelevant musings. Relevant or not, they are the musings that *Leviathan* prompted in me when I first read it, greedily, and are prompted in me every time I re-read it, with deepening satisfaction. Unlike mass-market fiction, it makes no attempt to tie up loose ends, or to fill every gap and crack with narrative plaster. What was Lillian up to in the daytimes, when she told Sachs she was working as a masseuse? Who knows? And – in a strictly non-cynical sense – who cares? Perhaps Auster himself could not provide the answers. Some questions are not appropriate; they are almost impertinent. It doesn't seem to me that *Leviathan* is a radically sceptical novel – it does not endorse Aaron's anxiety, and simply pronounce the sweeping verdict that 'nothing can be understood about anything'. It does, though, imply that, no matter how banal our lives, we all live deep in mystery. That there is only so much we can ever hope to know, even of the people we are closest to, even of ourselves.

And what is true of people is just as true of works of the imagination, like novels. Beyond a certain point, persistence in enquiry becomes boorish, silly, annoying. There are enigmas – 'secret dungeons' – in *Leviathan* that ought to remain so: the pleasure of a puzzle is that it must never be more than partly solved, which is why the *Giaconda* is one of the greatest hits of Western art. As a French poet once put it, the poem resists its annihilation into meaning. (Which is not to say that it is meaningless, but that it fights to preserve its most recondite treasures.) A good novel may reawaken us to the oddity and richness of the world, sometimes perceptible even at its most humdrum moments. *Leviathan* – I hope this much, at least, is clear by now – is an exceptionally good novel.

MICHAEL WOOD

I

In one of Ross Thomas's last novels, *Twilight at Mac's Place*, published in 1990, five years before his death, a man leaves a curious legacy to his son. The man is – or was; the story opens with his thinly attended funeral in Arlington, Virginia – a CIA operative and his legacy is a detailed memoir of his career. The son understands immediately. His father didn't have any money to bequeath him so he bequeathed him the means to get some. He is to sell the memoir to the highest bidder, who is likely to bid very high – not in order to publish the book but to make sure no one does. The bids start to come in straight away, and the narrative escalates into a series of murders and a proliferation of feints and disguises, including a second typescript of the touted memoir.

The set-up offers an elegant fable about the price and power of silence in certain circles; but the wit of the dead man's scheme goes much further. He has understood that in such situations the goal may be cash for silence but the true authority, almost the only indispensable player in the game, is rumour. To activate it you don't need to write a memoir, you need just to be thought to have written one. When the son and his lawyer open the box containing the supposedly troublesome text they find almost four hundred pages. On the first page there is a title, *Mercenary Calling*, and a note establishing copyright. On the second page there is an epigraph from Housman, giving a context for the title:

These, in the day when heaven was falling,
The hour when earth's foundations fled,
Followed their mercenary calling,
And took their wages and are dead.

On the third page is a dedication to the man's son. And on the fourth are the words 'Chapter One', followed by 'I have had an exceedingly interesting life and, looking back, have no regrets. Or almost none'. There is nothing else on the page, or on any of the other pages, although all of them are scrupulously numbered. We see the style of the man's mind in the form of the joke. Strictly, for the launch of a rumour, he didn't need a title, or a box, or paper. But he wanted to sign his non-existent book, he wanted his son not only to get the point and the money but also to share the intricate working of the trick. In this sense the memoir does exist; its blank pages evoke all the details the would-be buyers are afraid it will provide, and the epigraph seems to know all about the late twentieth-century adventures of the United States in Indo-China, which is where the man did much of his work, and where the not-to-be-known stories had their day.

This location (and this fear) remind us that rumour is not quite the only indispensable player. Someone has to worry about the rumoured revelation and to act on that worry. The memoir may be fictive or absent, but the tales it might tell must be true, and in need of disavowal.

No one explores and inhabits this shifting territory, where the imaginary gets entangled in the real because of what the real has been up to, better than Ross Thomas, at least in the territory's American mapping. He writes crime novels, not political thrillers, but his characters live on the edge of, or in the aftermath of, politics and war. Whether the institution is an intelligence agency, an American trade union, a police department, a newspaper, the army, or a congressional committee, there is always illicit money to be made, and there are often inducements even better than money – a hold over powerful people, for example.

Thomas seems to know just how such things are done, and he probably does, since after his wartime service in the Philippines he worked in American intelligence, in advertising, in union copywriting and in Washington and regional politics. Then at the age of forty – he was born in Oklahoma City in 1926 – he became a writer of fiction, and published twenty novels over the next twenty-eight years. Twenty novels as Ross Thomas, that is. He also published five under the name of Oliver Bleeck.

But the great interest of these works lies not in their inside knowledge, however real or unreal it is; it lies in the shape and movement of the world Thomas has made out of these scams, deals, capers and deaths, the fictional universe that is all his own. His tradition, as I have said, is that of the American crime novel, whose patron saints are Dashiell Hammett and Raymond Chandler, and whose archbishops are Ross Macdonald and Elmore Leonard. All of these writers can seem at times more gripping and urgent than Thomas is, but none has his ease or range or his almost scholarly sense of the varieties of moral corruption. He likes crooks – or likes to watch them at work and think about them. He suggests fine distinctions among devious modes of honour, and often allows us to contemplate the outrageous lack of any such notion. Even the seediest and nastiest of his figures commands his full, unmoralising attention. He paints no purely good guys, and is closest to Leonard in this respect. Where the chief characters of the other writers I have just mentioned are defined by unorthodox but unmistakable virtues, Thomas's heroes find their very virtues snarled in ruthlessness, and we are often alerted, early in the novels, to the coldness in their eyes. 'Down these mean streets,' Chandler famously wrote, 'a man must go who is not himself mean, who is neither tarnished nor afraid.' There is plenty of tarnish and fear in Thomas. His motto might be that only people we would call mean have any sort of chance on his streets, but some people are meaner than others.

In *Briarpatch* (1984), a man is described, by another character, as having to choose between his friend and his government, and choosing his friend. The speaker intends this description as a slightly stunned moral tribute, an American version of E. M. Forster's notorious and appealing hope ('If I had to choose between betraying my country and betraying my friend, I hope I should have the guts to betray my country'). The recipient of the tribute says, 'That's not a very big choice. That's hardly any choice at all.' He means that it's easy to get some things right but also that the moral complications of his decision, and the chances of real damage, are just beginning.

II

Eric Ambler says of Thomas that he 'is that rare phenomenon, a writer of suspense novels whose books can be read with pleasure more than once'. This amiable compliment is in this case perhaps more than merely amiable, since it acknowledges a response many readers may share: an appetite rather than a judgement. But then Ambler also seems to be making the familiar suggestion that one can't reread – or reread with pleasure – novels that are all plot, or all mystery and solution. One rereads Chandler, say, for the writing, even when one knows the story by heart. I don't find either of these claims convincing. I can happily reread novels that are all plot, if they are any good. And I reread Chandler, I hate to say, in spite of the writing. The point about Thomas, and what Ambler's comment catches for me, is that the considerable suspense in his novels is always linked to subtle and intelligent notations of human contact. His characters have histories, you hear it at once in their language. Sometimes they have histories with each other, going back to old criminal escapades or even childhood. And if they've just met, then a genuine history begins at once. A large part of the pleasure of reading Thomas is keeping company with these people, even though the company of their equivalents in real

life might be too much for us. Take the following exchange,
again from *Briarpatch*, between an ancient, usually drunk white
journalist and a black waiter at a Press Club in the Southwest of
the United States.

> 'Go away,' Laffter said. 'Go back in the kitchen and spit in the soup or
> whatever you do.'
>   'Spit in the soup?' Harry the Waiter said. 'Goodgawdalmighty, I nev-
> er thought of that! Lemme go and tell the other niggers.'

We know straight away that these men have known each other
for a long time, and we know Harry the Waiter is joking. What
we don't know is how to read the tone of the joke and its provo-
cation. It is possible for genuine affection to work through such
language; possible too for hostility to become a habit, even a
comfort, and have its traditions of wit. When Laffter has a heart
attack – more of this later, it is part of the story of ruthlessness the novel has to tell – Harry is the person who performs
artificial respiration, cursing the while. And finally we learn
that Laffter has left all his money to Harry. Does this settle the
question of affection or hostility? Not really. But it considerably
deepens our sense of this relationship, of how far back and how
far down it goes, and it tells us something about race relations
in a place resembling Thomas's native city.

III

I have mentioned *Briarpatch* twice, and I want to devote the
rest of my essay to this novel; to try to suggest how good it is
in itself, and how strongly it represents, in its loyalty to certain long and old preoccupations, both the genre novel and the
novel as a genre.

There is much to be said about this book – Thomas won an
Edgar award for it, and for *The Cold War Swap* (1966), his first
novel – but one particular sequence lingers in the mind, promising far more than it overtly displays, crying out for comment.

To put it a little cryptically for the moment, this sequence, like many moments in Balzac or Dickens, is about reading the material world, scanning a human habitat for the meanings it will deliver. I'm not associating Thomas with Balzac and Dickens in writerly stature, only saying that he is a skillful member of a large and inquisitive writing family. Not all novelists are inquisitive, and certainly not all of them devote so much conscientious attention to the litter of human signs.

We need a sense of the novel's story line before we go much further. Benjamin Dill is a thirty-eight-year old consultant for a United States Senate subcommittee. In the first chapter – after a brief prelude – he learns that his sister Felicity, ten years younger than he is, and a police detective in the Southwestern city where they both grew up, has been killed by a car bomb. She was plainly the target, not an incidental victim. Dill hears the news in Washington – the local police chief phones him – around 11.30 a.m. and by 4 p.m. he is back in his home town, and his tracing of an intricate tale of murder, politics and power begins.

Dill's question, of course, and ours, is, Who killed Felicity? But he has other questions too. Was she, as all the immediate evidence suggests, an accomplice in local crime, on the take? It says a lot about our expectations of the novel's genre that we are so sure she was not. This is what we want to believe, and genre fiction is usually quite eager to satisfy our plot desires. It says something about Thomas's use of the genre that Dill himself is not sure of his sister's virtue, although of course he wants to believe in it as much as we do. He has still other questions, which bring us to our sequence of readings of the material world. How did Felicity live? Where did she live? Dill's contact with her since he left the city has been regular and warm, but mainly by telephone and letter. He needs to know what he can of the traces of her life as a way of coming to terms with her death.

He is given the key to her apartment, the upper floor of the duplex she owns, and outside which the car explosion took place. Thomas, through Dill's eyes, takes us on a tour of the interior of this dwelling, developing a meticulous portrait of absence, detailing the markers and furnishings of a property where no one really lives. At one point Dill notices there are no scales in the bathroom and thinks that 'that might be significant; that it might even be a clue'. The possible clue is the detectable absence of a clue, and the discreet allusion, evoked explicitly elsewhere in Thomas's fiction, is to the dog that didn't bark in the Sherlock Holmes story 'The Silver Blaze'. Dill's conclusion actually precedes his exploration. He turns on the air conditioning and then, we learn,

> stepped to the center of the living room, glanced around, and found there was nothing to indicate his sister had ever lived there. Nor, for that matter, had anyone else with a shred of personality.

The description of his continuing scrutiny, however, takes three and a half pages. It begins:

> There was furniture in the living room, of course: a dark-green boxy couch, a matching chair, and a chrome-and-glass coffee table with nothing on it except last week's copy of *TV Guide*. On the floor, because there seemed no place else for it, was a small black-and-white Sony portable television set. There were no books, not one, which Dill found strange . . . There was a rug of a neutral sand shade on the floor, a few pictures on the wall that appeared to be cheap mail-order prints of Dufy, Cezanne, and Monet, and in one corner an inexpensive-looking Korean stereo so new it looked unused . . . The living room blended into a dining area where four chairs surrounded a drop-leaf maple table that looked as if it had been ordered by catalogue from Sears. A fake Tiffany lamp hung by a heavy golden chain over the table.

The visit continues through the kitchen, the main bedroom, another bedroom ('which turned out to be the den of someone who had run out of money') and into the bathroom with the missing scales. The dutiful dreariness of the description matches the intensely synthetic, low-budget feel of the place. We don't actually require more than a fraction of this account to get the point:

someone wants to persuade Dill that his sister lived here, when it's obvious that she didn't. But then, as with the mechanics of the memoir in *Twilight in Mac's Place*, we are shown that absence not only can do the work of presence but also has its own ways of presenting itself to our eyes. The dog barks and does not bark: the Korean stereo is as good a clue as the books that aren't there.

And the point we get so quickly turns out to be the wrong one anyway, a false inference. Felicity herself created the impression that she didn't live here – by not really living here. The duplex was a front for an investigation she was conducting; a place where she sometimes slept but which she chose not to mark with any sort of record of her personality. Of course you would have to know her as well as her brother does to register the tale of her absence; and you would have to have Dill's feeling for what actual human litter looks like to suspect the larger absence of any personal note.

Much later in the novel we find out 'where Felicity really lived', in Dill's words, and this apartment is described in great detail too, reversing the earlier effect.

> Dill . . . pushed the door open, went in, found the light switch, flicked it on, and knew immediately that Felicity Dill had indeed lived there.
>
> For one thing, there were the books: two solid walls of them, plus neat piles on the floor and in the deep sills of the four dormer windows that looked out over the alley . . .
>
> A couch stood against a wall. A coffee table was in front of it. There were also some chairs, a magazine rack (full), and a whatnot stand in one corner. None of the furniture matched, yet none of it seemed out of place.

In the kitchen there is 'a six-tier spice rack' and 'a four-foot shelf crammed with cookbooks'; the silver is polished and the bathroom comfortable and bereft of prescription drugs. Dill doesn't need to think as hard about this place as about the other one, or to query his own impression. 'She lived here', he says. 'And she seemed to like it. That's all I was after really.'

He wanted to know not just where she lived but that she really lived somewhere – in a setting where she wasn't camping or pretending. But the satisfaction is brief since all the questions return. Why couldn't Felicity live only in the apartment she seemed to like, what was she doing in the duplex she had bought 'by dint of some rather dubious creative financing'? The novel itself seems to invest in the disappointment since just before Dill arrives 'where Felicity really lived', the place is described as 'the two-story carriage house where the dead detective was said to have lived', and on its last appearance in the book is described as 'the garage apartment or carriage house where Dill's dead sister had sometimes lived'. These are fine distinctions. Felicity is said to have lived in two places, and in a modest, restricted sense, did actually live in both of them. The difficult declension is in the other phrases: she only sometimes lived where she really lived, and she died leaving the other apartment.

The great set-piece of the novel occurs between these two inspections, when Dill knows only about the first place. He asks the police detective Felicity was engaged to – this engagement is itself a surprise and a source of bafflement to him – where she lived. The detective names the address of the duplex. Dill shakes his head and says, 'I guess I didn't phrase it right.'

> What I'm asking, I guess, is where did Felicity really live? Your place? Is that where she spattered the stove with her rémoulade sauce, and read nine books at once and left most of them open on the floor, and smoked her two packs of Luckies a day, and weighed herself at least twice, and kept her kitchen stocked with enough food to last two months even if she knew she'd throw a lot of it out? That was my sister, Captain. That's how she lived. She wasn't obsessively neat. She didn't hang mail-order Impressionist prints on her wall. Give Felicity five minutes in a room, any room, and she made it look like she'd lived there forever.

Dill takes a deep breath and asks his question once again: 'So where did she live, Captain?' The detective tells him, and gives him the key. But the detective doesn't know why Felicity had two places, even though he was her fiancé. Dill glimpses something that is 'perhaps pain' in the detective's eyes. The reflection of a genuine sense of loss, surely; but also a feeling of exclusion from Felicity's secrets; and other worries too, no doubt, since this man, like almost everyone in this city, is playing for at least two sides at once.

But of course what matters here, and what distinguishes this scene from the visits to the two apartments, is the irrepressible life of the dead Felicity. She is her habits and tastes; she is what she liked to do. We hear Dill's affection in the very detail of his evocation of her style, and if his visit to the carriage house is a disappointment, even an anticlimax, it's because we know the real question is not where she lived, even if that's the one Dill insists on, but how she lived – and he has himself just given us the answer to that. There is a kind of resurrection in this memory – in this memory transformed into a troubled question – and it is because Felicity returns so vividly in this form that her death is more than a mystery to us. It is a loss.

Dill catches this sense perfectly when he returns to the phrase 'in vain', spoken by a well-meaning but shallow speaker at Felicity's funeral. 'When the young minister uttered the inevitable words "in vain", Dill quit listening as he always did when anyone spoke those words. They always came right after "sacrifice", another word that sent Dill's attention wandering.' 'If Felicity didn't die in vain,' he thinks, 'I don't know who did'. And yet at the end of the novel, when he has discovered how deep the many duplicities of the local characters go, and how difficult the investigative task was that Felicity had set herself, he finds a new use for the phrase:

> They all killed her in a way, he thought, and now all will pay just a little something on account. Otherwise, the preacher was wrong and she will have died in vain, although dying in vain isn't really all that bad since nearly everyone does it. It's the living in vain you really have to watch out for, and Felicity never wasted a day doing that.

IV

Detection is always a work of material memory, a reading of the remains of habits and actions, the mess left by various forms of life. But in much, perhaps most, crime and mystery fiction, the main mess belongs to the criminal, and the detective's job is to trace it to its origin, and even clean it up. Memory disappears into motive and explanation. In Thomas, the mess is called living, and, affectionately regarded, it can, as we have just seen, prolong or bring back a life. There are writers, like Michael Dibdin and Ian Rankin, who are less interested in who committed a crime than in what to do about the consequences. Thomas is too attentive to the idea of the person to go as far as that, but he also cares about ripples and reverberations rather than reasons. When you have made the relatively easy choice of your friend over your government, what is your next choice? At the end of the novel Dill has resolved the question of responsibility for his sister's death – although there seem to be more offenders than he or we can quite count – but he now needs to think about what to do about what he knows. He has been lucky enough to meet a wonderful woman, Felicity's lawyer. They may even have a future together, if he has a future. In a few minutes he will be interrogated by a pair of 'government agents', although he doesn't know which of several possible agencies they represent. He has time to call his new friend, and the last words of the novel are:

> As the phone rang, Dill wondered how good a lawyer she really was, and whether she would like Washington. Most of all he wondered whether she could keep him out of jail.

Dill is in trouble because of what he knows, because of who is involved in what he knows (an old friend, the local police chief, a high-ranking CIA officer, a Washington lobbyist, a White House chief of staff, and a US senator, for starters), and because he did not inform the FBI of what he knew, as was his legal obligation, at any of the several moments when the opportunity arose. He has the goods, in other words, on people who have the goods on other people. If it doesn't get him locked away or killed, this may help him a lot.

The chief crooks in this story, and therefore the most intriguing figures, are Jake Spivey and Clyde Brattle, former colleagues in various forms of government-endorsed skullduggery in the East, or as Spivey himself puts it when giving official testimony, 'duties . . . performed in Vietnam, Laos and Cambodia whose exact nature I am prevented by my oath from disclosing'. The duties included quite a lot of killing, and Spivey doesn't like to think about what he calls the 'stuff' he did, even though he likes the money he made and is still richly living on. He is a dodgy version of the poor boy who made good, Dill's old schoolfriend who now lives in a vast mansion once owned by a famous magnate in their home town. His house, he says, is his briarpatch, prickly with armed guards, but safe, as he thinks, and certainly luxurious and a source of great pride and pleasure to him.

The snag is that Brattle, once Spivey's supervisor in those distant activities, is no longer in the CIA or under its protection, and is worrying, as characters in Thomas's novels so often do, not about any possible harm to his reputation but about the probable harm his reputation can do to him. He is especially concerned about what Spivey might now choose to say, and is planning, it seems, both to have Spivey killed and to sell to the right buyer a whole lot of different secrets about other people. Dill also knows Brattle – met him no doubt on some unmarked occasion in his own nefarious past – and thinks of him as resembling 'some long-vanished Roman consul'. He does have lots of style, and we might regard him as something like a cross between Marlon Brando and Sidney Greenstreet. When Spivey steps behind him, unseen, and sticks a gun in his back, Brattle says, 'Well, Jake, how nice to hear from you again.' It is Brattle who eloquently recalls 'Mr Nixon's rather sodden farewell'. And

the deal Brattle wants to make, quite apart from his plan for
Spivey's death, is magnificent. He is the one who has the goods
on the figures I mentioned, and it is Dill's acquiring of this
knowledge in turn that puts him at risk. The deal is so subtle
that when Brattle proposes it to an ambitious Senator – not
the one involved with the CIA but the one Dill works for – the
man's own legal counsel doesn't get it. The lawyer thinks the
idea is that Brattle will get immunity in return for allowing the
Senator to play a role in the arrest and exposure of these men.
But Brattle knows better, and so do Dill and the Senator. Dill's
guess is elegantly framed as a mock-recommendation:

> Dill felt he knew which way the senator would go. Nevertheless, he
> gave him some silent advice. Put important men in jail, young sir, and
> you gain but fleeting fame. Keep important men out of jail, and make
> sure they know it's you who're keeping them out, and you gain im-
> mense power.

Dill and Spivey make an extraordinary pair, friends whose
infinite and justified suspicion of each other doesn't cancel out
their friendship. Dill likes Spivey in spite of his regrettable past,
and Spivey is pleased to see Dill even if his curiosity poses a
major threat to the whole scheme of his protected world. This is
where the title starts to echo around the book. Spivey is planning
to make sure the police chief becomes the mayor of the city. Dill
smiles and Spivey says, 'What I figure I'm really doing is growing my own briarpatch. Grow it high enough and thick enough,
there ain't nobody gonna come poking around in it.' Later Dill
asks him why he came back to the city. 'It wasn't just to grow
yourself a briarpatch. You could've done that anywhere.' Spivey
agrees, and says he probably came back for the same reason Felicity never left. 'It's home'. Dill always hated the place, couldn't
wait to leave. But for Spivey it's the only place where success
means anything. 'I guess home is where I wanted to grow my
briarpatch and show how rich poor little Jake Spivey done went

and got.' Later still, Spivey gives another meaning to the term and ostensively defines 'the ultimate briarpatch': knowledge so damaging to important people that he 'won't even have to *think* about going to jail'. And it's when Dill lays his hands on this knowledge that Spivey thinks he is going to have to kill him. It would be easy and safe. His friend the police chief is standing by and he's not going to cause any trouble. Spivey points the gun at Dill.

> As he aimed it, an expression of genuine sorrow spread slowly across his face. Dill wondered whether he would hear the gun fire. The sorrow then left Spivey's face and regret seemed to replace it. He slowly lowered the automatic and said, 'Shit, I can't do it.'

The writing is extremely careful here. Is an expression of genuine sorrow the same as a genuine expression of sorrow? And if regret only seems to replace sorrow what might really be lurking there in its place? In one register Thomas is offering us a moment of high virtue in unlikely circumstances. If Dill earlier chose his friend rather than his government, here Dill's friend chooses friendship over self-interest, a much tougher call. But the register of doubt, the sense of reading a face rather than knowing what the person feels, suggest something starker and simpler, although still impressive: there are killings that even killers can't do, whatever the reason for their restraint.

Brer Rabbit's briarpatch was also his home. He was 'bred and born' there, as he says when he taunts the fox. His triumph was to persuade his enemy that the worst thing he could do to him, the most horrible and terrifying of all torments, would be to fling him into a place of perfect safety and familiarity. The story is always rightly taken as showing the victory of brains over force, and of wit over awful odds. But in Thomas's reading it acquires another dimension. You don't need to be thrown into the briarpatch, because you're already there – even though you did make it yourself, it is precisely the riches and grand manner you were not bred and born to. And in another sense you can't be thrown into the briarpatch because, like the detailed memoir in *Twilight at Mac's Place*, it doesn't exist in actual space. Wherever people throw you will be your briarpatch. It is the name of your security, and a question of your relation with others. It is what you know about them, and it can lose its strength and comfort only if you let it go or use it badly. Here Thomas's interpretation happily rejoins the traditional one; we are talking about wit after all.

v

The city in the novel is not named, but that doesn't mean that we don't know it or that it can't create questions about knowledge. There are suggestions of Oklahoma City, since the parking meter is said to have been invented there, and is mentioned as a local achievement in the novel. Kansas City is described as 'up there' and 'back east'. There is a 'rival upstate city' that might be Tulsa. But then there are streets that seem to belong to Chicago and a bridge that is to be found in Saint Louis, and the William Gatty international airport seems to have been invented. The 'world' airport in Oklahoma City is named after Will Rogers; although there is a Wiley Post airport there commemorating the first man to fly solo round the world, and his navigator was called Harold Gatty. It is at about this point that historical detection begins to look like the wrong track. Thomas is quietly suggesting that this city is a real place (within this fiction) and could also be any one of several other real places in the Midwest or Southwest: big enough to matter in all kinds of respects, and far enough from either coast to seem a little out of the way, especially if your chief view is from Washington. The sheer details, street names, old hotels, evocations of neighbourhoods and local legend, create the double effect of a place of memory – Dill's memory, Spivey's home – and a sober historical reconstruction. Anything that happens here will seem a little more ordinary than it has any right to be, and the story of the governor who was impeached twice ('the first time for graft, which he beat by generously bribing three state senators, and the second time for the bribes themselves') certainly sounds as if it could easily migrate around the region.

Dill's new friend the lawyer is shocked when he cracks a man across the knee with a revolver to get him to talk. 'It is an act, isn't it?' she says. Dill says 'Sure', but he doesn't know whether it's an act or not, and a little later we see his genuine ruthlessness in action. Like everyone else in this novel he will do almost anything for information – the 'almost' being a moral qualification of some refinement. He needs to get the hard-bitten, hard-drinking journalist Laffter to tell him a thing or two, and threatens him not with violence but a lawsuit for libel. Laffter is sceptical, then recognises that Dill is not bluffing, and that he could lose all his savings to the court. Dill grasps at once that he has won, 'and almost wished he hadn't' – that crucial almost again. Laffter tells Dill what he wants to know, and promptly has a heart attack. This is where Harry the Waiter springs into action, and he and Dill manage to keep Laffter breathing until the paramedics arrive. Later he dies in hospital, another of this novel's many victims of the quest for knowledge. Of course Dill has not directly killed the old man, but the event tarnishes him, to use Chandler's word, and reminds us how mean the streets (and the press clubs and the mansions and the hotels and the apartments) are in this emblematic city. We can't start disliking Dill at this stage, and of course we want to know what he wants to know. We can't really disapprove of him either – or rather we can but our judgement is neither here nor there. What we do have to do is wonder who he is and where our liking has taken us. We knew that he too had his briarpatch, but perhaps we weren't ready for the quantity of thorns.

ROBERT MACFARLANE

The Line of Beauty is that rare thing: a deep novel about shallowness. It concerns the rise and fall during the 1980s of an upper-class English family, the Feddens, whose paterfamilias – the buffoonish Gerald – is a Conservative MP of limited intelligence but boundless ambition. Into the Feddens' world of mingled wealth, aestheticism and vulgarity comes the carefully named Nick Guest, a lower-middle-class boy from the provinces, and an Oxford friend of the Feddens' son. Nick has 'a certain shy polish' and a 'gravity' of manner, and after graduation it is decided that he should become a lodger with the Feddens in their Notting Hill house, while he pursues his doctoral studies into 'the style of Meredith, Conrad and James'.

Nick finds himself at once repelled and fascinated by the culture to which he has gained unexpected access: repelled by its affluent crudeness and solipsism, fascinated by the moments of aesthetic nonchalance which wealth enables (the Cézanne hung idly on a wall, the Gauguin given diffidently as an anniversary present). The novel follows Nick's social and erotic fortunes: at its opening, he has recently accepted his homosexuality, and is eagerly joining the gay world of 1983, a year when neither AIDS nor public tolerance of gayness were plainly in evidence.

As the hint of felony in his first name suggests, Nick is transgressor rather than visitor in the Fedden household. At once acquisitive and innocent, he takes more than he gives back, and is never able to assimilate himself completely into the aristocratic world of his hosts. Among the drivers of this curiously plotless novel, indeed, is the reader's unease at the impropriety of Nick's presence in the Fedden's house. One experiences the nervous awareness of a sustained trespass being committed, and of the exposure and eviction which will surely at some point come.

It is clear that Hollinghurst conceived of his novel as an inquest into the complicated relationship between beauty and goodness as it played itself out at the high noon of Thatcherism. Clear, too, that he trusted his novel not only to investigate but also to censure what one character calls the 'bloated excess' of those years. A stylistic difficulty confronted Hollinghurst, however, once he had settled upon these ethical ambitions and upon the brittle milieu of his novel. How was he to gain both a literary and a moral purchase on a venal world? What style would permit him at once to evoke and to indict a culture whose understanding of aestheticism was blighted by greed, and whose ethos was blighted by its understanding of aestheticism? How could he make a deep fathoming of people who were – in Gore Vidal's unforgettable description of Ronald Reagan – as shallow as spit on a rock? It is no coincidence that the recurring motif of *The Line of Beauty* is the mirror, for the compelling paradox of a mirror is that it is simultaneously planar and three-dimensional: that it both registers depth and insinuates flatness. Hollinghurst's novel needed somehow to possess just such a doubleness of aspect.

His solution to the problem – his formal equivalent to the mirror – was the free indirect style. The exceptional potential of the free indirect style to the novelist-moralist is that it permits twin compulsions to be contained within a single utterance: that it allows a character's consciousness or action to be simultaneously traced and judged. When, for instance, the narrative voice observes that the jacket of Lady Partridge – *a grande dame* of Wildean comic malevolence – is 'heavily embroidered with glinting black and silver thread, [and] had a scaly texture, on which finer fabrics might have snagged and laddered', a sense is instantly conveyed of Lady Partridge's appearance, but also of her abrasiveness and coarseness, as well of her perniciously serpentine nature. When, at a grand dinner, Gerald Fedden smiles at the person beside him with 'the fine glaze of preoccupation of someone about to make a speech', much is learnt about Gerald: his preference for hearing his own voice over that of other people, how his solipsism leads him to mismanage people, and how easily, in him, manners sag into mannerism. Again and again in the novel, Hollinghurst succeeds in both evoking and in pitilessly parsing high Tory society. As a reader, one learns both to admire and to be wary of the velveteen ferocity of his sentences.

Hollinghurst's scrupulous severity recalls that of Henry James, a comparison which the novel itself repeatedly asks us to make. For James, too, settled upon the free indirect style as the best form with which to suggest and to judge the elegant, moneyed atmospheres in which his novels thrived. There is no other novelist who knows better than James that style's potentials and perils and, in particular, how it is able to dampen but also to ignite desire in the writer. It was in *The Golden Bowl* – the novel which *The Line of Beauty* yearns to resemble – that James's free indirect style managed most brilliantly its coincident tasks of evoking and judging. In that novel the cast of mind of the wealthy American industrialist Adam Verver is enacted in the proportionally claused and tightly audited free indirect sentences which report him. Sometimes this enactment occurs at the level of a single word; one thinks of the moment in the First Book when Adam realises in a sudden burst of ethical clarity that he might marry Charlotte, and therefore solve the quandary in which the four main characters find themselves. The narrative records that it was at this moment that Verver's 'moral lucidity was constituted'. How perfectly that last verb is chosen by James – how it appraises Verver even as it emanates from him. For while Verver thinks that he has settled upon a flexible and egalitarian moral solution to the quandary, the verb 'constitute' (a verb we have heard

Verver use several times before), with its legalism and implied rigidity, betrays his failure to have done so. The etymology of the verb, too, which enfolds both the word 'statue' and the word 'statute', also points to two of James's warnings in his novel: the moral dangers of conceiving of human beings as art objects, or of ethical structures as contractual obligations.

Much else marks Hollinghurst out as James's contemporary successor or dauphin, beyond a shared affinity for the free indirect style. Like James, he is interested in knowing the ways in which people think of money, and the ways in which having money makes people think. And like James, he is a connoisseur of civil savagery – the little poison darts of the tongue, the put-downs which are handed out as compliments or harmless aperçus, only to writhe on closer examination into aspish life.

There are differences, of course. James's art is so often the art of omission, of partiality of knowledge, and of the unsaid: the eponymous spoils of Poynton, for instance, the 'old things' over which mother and son fight to the death, are never themselves specified. In Hollinghurst's novels, by contrast, almost nothing is left out. Hollinghurst practises the more ruthless art of the flenser. He works to lay bare the bone of a situation or person. His method is to allow a character to speak a line, make a gesture, or think a thought, and then to pare it mercilessly back. Perhaps, though, this mercilessness is an affinity between the two writers: one remembers J. M. Barrie's description of the smile that Henry James used to mark time in a conversation while he was searching for the right words with which to deliver a riposte to an interlocutor: 'They certainly were absolutely the right words, but the smile's enjoyment while he searched for them was what I was watching. It brought one down like Leatherstocking's Killdeer.'

One of the achievements of *The Line of Beauty* is its commitment to its vision. Nick is the character on whom the free indirect style is focalised throughout; it is his consciousness that we occupy without exeat during the novel. So it is that one understands what it means to see the world exactly as Nick sees it. We perceive with a particularity and prejudice of detail which is compellingly real: we are brought to experience, if not to sympathise with, Nick's lingering visual appraisals of cock through cloth, his physical disinterest in women, and the little twitches of misogyny which he cannot conceal, and which stir the ethical air of the prose. We feel, too, the tacitly hostile mood of Thatcherite London towards gayness: the faint tone of 'heterosexual menace' in the pub where Nick meets Leo, his first lover, the jeer and horn-blast from a passing car as they embrace in the street, and the oppressive presence of the 'efficiently reproductive species' from which Nick knows himself to be a dissenter, but which surrounds him socially.

Making Nick the dominant consciousness of the novel also allows Hollinghurst to investigate one of the things about which he writes and thinks best: nostalgia. The characteristic tense of all of Hollinghurst's novels is the future perfect, the will-have-been. His main characters – William Beckwith in *The Swimming-Pool Library*, Edward Manners in *The Folding Star* – love to cast their minds forwards to a point from which they will remember the ongoing present. They enjoy, too, the impossibility of return from that imagined future, the frisson of exclusion from a past that was once lived. As such, they remind us of the exquisite and implicitly erotic nature of nostalgia as frustrated desire. It was precisely this love – this eroticism – that Evelyn Waugh sharpened and formalised into an aesthetic in *Brideshead Revisited*, where it was shown to be fatal for its infantilising effect and for its corrosion of morality. As with Waugh, one suspects that Hollinghurst is only able to write so well about this particular kind of nostalgia by having been half in love with it as a feeling himself.

Hollinghurst is an aesthetically minded stylist, but not an

aesthete: his sentences are always aware of their own beauty, but are not devoted exclusively to its achievement. His care for prose rhythms, his understanding of how feeling can be delayed and relayed through the order and pacing of clauses, is one of the qualities that make him such a fine writer about nostalgia, itself a function of timing. Midway through the novel, having returned to the Midlands market town in which he grew up, and standing in its main square one evening, Nick recalls his 'long adolescence, its boredom and lust and its aesthetic ecstasies, laid up in amber in the sun-thickened light of the evening square'. The sentence is beautifully made, with the repeated 'ands' and 'ins' catching the strange, disconnected repetitions of the period of life which he is recalling, and with the image of amber lending its thickness to the already thickened light: a light which implicitly falls both in the moment of recollection and the moment being recollected. Later in the novel, Nick hears a piece of music which reminds him of his Oxford years. The memory, he thinks, 'confirmed and deepened the regretful longing which seemed now to have been the medium he lived in'. Nostalgia is here, again, concentrated upon nostalgia: Nick experiences regret for the passing of a regret which was once felt. Repeatedly in the novel we encounter such double-distilled nostalgia; a sepian liquid which fills the spaces of Nick's memory, and tints both his present perceptions and language. When he observes how, at evening time in the city, 'the street lamps brightened', we note that he says 'lamps' and not 'lights', and we understand that he is relishing the Victorianism of the word, the idea of 'street-lamps' – with their hints of wrought iron and candled glow – rather than the glaring pragmatism of 'street-lights'. Near the end of the book, a memory strikes Nick 'in a flash of acute nostalgia, as though he could never visit that scene of happiness again. He waited a minute longer, in the heightened singleness of someone who has slipped out for a minute from a class, a meeting, ears still ringing, face still solemn, into another world of quiet corridors.' It is an exquisite sentence, particularly in the way it develops, or is improvised, as it goes along, so that the experience of nostalgia is enacted rather than being only described. Nick is first pained by the nostalgia, but then recalls the strange pleasure of that sensation, and so deliberately protracts the experience ('a minute longer'), a protraction which allows him to elaborate the sensation into metaphor, thereby enabling the gorgeous languid parataxis of the closing clauses, ending in the 'world of quiet corridors'.

One of the distinctive marks of Hollinghurst's style has always been its easy evocation of spaces, both interior and exterior. His imagination naturally inhabits and finds feeling in the aerial shapes of rooms, buildings, streets, parks, skies. He is, in fact, a far finer writer of the outside than Henry James. James is happiest indoors, in the class- and taste-inflected spaces of houses, and when he does permit his characters outside, it is often to hurry them through the streets, before ducking back into the dark interiors of shops or houses. For Hollinghurst, though, the urban outside – street markets, parks, gardens – is a place of exciting and often sexual freedom. It is outside that Hollinghurst's narrative eye settles so readily upon forms of beauty which are déclassé, quotidian, available to all: the abstract tonal elegance of a dawn or dusk sky seen above trees, or the gleaming spin of a bicycle wheel, or the inscape of a slope of grass. Dusk, in particular, is a favourite Hollinghurst time, with its crepuscular promise, and its hints of illicitness, liminality and lust – of work ending and pleasure beginning. An exemplary dusk scene comes early in the novel, when Nick is standing on the balcony of the Feddens' house, looking out over the communal gardens as the night thickens:

> Someone was walking a small white dog, which looked almost luminous as it bobbed and scampered in the late dusk. Above the trees and rooftops the dingy glare of the London sky faded upwards into

weak violet heights. In summer, when windows everywhere were open, night seemed made of sound as much as shadow, the whisper of the leaves, the unsleeping traffic rumble, far-off car horns and squeals of brakes; voices, faint shouts, a waveband twiddle of unconnected music. Nick yearned for Leo, away to the north, three miles up the long straight roads. He felt hollow with frustration and delay. The girl with the white dog came back along the gravel path, and he thought how he might appear to her, if she glanced up, as an enviable figure, poised against the shining accomplished background of the lamplit room. Whereas, looking out, leaning out over the iron railing, Nick felt he had been swept to the brink of some new promise, a scented vista or vision of the night, and then held there.

There is much to admire here: the way that sound is used to give form and depth to the dusk, the discreet excellence of that 'waveband twiddle of unconnected music', the way that Nick's yearning for Leo, his first lover, is given a spatial correspondence, the way that a hint of the word 'polish' is brought out of the word 'accomplish' by its proximity to 'shining' and 'lamplit'. One notices, too, how subtly Hollinghurst registers Nick's changing knowledge of the scene before him. In the first sentence, the dog-walker is a 'someone'; by the time she returns along the gravel path, Nick has realised it is a 'girl', but the moment of that realisation goes unexpressed. The discrimination occurs in the real time of the prose, and is unremarkable to Nick, and is therefore unremarked upon. One also notices the revisions in the last line of 'looking out' to 'leaning out', and of 'vista' to 'vision'; these amendments, of course, record the act of Nick thinking, his aesthete's refinement of his own image, as he realises that to 'lean out' from a balcony is more riskily glamorous than merely to look out, and that a 'vision' is more alluring than a 'vista'.

At moments or scenes such as this, when Hollinghurst's prose inhabits so thoroughly a mind and a moment, when style is made finely attentive to the nuances of the lived moment, *The Line of Beauty* proves itself a historical novel of a high order:

that is to say, a novel which does not occupy a historical period, but instead occupies a mind occupying a historical period. Milan Kundera in *The Art of the Novel* proposed that a novel should examine 'not reality but existence. And existence is not what has occurred, existence is the realm of human possibilities.' Hollinghurst's novel is, at its best, an account not of what was, but of what might have been, in his chosen era. The good of this novel is that it offers, in Michael Wood's phrase, a record not of 'the fictional lives of real people but of the real lives of people who came extraordinarily close to existing'. One thinks of the moment when Nick notices the Miss Selfridge's label which is turned out on the blue shirt of Leo. He is struck with a pang of fondness for Leo's scruffiness, and longs briefly to tuck the label back into Leo's collar. Here, a specific period reference does not seem like an opportunistic product placement – the kind of heavy-handed retail-dating which characterises so many 'historical' novels – but is instead stitched into the emotional fabric of the novel.

Such subtleties of touch make the novel's occasional clumsinesses even more apparent, and more curious. Frequently, and for reasons that are not clear, Hollinghurst seems set on nudging his characters out of the realm of possibility and into that of caricature. Gerald's buffoonery is played too large at times, and one wonders here and there if Nick – a conversationalist of often arresting banality, whose favourite words are 'fascinating' and 'wonderful' – is really so acute a social observer as the free indirect style implies him to be. One wishes Hollinghurst could have resisted his Dickensian habit of naming-as-destiny. Do the ungenerous Sir Maurice and Lady Tipper, who visit the family in the south of France, require that particular surname? Does Wani Ouradi's have to carry its submerged hint of 'Uranus'? Does Nick Guest's name deepen or refine our understanding of his interloper status? In a novel which is concerned with delicacy of touch, and refinement of category, these allegori-

cal namings seem like large hands pointing in the margins of
medieval manuscripts, drawing attention to that which is already apparent.

In interview, Hollinghurst has described *The Line of Beauty* as a
fiercely political book: an indictment of what he called 'the new
depths of poverty' plumbed by Thatcherism, and the 'spurious
fantasy of elegance' that was conjured up by wealth in the 1980s.
Certainly, the novel has observations to make concerning the
prejudices of racism, homophobia and snobbery during that
decade, and how happily these three grim biases nested together in the minds of what Gerald – intending it as a compliment –
calls 'the property-owning democracy' of the decade. And there
are, it is true, little hints of political venom – brief flickers of
Hollinghurst's snake-tongue – as when Bertrand Ouradi praises Thatcher as 'a very kind woman'. 'Bertrand had,' writes Hollinghurst with delicious savagery, 'the mawkish look of a brute
who praises the kindness of another brute.' However, while we
pass most of our time in the novel within the house and family
of a Tory minister, politics as one would conventionally recognise it, and the consequences of politics, happen off-stage. The
social and personal devastations of Thatcherism are alluded to
in passing, never witnessed.

As we read on in the novel, we realise that what Hollinghurst
truly loathes about the Thatcher years is not the social consequences of its economic policy, but the coarseness of taste which
it licensed. The true crime of the age, according to Hollinghurst's
audit, is its combination of so much appetite with so little taste.
Gerald is the chief of sinners in this respect: Hollinghurst lav-
ishes contempt on Gerald's 'facetious boom', his 'taste for the
splendid' – which is not to be confused with the beautiful – and
his comic nervousness in the face of artworks to which he knows
he is meant to respond. 'I don't see what's so vulgar about being
glorious,' Gerald woundedly protests, after Nick has criticised

his love of Richard Strauss. The problem with Strauss, Nick thinks to himself, is the 'colossal redundancy' of his music, 'the squandering of brilliant technique on cheap material, the sense that the moral nerves had been cut, leaving the great bloated body to a life of valueless excess.' It is to precisely this conclusion that Hollinghurst's novel seems to want, morally, to commute: that the sundering of the aesthetic and the ethical will always lead first to vulgarity, and then to catastrophe.

The Line of Beauty is a novel which thinks at the level of metaphor, as well as of style; which makes its propositions by patterns of images, as well as by dialogue and argument. One of the most conspicuous of these patterns is that of reflection and self-admiration. The novel's epigraph is taken from Lewis Carroll, and looking-glasses are everywhere in the novel. Almost every surface gleams: lustrously polished wood, glinting surfaces of water, car bodyworks, 'high hall mirrors', 'gilt-framed mirrors'. Walking alone through the Fedden's house, Nick trails his fingertips over 'the dark polished wood' of the furniture, and sees himself 'partnered by reflections as dim as shadows' in the veneer. Reflective sunglasses lie about on table tops and sideboards, impassively registering the world (one remembers Nabokov's association of sunglasses with venality in *Lolita* – the 'lost pair of sunglasses' which is 'the only witness' to Humbert's near-ravishing of his childhood sweetheart, Annabel, on a beach). Everywhere, too, are the verbs and nouns of lustrousness: 'shimmer', 'sheen', 'glaze', and 'gleam' occur scores of times in the novel. Nick's eye is caught by the 'glassy polish of the table top', the 'gleaming slippage' of a loose pile of books, 'gleaming red veneer', 'gilt ballroom chairs'. When Nick and Wani slip into the bedroom of Wani's parents for an illicit fondle, and the free indirect narrative notes that 'the richness of the room was its mixture of shiny pomp, glazed swagged curtains, huge mirrors, onyx and glaring gilt', it is only one of dozens of puns on the word 'gilt': puns which compact and reinforce the idea that an excessive venera-

tion of appearance has led to an abolition of moral depth. Nick
goes to look at himself 'in the high gilt arch of the hall mirror',
in the Feddens' house; a cabinet bookshelf is 'a gilded cage', and
people sit on 'little gilt chairs'. So thorough-going and influential
is this lustrousness that it comes, after a while, to provide the
texture and finish of Nick's memory: he puts 'a bright gloss' on
an idea, entertains the 'gleam of a new possibility', and recollec-
tions come 'gleaming out of the blur of memory'.

Hollinghurst also tropes the era's obsession with style over
substance in the novel's eponymous motif: the ogee curve, or
'line of beauty'. The ogee is first found in William Hogarth's
Analysis of Beauty (1754), where Hogarth identified the sinu-
ous S-shaped double curve as an exquisitely elegant form: 'a
sort of proportion'd, winding line,' wrote Hogarth, 'which will
hereafter be call'd the precise serpentine line, or line of grace.'
Hollinghurst's version of the ogee, of course, is a line of 'beauty',
not a line of 'grace', and this secularising revision of Hogarth's
phrase is significant. For the ogee appeals to Nick – and comes
to represent the decade – precisely because of its functionless-
ness, its disinterest in purpose or ethics. The ogee is, for Nick,
an inscape of elegance, an expression of pure aestheticism. As
the novel proceeds, Nick's primed attention begins to find the
ogee curve everywhere, in the 'black and gilt S-shaped balus-
ters' of the Feddens' house, in 'mirror-frames and pelmets and
wardrobes', in the lines of cocaine which are chopped and ar-
ranged on the 'polished' glass tables and which Nick so keenly
snorts, and of course in the 'curve of the lower back and mus-
cular bottom' of men – the line of booty. The ogee echoes, too,
the cambers of Hollinghurst's own fine sentences, and the rise
and fall of the 1980s themselves.

'Ogee', of course, swerves suggestively close to 'orgy', and the
word thus registers a shadow of the decadence that exists in
elegance. Certainly, the self-devoted and useless aestheticism
represented by the ogee curve is, in one respect, precisely what

Hollinghurst devotes his novel to warning against – a commitment to beauty so sharp that it snips 'the moral nerves'. Yet for all his moral suspicion of aestheticism, Hollinghurst never manages fully to disavow or to denounce its claims and charms. This, perhaps, is his strongest affinity with Henry James: that Hollinghurst finds himself dismayed by the effects of aestheticism, yet also compelled by it. Both writers simultaneously desire and distrust absolute beauty.

What makes *The Line of Beauty* most interesting, perhaps, is watching the play of longing between Hollinghurst and the world he is bent on criticising: the intermittence of control on his part that is exposed during those parapraxic moments when the novel comes to know more about him than he about it. Repeatedly in *The Line of Beauty*, Hollinghurst reveals himself to be more in love with the careless style of the aristocracy, and the languid beauties made possible by wealth, than he can acknowledge or even sense. The novel's tone frequently lapses into a bitchy rapture for the Thatcher era: the one compulsion (to judge, critique, censure) collapses into the other (to evoke, describe, celebrate). At times, Hollinghurst becomes so involved with precisely cataloguing the material attributes of his characters – their paintings and furniture, their buildings and their estates – that he seems to slide into a gilty [sic] reverie. Like a mesmerist who has mistakenly looked in a mirror, he manages to enchant himself with his own incantations. This is, in part, a consequence of the demandingly subtle ethics of the free indirect style, which yields much to the writer in fluency and perspective, but which can claim a toll in the coin of moral compromise.

Hollinghurst's uncertainty over whether to despise or to crave his wealthy world finds one of its expressions in his use of the word 'lustre', which appears scores of times in the novel. Hollinghurst is aware, of course, of the buried hint of concupiscence in the word, and plays knowingly on this, but he seems less sure as to which of the word's two opposed main meanings he wishes to invoke by it. For 'lustre' can connote on the one hand a tawdry superficiality of light, and on the other a deep sustaining refulgence. Hollinghurst's use of the word often hovers indecisively between these meanings, or rocks inconsistently back and forth between consecutive uses: he appears uncertain whether the 'lustre' of the novel's world should be condemned or praised. This uncertainty stands in contrast to the decidedness of James, who uses the word 'lustre' dozens of times in *The Golden Bowl* – but only ever to indicate a superficiality of thought or a falsity of appearance.

'What would Henry James have made of us?' wonders a character halfway through *The Line of Beauty*. James would, one thinks, have recognised and sympathised with the moral struggle that we see occurring in *The Line of Beauty*; the struggle, that is, between Hollinghurst's aestheticism and his moralism. For James, too, was morally wary of wealth, but also powerfully attracted by it, in particular by the deep sincerity of old wealth. James had little problem censuring new wealth (like that of Adam Verver), but the allure of old money – like that of old knowledge, and what in *The Ambassadors* he calls 'antique order' – gripped him strongly despite himself.

The best way to understand the nature of Hollinghurst's ambitions and failures as a moralist is to measure him against James. In *The Golden Bowl*, his most sustained investigation of the relationship between beauty and morality, James suggested that aestheticism of any sustained kind is profoundly hazardous. Hollinghurst, however, can never quite bring himself to a declaration of this totality. He tries to goad himself to such a conclusion, only to find himself drawn away from making it by his finger-trailing fondness for the beauty of beauty.

The conspicuously abrupt ending of *The Line of Beauty* seems to be a function of Hollinghurst's belief that he must moralise: that the ethical must, ultimately, be seen to supersede

the aesthetic. After the novel's long, indolent central sections –
which tell of holidays in the summer house in France, of great
parties in country houses, and in which the plot pools almost
to the point of stillness – the swiftness of the closing chapters,
their rapid tumble of events, surprises the reader. Gerald's affair
with his assistant is exposed, as are certain irregular financial
dealings in which he has been involved, and the press also sniff
out Nick's relationship with Wani, a scandal which further con-
tributes to the public disgrace and political undoing of Gerald.
Inside the house, Nick finds himself no longer welcome: there
is a sudden contraction of hospitality into hostility, and he is
brusquely evicted.

As Nick shuts the great blue door of the house behind him,
and slips the keys back through the letter box, he is returned
to the Notting Hill street where his adventure had begun four
years earlier. The implication, to which we have abruptly been
brought, is that the nuanced aesthetic taste which we watch
Nick finessing and enjoying throughout the novel means nothing without a similarly finessed ethical sense: that the apprehension of appearance must be joined with an apprehension
of consequence. There are echoes, here, of James's own ritual
renunciation of wealth and beauty at the end of *The Ambassadors*, when Lambert Strether – the character who most resembles James – rejects all that Europe has to offer him, and returns
instead to America. The ending of *The Line of Beauty* can be
seen to offer a similarly pentecostal resolution, in which – in
James Wood's phrase – the novel decides upon an 'extremity of
. . . moral turn, [such that], as it were, the story itself must turn
on its beautiful creations and devour them in moral flames.'

And yet in the poised, ambiguous final paragraphs of the
novel, there is a hint that nothing at all has been learnt, that no
such devouring has occurred. For Nick's response to his eviction is entirely in keeping with the aesthete's nostalgic reading
of the world which has brought him to this point. As he walks

slowly and stunnedly down the street, unable to contemplate the present, he imagines instead that he has contracted Aids, and that he will die of the disease, and he casts his mind forward to the point of his death, trying to imagine how he will be remembered by the friends who survive him: 'The emotion was startling. It was a sort of terror, made up of emotions from every stage of his short life, weaning, homesickness, envy, and self-pity; but he felt that the self-pity belonged to a larger pity. It was a love of the world that was shockingly unconditional.' Then, suddenly – this future nostalgia having been comfortingly wallowed in – Nick's mind recurs to the exquisite irrefutability of the present. He gazes at the light falling on the stonework of a building ahead of him, and the novel ends with a word and a sentiment against which it has ostensibly been briefing throughout: 'It wasn't just this street corner but the fact of a street corner at all that seemed, in the light of the moment, so beautiful.'

BENJAMIN MARKOVITS

Henry James makes a brief appearance towards the end of Colm Tóibín's first novel, *The South*. The book tells the story of Katherine Proctor, a Protestant Irish woman who has left her husband and young son and moved, with uncertain purpose, to Spain. She begins to paint again, falls in love, gives birth to a daughter, and loses both lover and child in a car accident. Revolutionary politics plays a role in the story, the struggles of the communists and the struggles of the unionists. What gives a shape to the novel is the slow emergence of Katherine's career from the fragments of various halfwilled decisions and strokes of fortune. Her mother, an Englishwoman who also left her husband and child to live in London, takes her daughter on holiday to Portugal: she brings with her 'a lot of Henry James's novels', including *The Ambassadors*. Katherine, in a letter to a friend, compares herself to its protagonist: 'I am like Chad, still starry-eyed at the sight of the new. I am like Chad who wants the opportunity to see more, to do more. I do not want everything to be over with me. There is more. There is more.'

The allusion stands out, in part because the novel itself seems so unJamesian. The comparison to Chad makes clear how *unlike* Chad she is: the unembarrassed repetitions, the straightforward sentence structure. Her letter shows a lack of embarrassment all round: about optimism, about the bluntness of her comparison, about the simplicity of her reading. James, in his late preface to *The Ambassadors*, remarked that he never felt so sure of his ground as he did composing it. I imagine that

The South was a harder novel to put together. Sections are separated by date and place; the connections between them are often skipped. It is made up of fragments in part because it follows no narrative line. Katherine drifts from episode to episode, not quite thoughtlessly, but without much conscious effort. Things happen to her. Between the fragments, holding them together, we have a sense of the real world – the world that hasn't been made up. James himself would never appeal to it, which makes it notable that Tóibín has appealed to James.

His work seems to owe more to Raymond Carver. Short direct sentences. An emphasis on the plausible. A matt emotional finish. One of the odd side-effects of 'modest realism' is that it produces so much misery: that's what tends to emerge when you strip a plot of its extraordinary, satirical, and suspenseful elements. It certainly emerges in Tóibín's work. James, by contrast, has the light touch of artifice. Fiction plays games, and even at his tragic best, he manages to impart a consoling aesthetic delight. His heroines suffer beautifully. Not that Tóibín's novels seem uncrafted. *The South*, *The Heather Blazing*, *The Blackwater Lightship* suggest the thankless effort required to get small details right. He has said that you shouldn't read more than one or two of them: they're too grim. What he does impart in each of these simple and difficult books is the sense of a long and serious argument being made. We have an impression of his control, of a large overarching intention – but little sense of the small particular intentions, passage by passage, line by line, that make it up.

Simplicity is one of his tricks, though his prose is not as simple as it first appears. Or maybe it's truer to say, that there's more to it than simplicity. His sentences aren't *that* short; he's capable of sketching his ideas with a fine-tipped pen. In *The Heather Blazing*, a judge, an important man, has returned to the sea in which he swam as a child:

Each time a wave rolled inwards it unsettled the small stones at the shoreline, forcing them to knock against each other. They made a clattering, gurgling sound as each wave hit them and then retreated. He listened for it as the waves came in, a sound unlike any other, definite and oddly comforting, like two hollow objects being banged against each other, except that this was more modest, intimate.

What Tóibín avoids, for the most part, are metaphorical flights and grammatical complexities. Even here, the simile demands from us only a slight imaginative effort: the sound of wave on stone is like the sound of two hollow objects making contact. When he runs on, he runs on unashamedly, connecting the parts of his thought with nothing more elaborate than a few commas. He balks at elegant variations, and has never taken seriously Nabokov's advice, to avoid starting successive paragraphs with the same word. Subject + verb suits him fine. Children tell stories by saying, this and then this and then this; his novels are enormously complicated versions of their technique. The effect can be relentless, but his relentlessness is also deeply persuasive. Modesty is the proof he gives us of his realism.

James, famously, is a master of just those tricks that Tóibín forswears: metaphorical flights, grammatical complexities, elegant variations. Which makes that brief allusion in *The South* all the more suggestive. What is his debt to James? *The Master*, Tóibín's fifth novel, doesn't offer an easy answer to the question, though James is its hero, and his life is its subject. Like *The South*, it is separated into sections, which are introduced by a time and a place. Like *The South*, it is shaped by the vague irregular outline of someone's life. James drifts from episode to episode, not thoughtlessly, of course, but without much conscious effort. Things happen to him. The novel opens with the opening of his play *Guy Domville*. Like Chad, he is starry-eyed at the sight of the new. He wants the opportunity to do more, to see more:

> He was ready now to change his life. He foresaw an end to long, solitary days; the grim satisfaction that fiction gave him would be replaced by

a life in which he wrote for voices and movement and an immediacy that through all his life up to now he had believed he would never experience.

The theatre offers him a chance to take his place on the public stage. The story that follows describes his failure to make good on that chance – because of bad luck, because of his hesitations, his cowardice, because of the unchangeable tendencies of his character. His sexuality, or rather its suppression, has something to do with it. *Guy Domville* is about a man, the last of his family line, forced to choose between marriage and a life of contemplation – he wishes to retire to a monastery. I have said that Tóibín is good at covering up the tracks of his intentions. It looks at first as if he has made them clear here. A series of conversations, between James and an old friend, whom he knew in Paris, between James and Edmund Gosse, suggest that his homosexuality has been acknowledged, as a fact, as a problem, within his circle of acquaintance. We see him standing in the rain outside the Paris flat of his friend Paul Joukowski, hesitating, wondering whether to go in; later, remembering his own hesitations, his turning away at last. Someone mentions having seen Joukowski, greatly changed, aged; James refuses to admit his interest in him. This is a novel, it seems, about a man who cannot come to terms with the fact that he is gay.

The trouble with such a novel is that it makes us, as readers, much wiser than James: if only he could accept what everyone knows, his life would have been happier and more complete. I say 'trouble' – it's a line many writers would have taken. (I should say now that Tóibín hasn't.) The fact that James, as a historical figure, was enormously self-aware, enormously sophisticated, should undermine, a little, our confidence that we can understand him. But the truth is that most people are very good at their lives. They understand them much better in some ways (the work they do, the habits that sustain them, the content of their memories, the nature of their relations with

friends, parents, lovers) than any novelist can hope to. Which
makes the novelist's task almost impossible: to let us into the
lives of others, without violating our sense of the fact that what
interests us about them is their privacy, or, to put it another
way, their own superior understanding of themselves.

Tóibín's James, in fact, spends much of his novel resisting
the attempts of others to make sense of him. He rebuffs Gosse,
when, after the trial of Oscar Wilde is over, Gosse dresses up a
little of his curiosity as a piece of concern:

> 'It is advised, I think, that anyone who has been, as it were, compro-
> mised should arrange to travel as soon as possible. London is a large
> city and much can go on here quietly and secretly, but now the secrecy
> has been shattered.'
>
> Henry stood up and went to the bookcase between the windows and
> studied the books. 'I wondered if you, if perhaps . . .' Gosse began.
>
> 'No.' Henry turned sharply. 'You do not wonder. There is nothing to
> wonder about.'
>
> 'Well, that is a relief, if I may say so,' Gosse said quietly, standing up.
>
> 'Is that what you came here to ask?' Henry kept his eyes fixed on
> Gosse, his gaze direct and hostile enough to prevent any reply.

It's an important moment – no one in the book comes closer
than Gosse to raising the question, openly, of James's sexuality. Tóibín allows James to express his own resistance to this
line of inquiry. He does not himself enter into his character's
thoughts, though he is willing enough, elsewhere, to make the
attempt. Henry stands up and Henry stares – as much at us as
at Gosse. We see what his friend sees. He seems to be staring at
Tóibín, too.

Other people in the book also resist James's attempts to turn
them into his own characters. Writing, its effects, on both the
writer and the people he uses for his writing, is in some sense
the subject of *The Master*. I have said that the novel borrows
its structure from *The South*: a series of episodes defined by
the time and the place in which they are set. James's history,

however, progresses very differently from Katherine Proctor's. In her case, the structure of the novel reflects the fact that she feels imprisoned inside each stage of her life. In her marriage, from which she escapes to Barcelona; in the narrow round of expatriate life, from which she escapes, with her lover, to the Pyrenees; in the Pyrenees, from which she escapes, at last, after the death of her lover and child, etc. The narrow timeframes of each chapter serve as the walls that she can't see over, which keep her from making out the shape of her life. James, by contrast, spends very little of each chapter in the moment in which they are set. Tóibín allows him to range freely, backwards, into his memories, and forwards, into the stories he hopes to build from the scant materials of his personal experience. The setting of each chapter is really only the pivot on which he turns, to look both ways at his life. What moves the story forward, page by page, is the evolution of his work.

The failure of *Guy Domville* in January of 1895 – James is booed when he appears on stage after the first night – forces him to give up on his public ambitions. What follows is an account of the private revolutions that enable him, by October of 1899, to write the remarkable sequence of late novels that begins with *The Wings of the Dove* (first published in 1902) and ends with *The Golden Bowl* (1904).

> He took up his pen again – the pen of all his unforgettable efforts and sacred struggles. It was now, he believed, that he would do the work of his life. He was ready to begin again, to return to the old high art of fiction with ambitions now too deep and pure for any utterance.

His is an extraordinary ambition; I mean, Tóibín's. Great men are hard to write. Most people are very good at being themselves; the great are great in part because they are uniquely good at it. Novelists can tackle the problem in different ways. The simplest is to build a frame around their protagonist – to present him only as he appears in the more writable perspective of other people. Tóibín does not shy from the defining feature of James's greatness, his creative genius; in fact, he attempts to account for it, in each episode of *The Master*, and often with unembarrassed directness. In Ireland James observes a very pretty girl, the daughter of guests at the house in which he is staying, play up sweetly to the admiration generally felt for her. He wonders what will become of such precocious, such conscious innocence – he holds it up, as it were, in different lights, to see what he can make of it. Later, he recalls a story told him by the Archbishop of Canterbury, about two children left in the care of a governess. The house is large and the governess has been instructed not to contact their guardian 'under any circumstances'. Gosse asks him for the details of a rumour once reported about his father, that he had a vision of a terrible black bird, which reduced him to inconsolable helplessness; he needed months to recover. Henry had been too small to remember the incident, but Gosse suggests to him, on the strength of recent theories, 'that a child can take in everything, hold it but not absorb it in what they call the unconscious'. Various ideas dovetail, and he begins to form a plan for, among other tales, *The Turn of the Screw*.

Gosse eventually becomes suspicious of the uses to which Henry puts his gossip. He believes that 'writing a story using factual material and real people' is 'dishonest and strange and somehow underhand'. It reduces the art of fiction to 'a cheap raid on the real'. Gosse's objections apply as much to Tóibín's manipulation of James's biography as to anything James attempts himself. What drives the story along is the effect of such 'dishonesty' and 'underhandedness' on the author. How much has he sacrificed for his art? Whom has he sacrificed? The novel begins with an account of James's dreams, in which the dead he has loved return to him with an air of 'beseeching'. At various points, members of James's circle reproach him for the way he has detached himself from those who needed him. From his cousin Minny Temple, who wanted him to accompany her to

Rome when she was sick with tuberculosis. From his friend, the novelist Constance Fenimore Woolson, who killed herself in Venice, after James had failed, as he once suggested he might, to pass the long Venetian winter with her.

Their reproaches touch him in part because they force him to reflect on his own emotional defenses. Europe has taught him the power of privacy. 'Everyone he knew carried with them the aura of another life which was half secret and half open, to be known about but not mentioned.' Americans, by contrast, interest James for a different reason: 'their yearning openness . . . their readiness for experience'. James himself wanders between the two worlds: he wishes to be neither open nor secretive. That is, he wishes to be both at the same time, which can only be achieved at the expense of a private sphere. 'He himself learned never to disclose anything, and never even to acknowledge the moment when some new information was imparted, to act as though a mere pleasantry had been exchanged.' The suppression of his sexuality and his 'raid on the real' are related: James resists entangling himself in any relation that might expose him to his own talent for curiosity. 'There is nothing to wonder about,' he tells Gosse; it might be the refrain of the novel. Again and again, he consoles himself with variations on it. 'He worried about his privacy, but assured himself that there was nothing in his correspondence which was entirely private.'

The effort is exhausting, and the second half of the novel is occupied by his search for some kind of place of retreat. For James, the discriminating middle-class materialist, it takes the form of a permanent address. 'It was as though he lived a life which lacked a façade, a stretch of frontage to protect him from the world. Lamb House would offer him beautiful old windows from which to view the outside; the outside, in turn, could peer in only at his invitation.' Invitations duly follow. Guests visit him there, friends from Boston, Lily Norton, Oliver Wendell Holmes; Henrik Andersen, a young man he picked up in Rome, a sculptor, handsome, ambitious, awkward, slightly ridiculous; his brother William, William's wife Alice, their daughter. But James always reserves the mornings for his writing. When his hand fails him, he hires an amanuensis, a dour Scot named MacAlpine, to take dictation from him, and discovers, to his surprise, the pleasure of composing on his feet. Even in the midst of his inspirations, he is not alone; he presents a kind of public face to the blank page.

James, in Tóibín's novel, suppresses his sexuality (in this context, it doesn't matter so much whether he's gay or straight), not out of any delusion or failure of courage, but because it might interfere with his work. That, at least, is the account of himself he wishes to make, and the progress of his work allows James to argue for the sort of life he has chosen. His self-defence depends in part on something his cousin Minny once said to him. She served their group as a touchstone of spontaneous wisdom, and was courted, one summer, by his friends John Gray and Oliver Wendell Holmes. On the way up to visit her, James spent an awkward and intense night with Holmes, sharing a bed at an inn. Unlike James, Holmes had fought in the war; he had taken their enforced intimacy very coolly. Henry, for whom the experience remained one of the most passionate of his life, was amazed at the way that Holmes's fearlessness had entered 'so completely into the private realm'. In any case, they never shared a bed again. Holmes subsequently fell in love with Minny, but it was to Gray that she said, in a letter, 'you must tell me something that you are sure is true'. These words, Tóibín remarks, mean more to James than any other, including those he has written himself.

Many years later, after Henry has installed himself at Lamb House, Holmes comes to visit him. Minny had chosen Gray over Holmes; in any case, she died before she married. Holmes has changed a little: he has become a public man and can 'be pompous and intimidating' when he pleases. After dinner, Holmes brings up that summer after the war, during which they had shared, as Minny called it, 'the famous bed'. Holmes's fearlessness, it turns out, was really only a kind of death: he had lost a part of himself in battle. 'I felt sometimes as if I were under water, seeing things only in vague outline and desperately trying to come up for air.' The time they had spent together grew clear only in his memory, but it inspired him nonetheless to 'drink up the life that was offered to us then as those wonderful sisters did. I longed to be alive, just as I long for it now, and the time passing has helped me, helped me to live.' Henry is conscious of having been matched, in the kind of honesty he prized; conscious, too, of the fact that he has 'no confession of his own. His war had been private, within his family and deep within himself . . . He lived, at times, he felt, as if his life belonged to someone else, a story that had not yet been written, a character who had not been fully imagined.'

The comparison suggests James's famous remark about the origin of his stories, from his preface to *The Portrait of a Lady*:

> I have always fondly remembered a remark that I heard fall years ago from the lips of Ivan Turgenieff in regard to his own experience of the usual origin of the fictive picture. It began for him almost always with the vision of some person or persons, who hovered before him, soliciting him, as the active or passive figure, interesting him and appealing to him just as they were and by what they were. He saw them in that fashion, as *disponibles*, saw them subject to the chances, the complications of existence, and saw them vividly, but then had to find for them the right relations, those that would bring them out.

James, then, in Tóibín's words, feels like someone who has yet to be 'brought out'. What's interesting about James's remark is that it glosses over the distinction between 'the complications of existence' and the 'right relations'. Nor is it clear whether the phrase 'just as they were and by what they were' describes these 'fictive' suppliants before they had been subject to the chances of life, or after. The difference is significant. What's at stake is the possibility that a character can have an essence, a real existence independent of those complications and relations – if it can exist entirely for itself. This, at least, is the possibility that James, in Tóibín's novel, has pursued.

Holmes hasn't finished, and before he retires to bed, brings up *The Portrait of a Lady*, which he calls a 'great monument' to Minny, though he did not care for the ending. 'I wish she were alive now so that I could find out what she thought of me.' Henry's response is simple and faintly ironic. 'Yes, indeed.' Holmes refuses to be put off. 'Do you ever regret not taking her to Italy when she was ill? . . . Gray says she asked you several times.' Henry still evades him – 'I don't think ask is the word . . . She was very ill then. Gray is misinformed' – until Holmes is forced to make his reproach insultingly clear:

> 'When finally she knew no one would help her she turned her face to the wall. She was very much alone then and she fixed on the idea. You were her cousin and could have travelled with her. You were free, in fact you were already in Rome. It would have cost you nothing.'

In fact, the real James, after her death, responded more coldly still. He wrote in a letter to his brother William: 'You will all have felt by this time the novel delight of thinking of Minny without that lurking impulse of fond regret and uneasy conjecture so familiar to the minds of her friends.' The choice of 'novel' in this context is unlikely to be accidental. And he continues: 'The more I think of her the more perfectly satisfied I am to have her translated from this changing realm of fact to the steady realm of thought.' Death has provided for her exactly the right relation, and he uses it, too, if not in *The Portrait of a Lady*, then in *The Wings of the Dove*.

Tóibín, in *his* novel, has chosen not to make use of this material, but the upshot of their little confrontation does depend, in the book, on letters and on a kind of literary question. What had Minny written? 'He was aware that Gray had kept her letters, and he too in his apartment in London had stored away those letters which Minny had written to him in the last year of her life. He knew that she had accused him of nothing, but he now wished to know what terms she had used all those years before in her expressed desire to go to Rome.' The letters begin to obsess him, and he stops writing and travels to London to examine them. For the first time since the disaster of his play, he feels that the 'equilibrium he had worked so intensely to achieve has disappeared'. Henry has been used to observing the biases of others, including Holmes, from his own superior detachment. 'Tell me something that you are sure is true,' Minny had said, and James has devoted himself to living the kind of life, independent, uncompromised, unimplicated, that might enable him to. His own detachment, it turns out, has involved him in a form of bias, too:

> He put the letters aside and sat with his head in his hands. He did not help her or encourage her, and she was careful never to ask outright. If she had insisted on coming, he forced himself to complete this thought now, he would have stood aside or kept his distance or actively prevented her coming, whatever was necessary. He had himself, in that year, escaped into the bright old world he had longed for. He was writing stories . . .

James, in real life, was equal to the same acknowledgment: 'While I sit spinning my sentences she is dead: and I suppose it is partly to defend myself from too direct a sense of her death that I indulge in this fruitless attempt to transmute it from a hard fact into a soft idea.' There is a difference, of course, between Tóibín's James, who sits with his head in his hands and privately 'completes' a thought, and the other James, the real one, who turned his own literary predations into an object of curiosity, and polished it into a confession for his brother. A significant difference: between a gossipy, fluent and charming socialite, and a passive, introverted observer of the scene. It isn't always clear how much that difference matters, whether the novel depends on anything like biographical accuracy. Not much, I suspect. It's a novel, after all, though one of the interesting games that Tóibín plays in it involves gesturing at the gaps that history can supply. Edmund Gosse is introduced mostly as Edmund Gosse or Gosse, as if he were real, which, of course, he was. If we wanted to, we could look up his biography. But Tóibín has taken this line before. Katherine Proctor's friend, and occasional lover, in *The South* is always referred to as Michael Graves – as if he, too, were real.

Still, the history matters, if only because Henry, as a character, is the author of the books that the real James wrote. This makes a certain amount of correlation between the two necessary, and Tóibín, in this novel, comes closer to writing in the style of his protagonist than he ever has before.

> Holmes began by believing that Minny did not like Gray, which pleased him, and then became aware with flashes of alarm that Gray was winning. Holmes's alarm made a sound that Minny and her sisters and Gray were too distracted to hear, but which Henry picked up easily and stored and thought about when he was alone.

He has teased out, from the word 'alarm', its metaphorical content, and casually reinstated its poetic power. A typically Jamesian move, the reinvigoration of idiom, though this example suggests the earlier and simpler James style, and even then he might not have permitted himself the slightly awkward transition from a 'flash' of alarm to a 'sound'. The directness, the plainness of the last half-sentence is pure Tóibín, and it's worth remembering that *The Master* tells the story of the late James, of the internal evolutions that produced his grandest and most assured complexities of style.

There is a great gap between those flashes and alarms, and this, taken almost at random from *The Golden Bowl*. James is comparing the character of Adam Verver, and its internal workings, to a church with a light in it:

This establishment, mysterious and almost anonymous, the windows of which, at hours of highest pressure, never seemed, for starers and wonderers, perceptibly to glow, must in fact have been during certain years the scene of an unprecedented, a miraculous white-heat, the receipt for producing which it was practically felt that the master of the forge could not have communicated even with the best intentions.

It would be impossible, of course, to 'do' late James; even if you could, the likely effect would be satirical rather than serious. But the question remains, how can you get James right, as a character, without getting right his own inimitable style of thought? I don't know that I can answer it, except by saying that Tóibín's James consciously and repeatedly resists being 'got right'. He refuses to enter into any relation that might 'bring' out his character. And 'for the sake of something hidden within his own soul' he abandons, when he is most needed, the friends who love him. Wandering through the Protestant Cemetery in Rome, by the grave of one of these friends, James decides that 'the state of not-knowing and not-feeling which belonged to the dead' is 'closer to resolved happiness than he had ever imagined possible'. Happiness, in his mind, is related to being unknowable. Tóibín even permits his hero a humorous little dig at himself, at his own careful attempt to make sense, after James's death, of his character, when Henry declares, to fend off one of his brother's suggestions, that 'the historical novel' is 'tainted by a fatal cheapness'.

All of which threatens to expose both Henrys, historical and fictional, to a charge of hypocrisy, for he continued to write and to invade. Unless, that is, you consider the evolution of his late style as a response to this problem, the problem of privacy. James found a way of exploring the subtleties of character without giving them away. The passage from *The Golden Bowl*, quoted above, describes in effect the operation of such privacy, in terms that preserve it behind a decent veil of metaphor, extended and draped upon itself, in hesitations and double negatives. Part of the point of the passage, in fact, is to declare that the real truth, about character, remains impenetrable to assaults both from without and within: to the starers and wonderers who fail to perceive its glow, and to Adam Verver himself, who cannot, with his best intentions, account for it by any 'receipt'. James's stories turn often on concealed communications and ambiguous facts, burnt papers and letters and uncertain flaws, so that, even at the level of plot, crucial pieces of information are denied us. One of the odd things about him is that he is enormously adept at describing inarticulate characters, at capturing the Maisies and the Miss Tina Bordereaus – in part because he is so good at giving a definite shape and outline to the things we cannot know about others.

This, I think, is what Tóibín owes to James: a respect for the fact that characters appear most forcefully and truthfully when they remain decently concealed. Tóibín makes simplicity do the work of James's complexity. His descriptions, clear and direct, sometimes have the effect of statements under oath. Not that they don't seem true; rather, we suspect that behind them a great many other truths, of various kinds, have been held back. Their styles approach each other most closely in the use of dialogue, in which the strangeness of other people, their surprisingness, can be developed. And in the setting of scenes: the extent to which they let physical dispositions, arrangements, stand for emotional ones. Henry in *The Master* watches a young girl listening in on a conversation between two lovers. 'He realized now that this was something he had described in his books over and over, figures seen from a window or a doorway, a small gesture standing for a much larger relationship, something hidden suddenly revealed.' Tóibín might equally be talking about his own work here, but it is important (for both of them) always to complicate such 'revelations': 'He had written it, but just now he had seen it come alive, and yet he was not sure what it meant.' It is the job of the novel to tell us what it is like to be someone else – and that involves conveying a sense of a character's ability to elude us.

Little happens in John McGahern's last novel. There are no chapter divisions, no structural breaks in the narrative, there is no plot, minimal theme and no character or incident is dominant. There is no access to any one's rich interior life and the narrator is no help either, offering almost no analysis of what happens. Within a mostly uneventful year in a remote, self-enclosed rural community near the border with Northern Ireland, some time after the 1987 Enniskillen bombing, the novel's only dated political event, the overall tone is serene, often subdued, frequently still.

No character in this sparsely populated region seems that memorable either. After many years in England, Joe and Kate Ruttledge, a childless middle-aged couple, have returned to tend a small farm by the lake. He is a part-time copy-writer, she a sometime artist. The lake touches every life: the life of the Shah, Joe's entrepreneurial uncle, Patrick Ryan, an odd-job man, John Quinn, a sexual predator and first-class crank, Bill Evans, an emotionally maimed peasant, 'like something out of a Russian novel'. And principally Jamesie and Mary, the Ruttledges' nearest neighbours, the couple through whom the Ruttledges maintain contact with their community.

From an initial 18,000 (eighteen thousand) manuscript pages, McGahern chiselled an acclaimed, international best-seller, a drama-less novel about a resolutely provincial townland. Reviews compared the work to Chekhov while McGahern was anointed a member of the apostolic succession of Irish literary greats: for John Sutherland in *The New York Times*, 'McGahern ranks with the greatest Irish writers.' Twelve years in the making, it is perplexingly hard to summarise because so little happens to summarise. The narrative barely retains the structure of a novel, being by turns anthropological and, like some richly textured memoir, a loving evocation of a beleaguered community facing the challenge of passing time and time passing. It often resembles a series of short stories, forensically examining the particles of individual lives in the percussive roll of singular moments onto one another. Time, Death and Nature are certainly central concerns. So too is the price of cattle, the swarm of bees that 'ate the arse' off Patrick Ryan, drink – McGahern's seasoned descriptions ('the dark whiskey had a slight taste of port from the cask and looked beautiful in the clear glass of the unlabelled bottle') are memorable sorties against the dangers of temperance – harvests, conversation, emigration, the grammar of hospitality, the building of a shed, the laying of a table, the preparation and burial and the resurrection of the dead.

What inspires these delicate, miniature, arable portraits is the overwhelming fact that time passes and must, somehow, be remembered in mostly fixed lives lived each day knowing that what happens is, mostly, repetition. That when all is said and done, what can be said and done about those left behind? How does one live with the knowledge that each day passes? From the paring or purging of that 18,000-page script, McGahern's technique is to impose on key words this impossible existential freight. In a novel about the overwhelming and the ordinary, life becomes a sentence, and the style of each sentence is a calibrated mix of the aesthetic and the ethical. The good of this novel derives from the goodness it contains.

One fundamental distinction scores this world: Meaning is always secondary to Being. Life around the lake is not explained or unpacked or shown in cultural dialogue with something besides itself. This is part of its defiant provincialism. Instead of interpretation, the novel offers the chance to imaginatively participate in the daily experience of its unfolding seasonal rhythms. The only marker of social change imposed from without is at the novel's end, when telegraph poles begin to dot the landscape. All narrative is an imposition, so McGahern wants to present a world that has in some sense already narrated itself. Plot is absent because plot is a vehicle for theme and theme is imposed, by some dominant shaping consciousness that determines meaning for everyone in the world it creates. Here the gently rolling narrative structure forbids any determined attempt to understand life round the lake as meaning something other than itself. From within the world it chronicles, this subdued novel about a tiny, uneventful, isolated rural community emerged to rapture. Published near the height of Ireland's economic boom, a novel which could belong to the 1950s, 70s or 90s, and which fondly recounts the rituals of the rural poor, became a national phenomenon and a word-of-mouth global success. Shortly after publication RTE organised a free public reading and interview. Nearly 1,000 people attended, waiting till 11 p.m. to give McGahern a standing ovation. 'I think he was amazed by the reception he got,' said one journalist. 'He was like a rock star.' It is all a bit of a puzzle.

In the introduction to this book we quoted Milan Kundera:

> The sole *raison d'être* of a novel is to discover what only the novel can discover. A novel that does not discover a hitherto unknown segment of existence is immoral. Knowledge is the novel's only morality.

With no plot to advance or theme to tighten, words exist in *That They May Face the Rising Sun* to capture the numinous matter of lived experience. What McGahern's novel knows about the world is already well known. Time, food, being and death are accessible to all. These known segments of existence are introduced to an element of being which is not just being.

If life is a sentence for each character, lived out uniquely and within communal codes, it is words that distinguish each life. Functionally, the narrator only exists to register the earthen, implacable nature of reality: the narrator knows of no unknown segment. The experience of being in the world is a condition so miraculous that sentences become inventories or archives of the actual. When Ruttledge enters Patrick Ryan's house he sees:

> A bowl of sugar, unwashed cups, part of a loaf, a sardine tin, a plate with an eggshell, a half-full bottle of Powers, a bar of soap, butter, an empty packet of Silk Cut, red apples, a pot of marmalade, salt, matches, a brown jug, an open newspaper, a transistor radio, an alarm clock littered the table.

This list of a sentence contains in one visual screen the mute particles of Ryan's life, and this particularity is one way the novel captures reality. If the Romantic sublime implies that man can emotionally and linguistically transcend the limits of perception, McGahern's inspiration and material comes from what is implacably within those limits. The sublime is that which eludes our experience of art, so it is grasped in metaphors that allude to what exists beyond human and empirical experience. The sublime focuses on what is absent, on something more than the mundane. It is a mystery that defeats every effort of sense and imagination to picture it, so it is defined and described only in symbolic terms, which ironically means that it can't be captured visually.

McGahern presents Ryan's table as a study in still life, a frozen tableau that arrests the process of decay, so that even as it is mundane it has a simple mystery that comes from the empirical order of what is present.

This list of a sentence has a patient fidelity to the quotidian. It relinquishes any ambition to transform or transcend what it registers by abolishing any invasive style – 'littered' is loaned to the scene by the narrator – so that we in turn participate in its tactile details, the felt reality of Ryan's sensory being. It is a scene that would be vandalised by any syntactical or descriptive intrusion beyond 'littered'. Idyllic in its disorderly composition, the scene asks only that the sentence do no more than contain each mundane item that comprises it. 'Littered' does that by going just under the top.

Life round the lake is a mercilessly egalitarian world – 'No misters is this part of the world. Nothing but broken-down gentlemen,' says Jamesie to Ruttledge – so introducing individuals through this repetitive accumulation of singular things is also a style without social hierarchy or moral judgement. The novel pays tribute to this world but is not its tribune. It is a witness, not a judge. It does not try to reconfigure what it represents. Even after these domestic details, Ryan's private life remains just that, private, despite the solemn accumulation of his particulars. We know as much about him as the novel does. To adopt Kundera's terms, it would be stylistically unethical for this novel to excavate some unknown segment of Ryan's existence.

The good of this novel emerges, then, from McGahern's often beautiful fusion of ethics and nature, culture and cultivation, in the seasonal passing of time. Not much happens day by day yet the whole is entirely memorable. A serene and composed world, it is suffused by the fear that daily life may decompose. The title, *That They May Face the Rising Sun,* looks to the resurrection of the body in an eternal life to come, but it also, surely, alludes to a line from the book of Ecclesiastes, 'nothing new under the sun', a line Beckett also alludes to at the start of *Murphy* ('The sun shone, having no alternative, on the nothing new'), as does Hemingway in *The Sun Also Rises*. The full biblical quote is:

> What has been will be again, what has been done will be done again; there is nothing new under the sun. Is there anything of which one can say, 'Look! This is something new'? It was here already, long ago; it was here before our time.

To face each day the fact of the rising sun is also to acknowledge the impossibility of experiencing anything in life as pristinely new. Round the lake lives evolve in a mix of fixity and flux, ritual and repetition, the ordinary and the quotidian. Ruttledge's name, Rutt-Ledge, incorporates the static and catastrophic, the daily possibility of oblivion. Reality is a constant negotiation between the community's grounded needs and its founded and unfounded fears.

What McGahern's purged lyricism does is make sentences foray into the ineffable, that part of individual and collective identity where silence reigns and language disguises what is said. Around the lake news is the main means of exchange, a customised account of events that briefly enriches the speaker. Yet all the talk of news is scored by the 'tension in the call between the need to be heard and the fear of being heard'. It is from between fixity and flux, sound and silence, woman and man; between generations; between culture and cultivation, nature and the human; between the auditable, mute reality of daily life in its seasonal rhythms and the unfathomable otherness of death – it is from the space between Rutt and Ledge that McGahern discovers, in Kundera's term, those known and unknown segments that only the novel can know. Life is a sentence lived quietly, tactfully, in a daily embrace of the despotism of that repetitive fact. It is an exercise in restraint. Jamesie tells Kate, 'Right or wrong, Kate? There's nothing right or wrong in this world. Only what happens.' Every sentence, in other words, has to go just under the top so as to respect the horizon of what is.

When something does eventually happen, the tone is pitch-perfect, the sound of each sentence an audible actor in the momentary dramas punctuating life round the lake:

> Late in the day they heard a heavy motor come slowly in round the shore and turn uphill towards the house.

The strain of this sentence, in both senses of that word, enacts the engine's distress. For in this short sonorous clump of heavy extended vowel sounds – *late, day, heard, hea-vy, mo-tor, slow-ly, round, shore, hill, towards, house:* no word here can be hurried – we have travelled miles. This is lyricism as a form of precision, a lyricism where cadences combine to enact time, distance and even a mechanical condition. Within any given day, there are repeated encounters with an other-worldliness that we could call grace or the sacred, that element in being which is not just being. So too within a given sentence there can be orchestrated occasions of lyrical precision:

> Patrick Ryan's re-emergence into this slow mindlessness was like the eruptions of air that occur in the wheaten light of mown meadows in a heatwave.

This sentence is composed, its lyrical strain and precise still-ness offering an exquisite alliance of the aural and the visual. The aural impact is a rhythmic combination of sonic peaks and troughs – the clipped syllables of 're-emergence' and 'wheaten' swiftly descend into the deeper vowels sounds of 'slow' and 'mown' and 'meadows'. The syllabic parity and kinetic contrast between 'slow mindlessness' and 'eruptions of air' lifts this sen-tence, and Ryan's existence, into the poetic, so that the condi-tion of being looks itself like a cloth that veils another mystery of being. 'I'm only interested,' McGahern has said, 'in poetry, which occurs more often in verse than in prose.' Attending to the music of what happens in the moment of Ryan's re-emer-gence – the 'wheaten light', 'mown meadows', 'heatwave' – in-fuses his being with something more than being, a grace drawn from nature. These luminous and precise images of air in mo-tion, light and the colour of grain, the two wrapped together in an earthen warmth, establish layers of his existence that have been, in Kundera's formulation, hitherto unknown.

Style here has an ambitious purchase on known and un-known segments of reality. It aspires to inhabit the stillness in the muteness of things and objects, in each life round the lake. Silence itself is an aspect of this style. Style tries to establish the complexity of the concrete, to show how consciousness is grasped, amplified and best understood when it is mediated through what is actual, even if that is just a tin of sardines. In other words, words can become facts. It does not pay to ask if the experience of Ryan's re-emergence is true or not, because what style does here is reveal that hitherto unknown segment of Ryan's existence which is more than just existence.

'Will you look at the men? They're more like a crowd of women . . .' That image ended McGahern's previous novel, *Amongst Women*, as the three daughters of the deceased patriarch Moran stride away from their father's grave. Mary Robinson was elected president of the Republic of Ireland in the same year, 1990, so the image seemed, in retrospect, prophetic, a harbinger of dramatic political change to come. By 2002 and the publication of *That They May Face the Rising Sun*, dramatic social change had arrived. McGahern's novel was published during a period of unprecedented economic transition – the era of the 'Celtic Tiger' – that fundamentally transformed the Irish social landscape. As Dublin prospered, rural Ireland often seemed to function as a satellite sector for the city's insatiable growth. The rage for acquisitive advancement crushed many traditional values organised around the communal, and it accelerated the collapse of the Catholic church. If one is being celebratory, Ireland was at last matching, even surpassing European levels of prosperity. If one is being judgemental, the country lost the run of itself, because that boom has now emphatically gone. But what is undeniably true is that during the twelve-year incubation of *That They May Face the Rising Sun*, Ireland's self-definition was that of a creative, cool, entrepreneurial European state with a dash of Celtic colour added – about as far from the lake as conceivable. Diversity became the norm, with economic migrants bringing multiculturalism in their wake. In this context, McGahern's novel seems just that little more subversive. Even the title gathers together values and priorities that precede and outlast any economic boom. Some aspect of this provincial rural vision prompted that rock-star ovation in multicultural Dublin, but was it just nostalgia, the backward look longing for a time when communities were knowable and social harmony meant religious, maybe even ethnic homogeneity? Is it even fair to ask if McGahern's vision of life round the lake can cope with twenty-first century realities?

This novel's composed stillness does not derive from the category of the singular. In Joe Ruttledge, we have the fusion and occasional confusions of a man who is, Patrick Ryan thinks, sometimes like a woman: 'That pair in there are different. They never seem to go against one another. There are times when you wonder whether they are man or woman at all.' Ruttledge is a man who constantly blends two ways of being. A writer who trained to be a priest, his speech is unconsciously liturgical, full of delayed repetitions that discover a sacral realm in the quotidian. At Monaghan Day, the county's major cattle auction, Ruttledge commends his parish priest's work as a farmer: 'If his black gear hasn't a place in the cattle market it hasn't a place anywhere else either. It either belongs to life or it doesn't.' Kate's speech is oracular: 'When someone falls like Johnny, it guarantees suffering.' 'I think people are sexual until they die.' What little this painter utters always combines some version of the visual and the aesthetic: 'The past and present are all the same in the mind . . . they are just pictures.' Through these two sensibilities – writer and painter, the conversational and oracular, the once aspirant priest and the still aspirant artist – McGahern implicitly deciphers the elusiveness of reality around the lake. Patrick Ryan presses Kate on her painting:

'Do you think will you ever make that drawing you do pay?'
    'I don't think so, Patrick.'

'Why do you keep at it then girl?'
'It brings what I see closer.'

Closer is not necessarily better. Kate says to Patrick, 'You have an interesting face but you know that yourself. I don't think I ever got it right.' What Patrick Ryan knows is that the precision of Kate's 'right' is inimical to this place of blurred boundaries. The face registers human uniqueness, but in one of the novel's comic interludes, Patrick tells Johnny, the holidaying emigrant, of the Ruttledges' attempt to assimilate.

> You know yourself that you have to be born into land . . . Everything round the place are treated like royals. There's a black cat in there with white paws that'd nearly get up on its hind legs and order his breakfast. You'd not get thanked now if you got caught hitting it a dart of a kick on the quiet. The cattle come up to the back of the house and boo in like a trade union if the grass isn't up to standard. . . . They even got to like the sheep. There's no more stupid animal on God's earth. There's an old Shorthorn they milk for the house that would nearly sit in an armchair and put specs on to read the *Observer*. The bees nearly ate the arse off me an hour ago. She draws all that she sees. She even did a drawing of me . . . You wouldn't know if I was man or beast . . . Another thing that brought them here was the quiet. Will you listen to the fucken quiet for a minute and see in the name of God if it wouldn't drive you mad.

This is a subtle comic mockery of the Ruttledges' attempt to distinguish Patrick through art. Like the priest at the cattle fair, Patrick already is, in both senses of the word, distinguished by his relationship to the totality of his environment, whether that is the bees atein' the arse off him, the newly unionised cattle, or the fucken quiet. In a context where cultivation and commerce mingle across the seasons, the priest's religion and Patrick's unsentimental being both emerge from this elaborate fusion of man and beast.

What brings Patrick closer is not his distinguished face – there are no gentlemen here – but Ruttledge's slow accumulation of their first meeting. Patrick denies Ruttledge's account of that meeting with 'I disremember lad . . . I disremember that as well.' Similarly Bill Evans' anguish is overwhelming when pressed by Ruttledge about his early days with the Christian brothers – 'Stop torturing me!' And anguish awaits too when Bill Evans moves beyond the immediacy of the day to imagine the future:

> He was no longer living from moment to moment: from blow to blow, pleasure to pleasure, refusing to look forward or back: he was now living these bus rides on Thursday in the mind as well. The seeds of calamity were sown.

In this community, illegitimate memories are not suppressed, they are obliterated, made unborn, 'disremembered'. Only events participating in the liturgical rhythm of seasonal communal life experienced from day to day are sanctioned. And this public memory of seasonal events can, the novel insists, be brought closer. As Patrick and Ruttledge work on an unfinished, possibly unfinishable shed, Patrick demands to know what Ruttledge is staring at.

> At how the rafters frame the sky. How the squares of light are more interesting than the open sky. They make it look more human by reducing the sky and then the whole sky grows out from that small space.

The utility and fertility of scale – the whole sky growing from that small space – distils the vastness surrounding their existence, reducing it to little tableaux of light to humanise its overwhelming immensity. This is the sense in which McGahern's provincialism is aesthetically defiant: the framed square is more interesting than the open sky. The intensity and complexity of human significance is neither derived from nor transformed by this framing perspective, but the perspective seems to delay time in order to accommodate time. What happens around the frame of the lake is 18,000 pages of 'news that stays news', to use Ezra Pound's definition of literature, when it is reduced to the manageable frame of the novel we read. Or as Jamesie, forever addicted to news, puts it, 'I may not have travelled far but I know the whole world.' Distilling experience until it fits this minimalist frame makes it more potent, the process of reduction magnifying individual segments of existence so that even a sardine tin has its place.

This sense of time is minute. It never seeks to recapture some richer segment of meaning beneath the immediate surface of the everyday. In this McGahern's register is sharply different from his near neighbour and contemporary Seamus Heaney. In shape and structure, Heaney's famous bog poems are like little arrows or spears that plummet into and puncture the ground they explore. They produce a sense of time that circumvents the sectarian realities of the North by recourse to several different levels of experience. The bog poems' archaeological recovery of human and political history dreams of a fabulous sense of full and immediate presence. Time is at once immemorial and perennial and the gap between self and other is obliterated. Beneath surface events, deep in the bog, there resides a richer, residual meaning that can mediate and make whole again a divisive present.

McGahern's version of time is horizontal, repetitive and, ultimately, a register of bleak and lonely experience. Bogs, lakes, animals – the raw ingredients of Heaney's world are here, but that vertiginous sense of historical depth is not. 'How can time be gathered in and kissed?' the novel asks directly for the one and only time. 'There is only flesh' is the answer. The Shah is adept at 'turning each day into the same day, making even Sunday into all other Sundays'. There is no rift between experience and meaning because meaning in McGahern's world is never premature or already inscribed by some mythic sense of time that each has no choice but to inherit. Each day time is pixillated and minute. The consolation of any mythic realm of meaning is everywhere absent. Experience is ordered minute by minute, day by day by the lake, the dominant liturgical space around which life and death unfold.

And to continue the contrast with Heaney, of this dominant space only its surface is ever described. Its depths may be hinted at, but the lake does not contain some hidden level of meaning that precedes experience:

> The lake was an enormous mirror turned to the depth of the sky, holding its lights and its colours. Close to the reeds there were many flies, and small schools of perch were rippling the surface with hints of the teeming energy and life of the depths.

It is hard not to hear some echo of the play in *Hamlet* here. 'An enormous mirror turned to the sky' is not too far from 'the mirror up to nature' in Hamlet's speech to the actors:

> Suit the action to the word, the word to the action, with this special observance, that you o'erstep not the modesty of nature: for any thing so o'erdone is from the purpose of playing, whose end, both at the first and now, was and is, to hold as 'twere the mirror up to nature: to show virtue her feature, scorn her own image, and the very age and body of the time his form and pressure.

For Hamlet, the 'purpose of playing' is to hold 'the mirror up to nature'. Drama must be truth, a form without exaggeration, distortion, bombast or excessive sentimentality. In the theatrical mirror, virtues and vice are reflected back to us in their true shape, which is the moral function of theatre. Looking out towards the sky, the lake reflects all that happens, a reflection which the novel then intensifies through the precise lyricism of its reduced frame. These minimalist portraits reduce the sky, as Ruttledge put it, to undistorted, unexaggerated tableaux of light. The lake is a mirror up to nature, and it is the moral function of the novel to distil these lives to the essence of their being so as to capture that element that is not being.

From the lake a heron rises each time there is a passer-by. That heron is just that: a heron, not a mythical emblem of something beyond itself but a repetitive part of the repetitive experience of each day. If soil is what land becomes when it is invested or injected with mythic beliefs, the lake is immune to any kind of symbolic appropriation. Around its shores time remains ungraspable as an immediate or full presence:

> The days were quiet. They did not feel particularly quiet or happy but through them ran the sense, like an underground river, that there would come a time when these days would be looked back on as happiness, all that life could give of contentment and peace.

If, as Coventry Patmore says, the end of art is peace, part of the credo of this Irish novel, set near a volatile border, is that peace, in all its mundane, repetitive and unavoidably dreary reality, does not mean the end of art. Surface items – sardine tins, coffee cups, low flying herons – are not repositories of eruptive historical energies. The land around the lake remains arable and economically productive in a way soil never can. The experience of time is unique, lonely and always unwhole.

The full bleakness of this insight affects Johnny, the failed emigrant dreaming of a return to live with Jamesie and Mary. Redundant in Birmingham, the lake is that place where he imagines a full and harmonious presence. Like Bill Evans, Johnny begins to live in the future. The reality is that Johnny bores Jamesie and Mary and would ruin their family life. His dream is illusory. In Jamesie and Mary's house, time is a jigsaw of discrete moments that can never be gathered whole: 'No two clocks were the same or told the same time but all were running. Each one had its separate presence and claim.' The reality is that Johnny returns home for good only when he is dead. If happiness is possible, it is known only in retrospect. The 'separate presence' of each moment inscribes an unbridgeable gulf between meaning and being. Or, again, as Jamesie puts it, 'Right or wrong, Kate? There's nothing right or wrong in this world. Only what happens.'

Because they exist outside the seasonal rhythms pulsing through each day, the past and future are inaccessible zones. Because they work inside the seasonal rhythms contained in a single day, individuals can become curators of their own existence, caught up in some otherwise inexpressible exchange with the totality of their environment. Jamesie, Mary, Kate and Joe stack hay:

> The bales were too heavy for the child but the two women and Jamesie were able to stack them almost as quickly as the baler spat them out. Two bales were placed sideways, sufficiently close to be crossed by two other bales but far enough apart to allow air to circulate. The stack was completed by a single bale on top, the uncut side turned upwards to cast the rain. When they were all stacked, they stood like abstract sculptures in swept empty space.

'Abstract sculptures in swept empty space' – the image seems more suited to a landscape painting than a kinetic narrative. As a culminating image it is fixed ('stood') and it restores or extracts some idyllic version of harmony and order from the seasonal flux, and it shows how culture arises from the cultivation of the environment. Each character becomes the curator of their own existence in this communal aesthetic. It is hard not to think that the novel here is almost too full of goodness, the image coming too close to the top, almost more perfect than any McGahern could have witnessed. When they finish stacking hay, this intensely visual harmony shifts to domestic space:

> Inside the house a reading lamp with a green shade was lit on the big table. On the red-and-white square of the table cloth stood a blue bowl filled with salad and large white plates of tongue and ham, a cheeseboard with different cheeses, including the Galtee Jamesie liked wrapped in its silver paper, a cut loaf, white wine, a bottle of Powers, lemonade. There was a large glass of iced water in which slices of lemon floated.

After the public seasonal labour, the writer is witness to the implacable stillness and ordinariness of domestic objects. The narrator may not provide analysis of any character's psychology, but this is still a rich interior life. It is an example of what Amit Chaudhuri in his essay here calls the novel's 'special minority gift for the particular that is not to be found in any other form of discourse'. Each object already belongs to some numinous aura simply by being. The ritualistic provision of daily bread and cheese and whiskey and wine draws its aesthetic and sacral grace from a combination of the visual and literary, from Kate the artist and Joe the aspirant priest, from the seasonal context of time passing for these neighbours and the mute stasis of what passes in each moment of time. The table is an offering, an appropriate climax to the ceremony of stacking hay, and its stillness is one way of making time flesh, of arresting the process of decay.

The communal codes underpinning this collective life exist in 'that space between the need to be heard and the fear of being heard'. When Jamesie enters the novel and the Ruttledge home he is like a preordained presence, something silent and non physical yet still felt, a bit like the wind:

> Jamesie entered without knocking and came in noiselessly until he stood in the doorway of the large room where the Ruttledges were sitting. He stood as still as if waiting under trees for returning wildfowl. He expected his discovery to be quick. There would be a cry of surprise and reproach; he would counter by accusing them of not being watchful enough. There would be welcome and laughter.

And two pages later, in anticipation of Johnny's annual return,

> The house and the outhouses would be freshly whitewashed for the homecoming, the street swept, the green gates painted . . . Mary would have scrubbed and freshened all the rooms. Together they would have taken the mattresses from the bed on the lower room . . . the holy pictures and the wedding photograph would be taken down . . . his bed would be made . . . an enormous vase of flowers from the garden and the field . . . would be placed on the sill . . . the order for the best sirloin would already have been placed at Carroll's in the town.

The future perfect 'would' is one of those key McGahern words, and here it is freighted with anthropological weight. 'Would' means that experience always awaits its consummation as an act to be made flesh amongst individuals. The cleaning, pictures, flowers and steaks 'would' happen; they are all rituals, and what ritual tacitly communicates are the deepest values of all the individuals performing it. Ritual expresses wishes at odds with conscious experience – the ritual of hospitality disguises the boredom of Johnny's visits, for example. Ritual establishes separateness, a mode of individual and collective being whose deepest coordinates are derived from a distinct cultural identity. Ritual distinguishes life round the lake, exalting the primacy of place and race because its underlying patterns are accessible only to those already within the community. Or as Jamesie tells Kate, 'You'd nearly have to be born into a place to know what's going on and what to do.'

'Going on and what to do' – the phrase combines procedure and activity, life as an unending and renewable process. Johnny dies but Ruttledge delivers a calf and it is the 'beginning of the world' again. But with so little civic society – Patrick says 'Only for the football and the Mass and the *Observer* on Wednesday people would never get out of their frigging houses. They'd be marooned' – interaction becomes a focus for inaction and inactivity. Patrick Ryan's unfinished shed is a statement against closure, for closure would rule out contact, and round the lake talk not money is the primary means of exchange. So the shed is, like the novel itself, a structure in perpetual process. Like the novel, the shed mingles various genres – it is symbolic and substantive, a fertile source of gossip for Jamesie and the Shah on Ryan's uselessness, and something caught up in the commemoration of Johnny's being. 'Going on', Ruttledge realises early in the novel, is more important than getting it done. Patrick says to Ruttledge,

'I'll be round tomorrow. We'll finish that shed . . .'

'There's no hurry.'

'You were anxious enough to get building done once . . .'

'That was a long time ago.'

As the novel ends, Patrick is insistent on what needs to be done:

'Tomorrow we'll make a start, in the name of the Lord, and we'll not quit until that whole cathedral of a shed is finished,' he said in the same ringing, confident tone that had ordered Johnny's head to lie to the west in Shruhaun so that when he rose with all the faithful he would face the rising sun.

'There's no great need or rush with the shed, Patrick,' Kate said uncertainly, surprised by her own forwardness. 'Maybe it could be left there for another summer in deference to Johnny?'

This cathedral of a cattle shed is another abstract sculpture in swept space, an image through which to mediate belief in some element of being that is not being. And like ritual, this use of image as a means of devotion is drawn directly from Catholic practice. In the novel's concluding scene, Patrick asks Ruttledge for a definitive answer on the shed, yes or no, built or unbuilt, finished or forever unfinished, unwhole.

'What are you going to do?' Kate asked as they passed beneath the alder tree.

'I'm not sure,' he said. 'We can talk it through in the morning. We don't have to decide on anything till morning.'

Ruttledge knows that finishing the shed would impoverish a public segment of their existence. Kate and Joe as woman and man, artist and the once-aspirant priest, merge their uncertainties within nature, beneath the alder tree, and take solace from talk, that non-material means of exchange. Solace is the simple availability of another day, the chance to deflect Patrick's harsh certainties. The unknown segment of existence that only the novel knows is that, on this final page, Joe and Kate repeat

Jamesie's entrance to their home on the first page – 'He stood as still as if waiting under trees for the returning wildfowl.' The year ends in some echoing format of its beginning, nature a constant, human activity round the lake sheltered by it, experience cyclical and repetitive.

Kundera claims that 'Knowledge is the novel's only morality', but the economy of McGahern's style, and the layers of being it encodes, provide something more and less than knowledge. It is less a moral vision of how to live than a creed on how the enormity of life can be contained and conserved within each day. It is a creed that believes in something holy and still within the ordinary and also something ghostly and numinous beyond it. It derives its unconscious public practices from the Catholic use of ritual and image, and it gathers together a communion of individuals that looks to the resurrection of the body and the life of the world to come.

Is it too good to be true? A feature of life round the lake is the absence of children. Calves and sheep may breed but Jamesie's niece is the only child in the novel, and even she belongs to Dublin. Nature is endlessly fertile but this community is aged – the Ruttledges' childlessness is too sensitive for direct address, but it is still a feature of their relationship. The only overtly sensual moment between Joe and Kate is similarly indirect. Kate's cat kills a young hare. As Kate sleeps, the cat drops the leveret across her throat with Joe 'trapped in the fascination of watching':

> The flesh was still warm. A trickle of bright scarlet ran from the nostrils. There was a thin red stain along the white cover of the bed, like a trail.

This sacrificial offering of the hare is erotic because of its excess. Drawn from a wildness in nature – now tame, the cat had 'never lost her wildness completely' – it exceeds what Joe can aspire to. The once aspirant priest relishes this ideal, untamed image of seduction, the thin red stain against the white bed offering not just a vivid image of virginal possession, but also some reticent allusion to the Christian sacrifice in a wild setting. The point is not that this fantastic offering of warm flesh to his wife, the artist, is unavailable to Joe. The point is that this does not make the image any less potent. The point is that these sensuous energies – predatory, religious, dramatic – are present in this ostensibly inert, isolated environment.

It does not really matter if the scene is too good to be true. What matters is that it captures some of what would be lost if this community dies. To return to Kundera, the morality or good of this novel belongs primarily to a style that conveys something more and less than knowledge about the known and unknown segments of this world. Little happens, the people are aged, loneliness is an ever-present, death and the world to come a constant preoccupation. But it is still a novel of resistance. It resists incorporation into the values of status and consumption that mark the wider world it enters. It describes a version of freedom that does not need to be reconciled to what surrounds it. McGahern does not overtly write against the grain, of course (moving some of his cruder critics to describe him as 'retro'), but his novel does describe the ethical and aesthetic good of a community cultivating its environment and conserving grain and hay, of people passing on news and extending hospitality to one another, of enduring the 'fucken quiet' so that silence and stillness become part of life's texture.

Part of McGahern's attraction is his strange quotidian nobility. He conscripts the Yeatsian tradition of custom and ceremony for precisely the Catholic bourgeois class Yeats thought would ruin these virtues. 'I may not have travelled far but I know the whole world,' says Jamsie near the novel's end. 'You do know the whole word,' Ruttledge said, 'And you have been my sweet guide.' 'Sweet' is a discriminating word, one that captures Jamesie's ethical, aesthetic and civic goodness, and shows that goodness to be a matter of exquisite taste as well as a testament to what keeps people going day after day, knowing there is nothing new under the sun.

In this his last novel, written when McGahern must have known that the end of his life was near, McGahern's main character, Ruttledge, concludes with 'I'm not sure. We can talk it through. We don't have to decide on anything till morning,' phrases that find some resonance in Edward Said's description of late artistic style:

> This is the prerogative of late style: it has the power to render disenchantment and pleasure without resolving the contradiction between them. What holds them in tension, as equal forces straining in opposite directions, is the artist's mature subjectivity, stripped of hubris and pomposity, unashamed either of its fallibility or the modest assurance it has gained as a result of age and exile.

That heron no longer flies because of the telegraph poles dotted round the lake. The landscape is slowly changing, time and communication are being altered too, but still Joe is unable to contemplate deviating from the daily customs and ceremony of their existence. It was McGahern's 'power to render disenchantment and pleasure', his spiritual fusion of the ordinary and the uncanny, ritual and repetition, that moved those one thousand people in Dublin to greet him with such rapture.

Contributors

AMIT CHAUDHURI was brought up in Bombay. He has contributed fiction, poetry and reviews to numerous publications including the *Guardian*, the *London Review of Books*, the *Times Literary Supplement*, *The New Yorker* and *Granta*. His books include *A Strange and Sublime Address* (1991), *Afternoon Raag* (1993), *Freedom Song* (1998), *A New World* (2000), *The Picador Book of Modern Indian Literature* (editor, 2001), *Real Time* (2002), *D. H. Lawrence and 'difference': Postcoloniality and the Poetry of the Present* (2003), *St Cyril Road and Other Poems* (2005) *Clearing a Space: Reflections on India, Literature, and Culture* (2008) and *The Immortals* (2009).

JASON COWLEY is a journalist, magazine editor and writer. He is editor of the *New Statesman* and was previously editor of *Granta* magazine and of the award-winning *Observer Sport Monthly*. He is the author of a novel, *Unknown Pleasures* (2000), and of *The Last Game: Love, Death and Football* (2009), and is a director of Zamyn and a founding member of the council of the Caine Prize for African Writing.

TESSA HADLEY teaches literature and creative writing at Bath Spa University. She has published four novels, *Accidents in the Home* (2002), *Everything Will Be All Right* (2004), *The Master Bedroom* (2007) and *The London Train* (2011); she has had stories in *The New Yorker*, *Granta* and the *Guardian*, and brought out a collection, *Sunstroke and Other Stories*, in 2007. She has also written a critical book on Henry James, and writes for the *London Review of Books*.

MARY HAWTHORNE is a staff writer on *The New Yorker*.

KEVIN JACKSON is the author of many books including, most recently, *The Pataphysical Flook* (2007), *The Book of Hours* (2007), *Lawrence of Arabia* (2007) and *Moose* (2009). He has written widely on film, photography, modern art, literature, language and cultural history, and is the author of a biography of Humphrey Jennings.

ROBERT MACFARLANE is a critic, essayist and travel writer. He is the author of *Mountains of the Mind* (2003), *Original Copy* (2007) and *The Wild Places* (2007), and he writes for the *Guardian*, the *Times Literary Supplement*, the *New York Times* and *Harper's Magazine*, among other publications.

LIAM MCILVANNEY was born in Ayrshire. He is the Stuart Professor of Scottish Studies at the University of Otago, New Zealand. He won the Saltire First Book Award for *Burns the Radical* in 2002, and his work has appeared in the *Times Literary Supplement* and the *London Review of Books*. He lives in Dunedin with his wife and four sons. *All the Colours of the Town*, his first novel, was published in 2009.

BENJAMIN MARKOVITS is a novelist and freelance writer whose essays, reviews, stories and poems have appeared in *Granta*, the *New York Times* and the *London Review Books*, among other publications. He is the author of six novels, including a trilogy on the life of Lord Byron: *Imposture* (2007), *A Quiet Adjustment* (2008), and *Childish Loves* (2011). He lives in London with his wife and two children, and teaches at Royal Holloway.

ANDREW O'HAGAN's books include *The Missing* (1995), *Our Fathers* (1999), *Personality* (2003), *Be Near Me* (2006), *A Night out with Robert Burns* (editor, 2008) and a book of essays, *The Atlantic Ocean* (2008). His most recent novel is *The Life and Opinions of Maf the Dog, and of His Friend Marilyn Monroe*.

RAY RYAN is author of *Ireland and Scotland: Literature and Culture, State and Nation, 1966–2000*, editor of *Writing in the Irish Republic: Literature, Culture, Politics, 1949–1999*, and, with Liam McIlvanney, co-editor of *Ireland and Scotland: Culture and Society, 1700–2000*.

IAN SANSOM is the author of a number of works of fiction and non-fiction, including *The Truth About Babies* (2002) and *Ring Road* (2004).

FRANCES WILSON is a critic and biographer. Her books include *Literary Seductions: Compulsive Writers and Diverted Readers* (1999), *The Cour-*

tesan's Revenge: Harriette Wilson, the Woman who Blackmailed the King (2005) and *The Ballad of Dorothy Wordsworth* (2008).

JAMES WOOD is Professor of the Practice of Literary Criticism at Harvard University. His books include *The Broken Estate: Essays in Literature and Belief* (1999), *Selected Shorter Fiction of D. H. Lawrence* (1999), *The Book Against God* (2003) and *The Irresponsible Self: On Laughter and the Novel* (2004).

MICHAEL WOOD is the Charles Barnwell Straut Professor of English and Professor of Comparative Literature at Princeton University. His works include books on Stendhal, Garcia Marquez, Nabokov, Kafka, and films. He is a widely published essayist with articles on film and literature in *Harper's*, *London Review of Books*, *New York Review of Books*, *New York Times Book Review*, *New Republic* and others. His latest book is *Literature and the Taste of Knowledge* (2005).